# WHAT WERE YOU THINKING??

# WHAT
# WERE
# YOU
# THINKING??

**$600-PER-HOUR LEGAL ADVICE ON
RELATIONSHIPS, MARRIAGE & DIVORCE**

## MARK A. BARONDESS, ESQ.

ISBN: 1-59777-500-2

Library of Congress Cataloging-In-Publication Data Available

Book Design by: Sonia Fiore

All cartoons courtesy of cartoonbank.com

Printed in the United States of America

Phoenix Press
9465 Wilshire Boulevard, Suite 315
Beverly Hills, CA  90212

10  9  8  7  6  5  4  3  2  1

I dedicate this book
to my Father,
a man who exemplified
the better part of valor;
to my Mother,
a woman who has been there for me
during every step of my journey;
to my beautiful wife, Rose,
who must unfortunately endure me every day;
and to the joys of my life,
Andrew and Alec

# TABLE OF CONTENTS

# WHERE DO WE BEGIN?

*A few opening thoughts*

*"We are gathered here to join together this man and this woman in matrimony—a very serious step, with far-reaching and unpredictable consequences."*

"What were you thinking?" "What was I thinking?" These two haunting questions have probably been pondered by you or posed to you by your family or friends at one time or another. These are the questions that are the subject of lively discussion, maybe even debate, and more frequently gossip. They are the questions posed on the eve of, or in the days following, the demise of a relationship. It's the "I can't believe I dated him" or "I can't believe you actually married her—*what were you thinking?*"

Ninety-five percent of all Americans will get married at some point in their life—and half of us will get divorced. As such, marriage and the peril of divorce should certainly be topics of abiding interest to most people. What about you? When you honestly look back at your life or take a look ahead, should you have gotten—or get—engaged, married, divorced or remarried? Did a friend or family member get you this book (hint, hint)? The answers to these questions are inevitably up to you, and they should be made only after the most careful reflection on the experiences that you have had in your own life and the risks you are willing to take in order to enjoy the happiness that marriage or divorce can eventually bring. Life is simply too short to have to unnecessarily endure the misery of a divorce once, let alone twice or more.

This book is not a "how to" book about love, marriage and divorce. It is not *Divorce or Marriage for Dummies.* There are plenty of books like those. The best way to appreciate what is in store for you here? Imagine the following scenario: Before you considered getting married or divorced, wouldn't it be nice if you could sit down with a lawyer who ordinarily charges $600 per hour and talk openly about your marriage or divorce plans without having any concern as to the amount of the legal fees you would incur? Would it not be beneficial to be able to get some witty straightforward advice for yourself, a family member or friend who was contemplating marriage or divorce? Wouldn't it be helpful to know how lawyers and judges really deal with those whose marriages have failed? Wouldn't it be great to have to have a better understanding of the laws pertaining to marriage and divorce, as well as a few tricks in your pocket in the event that the joy of the "I do" becomes the agony of "I don't"? Now is your chance to blow the bank on legal fees without really doing so, to laugh a little and learn a lot.

As you read the book, you will see that I sometimes go off on rants about various subjects, especially the question of whether someone should get married. Please understand that it is impossible to have extricated clients from miserable marriages for 20 years and not feel opinionated about the institutions of marriage and divorce. I have also asked some of my friends to offer their individual perspectives on love, marriage and divorce, so you will be able to read their advice and views in their own words as well. Some of my friends you may already know, others you probably do not. In any event, each one offers a unique perspective on this important part of our lives, and I think you will probably be surprised by what all of them have to say and the advice they have elected to share.

Now, if you are a former client reading this book, you need not approach it with any apprehension that your confidences or secrets will be revealed. I have changed the names, places and other identifying facts to protect the innocent as well as the guilty. I have referred only to a few matters of public record.

Now if you are my wife and reading this book, please understand that it is easier for me to articulate the guidance provided in these pages as opposed to my actually following my own advice. As for those points that you may find somewhat controversial, I was really only kidding…

Many of life's biggest and very best rewards are bestowed upon those of us who take the largest risks. But before you take a risk, you should at least have a basic appreciation of the potential consequences of your decision. So pull up a seat, and let's have a candid conversation. No need to rush—the clock is not running.

Now, honestly, tell me: *What were you thinking?*

# CHAPTER 1

# THE PRIMARY CAUSE OF DIVORCE: MARRIAGE

"Look, I'm not talking about a lifetime commitment. I'm talking about marriage."

Allow me to offer a basic but important idea at the very beginning of this book: if you never want to suffer through the agony of a divorce, the wisest course of action is to *never marry*. Think about it—it is really quite plain and simple: you only receive a 100 percent absolute guarantee of no divorce if you do not get married. Nothing else works. Really. Now, if you insist that the road down perceived marital bliss is a journey that you must embark upon, you should at least educate yourself about exactly what adventures may lie ahead. After all, you probably would not decide to buy a car without first taking it for a test-drive and understanding the costs associated with the ownership of the vehicle. For instance, how much is the monthly payment? Does the car require premium or regular unleaded? Will your insurance payments go up? Is the vehicle easy to maintain, or does it require frequent service? What are the terms of the warranty, and exactly what does it cover? Are there any published reviews of the car? What do people in the auto world think about it?

The equation becomes even more complex when you consider a used vehicle. Do you know the prior owner (or owners)? If not, do you know if the vehicle was properly maintained? Are you buying the car from a newspaper classified ad or sight unseen and unproven, relying solely upon a few pictures and a description crafted by the owner on the Internet? Was the car ever in an accident? Was it a minor fender bender or is there potential structural damage that is not readily apparent on the surface? Are you willing to accept a warranty that may be limited or nonexistent? How has the vehicle traditionally performed in the past? Is it reliable?

After spending 20 years representing clients who were divorcing their spouses, it should not come as a surprise that one might become somewhat cynical about the benefits of the age-old institution of marriage. Does marriage work? Sure. Well, *sometimes.* About 50 percent of the time. Is marriage right for everyone? Of course not; in fact, there is just as good a chance that your marriage will fail as it will succeed.

Look at it this way: Let's say you spend months and months planning a fantastic vacation to the Bellagio Hotel in exciting Las Vegas. This trip is something you have envisioned in your mind for many years. You saw the hotel immortalized in the remake of *Ocean's Eleven.* The beautiful fountains, the nightlife, the opulent suites, the glamour, romance and excitement. When you arrive, proceed straight to the roulette wheel. Make sure that you go to the high-limit gaming area, because you are about to make a huge bet. Take everything you

> **LOVE IS AN IDEAL THING, MARRIAGE A REAL THING; A CONFUSION OF THE REAL WITH THE IDEAL NEVER GOES UNPUNISHED.**
>
> —*Johann Wolfgang Von Goethe*

own and really love and treasure (your children, company, bank accounts, cars, stock, jewelry, artwork, pensions and even your knives and forks) and tell the dealer that you want to bet it all. Everything. Red or black.

Once they spin the wheel, there is no turning back. In an instant, everything you love, own, worked for, sweated for and planned for is at risk. The ball is lively, energetic, and oh so unpredictable. The wheel spins fast at first, then slows down as time goes on. The seconds seem like hours, days, even years. Suddenly, you have the sense that things might not go as planned. The great idea that you had might not be so great after all. In fact, it might be an absolute disaster. The ball comes to rest, the wheel still spinning in the notch for the color black. Too bad you picked red. Welcome to the wonderful world of marriage, and its nasty next-door neighbor, divorce.

The biggest decision you will probably ever make in your life is the decision to marry. It is a time when you must reach deep into your soul and ask and answer many difficult questions, not only of yourself, but also of your prospective partner in life. Forget about all the effort and time that will be devoted to caterers, honeymoon plans and selecting china patterns. In the end, those issues have no meaning. Instead, focus on the questions that really will matter: what are the rules and regulations that will govern your relationship?

There should be a great deal of discussion about children, where you will live, and the end goals of your life together. Where do you see yourself in 10 years? In 20? What is the level of interaction going to be between the families? Are your values and morals consistent with each other? Have you been honest? Are you happy or just acting as if you are? Are there issues present in your relationship that you assume will be resolved *after* the marriage?

There are another set of issues to confront if either party already has a former spouse and children. These issues must be openly discussed and resolved before you take the final walk down the aisle. Once you are up at the altar, it is too late. Just a few words will forever change your life. For better, or for worse, but it will definitely change your life.

So what are the reasons that we get married? Well, they really do vary. Some people marry because society dictates that it is the right thing to do. You might marry because you want to have children and legitimize them, maybe even because you fell in love—though many people confuse infatuation with love. You might love certain things about a person, you might love how they look or things that they can provide for you, but that is not love. Love is only tested when things have totally turned upside down and everything is going wrong. When you place a major stressor on a marriage, then you test love. Moreover, more often than not, you find that the people were not really in love in the first place. It was just infatuation on steroids. Hence their divorce. Here's an example:

I was representing a young woman once in her divorce from a young man from a very wealthy, prominent family. They were extremely attractive, well spoken and highly educated, even though both were still in their early twenties. With their cooperation, they intelligently settled everything amicably. I only saw the husband once, when the parties had to make an appearance in court for their uncontested divorce hearing. After the quick hearing, I happened to walk out of court with them. The wife turned to the husband and said, "What are you doing now?" He said, "Well, I have a two o'clock meeting I need to get to." "Well, do you want to come over afterwards and f@%k?" she asked sweetly. He checked his watch. "Yeah, I could make it around five." "Great!" They smiled at each other, kissed and went their separate ways. I just shook my head. This was a perfect example of a couple who could not manage to live together. They liked to fornicate, but that did not a marriage make. You cannot base the foundation of your marriage on sexual attraction, which is much stronger when you are young. When you marry someone for their looks, nine times out of ten it will fail. *Looks are only a bonus.*

I represented another young, handsome man who was one of the heirs to a substantial interest in the stock of a major public corporation. He had left his wife and acquired a girlfriend since his separation, and he talked about his new girlfriend very lovingly. The young lady accompanied him to a meeting with me once and I was a little surprised, because she was not particularly attractive or sparkling. When we showed up at the final divorce hearing, I saw his estranged wife for the first time and was stunned. She was a knockout. I said to my client, "Look, I've got to ask you, what are you doing? Are you crazy?" He just looked at me and said, "*Beautiful* on the outside, *ugly* on the inside." That sums it up pretty well. If it is merely someone's physical beauty that attracts you, it is probably a mistake to base a marriage on it. Of course, there are plenty of people who are very attractive and very good people inside and out. However, we will not all always look the same way. Beauty should not be a defining factor in choosing someone with whom to spend the rest of your life. Look between their ears and into their heart—not at their anatomy.

---

## IF THERE IS ANY REALISTIC DETERRENT TO MARRIAGE, IT'S THE FACT THAT YOU CAN'T AFFORD DIVORCE.

—*Jack Nicholson*

---

Many people get married so they will not have to be alone, and then refuse to divorce for the exact same reason. When you have been married for a long time, you have presumably been completely out of the singles realm (or you may *not* have been, and thus understand divorce more clearly). People are afraid to reenter that world, but the truth is they do not really know *what* is out there. "No one will want me; I'm divorced and have two kids." I hear that all the time, and look, there are plenty of people out there who would be happy to marry someone with children. They do not necessarily want to go through the diapers-sleepless-nights-toddler stage, but would love to have a relationship with children, though they do not want their own. My father-in-law has a quote that sums up the bottom line: "*There's an ass for every seat.*" You can find someone out there. I do not accept the proposition that *anyone* has to be alone, or that anyone has to be married. However, the decision does require careful and prudent judgment.

Let's look at a prime example: Britney Spears. She apparently has no judgment, as she amply demonstrated in her first 55-hour marriage, her subsequent remarriage and hasty decision to perpetuate her genetic line. She is no different from Jennifer Lopez. If I remember correctly, it was only last year Marc Anthony was renewing his vows with his first wife. Then all of a sudden he's married to J. Lo? By the time this book is published, that situation may well have changed. These are people with serious issues. They do not have a clue what they are doing. Rich or poor, you can do whatever you want. Get divorced once, okay. Get divorced twice, still okay—things can certainly happen. Nevertheless, when you reach the third and fourth official dissolution of your marriage, you may want to take a hard look at yourself. There are probably fundamental relationship issues that are far from being resolved.

I have a friend who for discussion's sake I will call Valerie. Valerie comes from an affluent family and was married at a young age to someone who her family felt was the "right person." A few years into the marriage, her husband abandoned her and their two young daughters. The girls are now 16 and 18, doing extremely well, and Valerie remains a very attractive and intelligent professional who has never remarried. Has the experience made Valerie bitter towards marriage? No, just more realistic. Valerie's philosophy? "Men are better as rentals. The laws of economics tell you that when you buy something it depreciates. When a man thinks they own you, they do not take as good care of you as, say, a rental that you have to eventually return or risk forfeiture of a large security deposit. I just spin it around the other way. I treat men now like rentals—when I'm tired of them, I just turn them in and get another. No hassles of ownership, but almost all of the benefits."

So what is the key to the societal dilemma of securing a happy marriage? Clearly, there is no single answer, as the complexities of marriage present multiple conundrums. The motto of the Boy Scouts probably says it best: "Be prepared." But how can you prepare for something that you cannot predict or control? There may be several alternatives. Let's explore some, but first enjoy the following little essay on engagement rings.

# I WANT MY RING BACK!

For years and years, it has been ingrained in our consciousness that "a diamond is forever." We have been counseled how much we should spend on this symbol of commitment—the current marketing dictating that two months' salary is the correct amount. The problem is that while a diamond is forever, *marriages are not*. And sometimes, engagements are not either.

So let's assume that you have either received or presented a $20,000 engagement ring. Things are going along fine, but you have now read this book and decided that perhaps marriage is not right for you. You have decided to break off the engagement. Can you get the ring back, or do you have to give the ring back? It depends on where you live.

It used to be that engagement rings were considered gifts, completed at the time of delivery. But now, courts have divided their views into two separate camps, just like divorce: fault and no-fault. In fault jurisdictions, the courts look at who broke off the engagement and the reasons why. They then determine if you get the ring back. In no-fault jurisdictions, the courts do not examine the reasons why the engagement was terminated; they simply hold that if the marriage does not take place, the person presenting the ring gets the ring back.

I'm sure that half of the people reading this will find such a conclusion unfair. Well, get over it—the law is not always fair. The Supreme Court of Kansas examined this issue and their rationale for adopting a no-fault rule. Here's a little excerpt from *Heiman v. Parrish*, 262 Kan. 926, 942 P.2d 631 (1997):

*"What is fault or the unjustifiable calling off of an engagement? By way of illustration, should courts be asked to determine which of the following grounds for breaking an engagement is fault or justified? (1) The parties have nothing in common; (2) one party cannot stand prospective in-laws; (3) a minor child of one of the parties is hostile to and will not accept the other party; (4) an adult child of one of the parties will not accept the other party; (5) the parties' pets do not get along; (6) a party was too hasty in proposing or accepting the proposal; (7) the engagement was a rebound situation which is now regretted; (8) one party has untidy habits that irritate the other; or (9) the parties have religious differences. The list could be endless."*

I personally subscribe to the fault view, but I don't get to make the decisions. The safest bet is to still treat the ring like a gift. Once it is given, it is gone. That is, until a judge rules otherwise.

So now, back to the problem of marital breakups. Informed consent for marriage is an idea whose time has come. Every person contemplating marriage should be required to execute a legal consent before a marriage license is ever issued. Informed consent is a concept most of us are already aware of, even though we may not realize it. Whenever a patient undergoes elective surgery or enrolls in a clinical trial, they are asked to sign an informed consent acknowledgement. The informed consent generally includes a description of any benefits to the patient that may reasonably be expected from going through with the planned procedure—for example, the removal of your tonsils to alleviate throat infection. The perceived benefits of marriage, of course, are all that most people are thinking about as they make wedding plans. Nobody really considers what happens when the house of love collapses into poisonous rubble.

Some of the benefits of marriage may include the following: Formalizing a relationship with someone you consider your "soul mate." You might marry a person who understands you, loves you and sincerely wants to care for you for the rest of your life. Someone who is understanding and who accepts your faults as well as your positive attributes. You could marry someone who is a hard worker who wants to generously provide for you. Someone whom you can utterly trust and rely upon. Someone who picks you up when you are feeling terrible. Someone who is wonderfully helpful to your career and supportive of your goals. A person who introduces you to new people, places, things, hobbies and ideas that you never would have explored without them. Someone who opens your eyes and causes you to see the world a little differently. Someone who is a wonderful mother or father and lovingly raises your children. These are just some of the plusses, the *benefits* that most of us idealize before standing at the altar.

However, consider for a moment, if you will, what the rest of an informed consent for marriage would say, the part that describes the foreseeable, known or potential *risks*. You could be deceived and lied to. Your spouse may cheat on you. You could be lonely. You could be stolen from. You could be publicly humiliated and have your heart broken. Be physically or emotionally abused. Spend 25 years in a relationship and when it ends against your wishes, receive absolutely nothing from it. Wind up as a caretaker to someone stricken for many years with Alzheimer's or another equally devastating disease. You could discover that your spouse

> **EVERYTHING IS SWEETENED BY RISK**
> —*Alexander Smith (1830–1867)*

is gay. Or transsexual. You could have children. That is plenty in and of itself, but you could have children who are born handicapped or disabled. You could contract AIDS or another sexually transmitted disease through sex with your spouse and die. On the other hand, they might kill you some other way. And these are just a few of the obvious possible risks you take by entering into marriage.

An informed consent also typically states the extent to which the confidentiality of records concerning the procedure will be kept. The contract of marriage basically amounts to an absolute abandonment of all personal privacy. The most intimate details of your life are prone to disclosure. Anything you thought you and your spouse had done together, privately and consensually, may someday be out there for the world to see and judge. Just ask Jack Ryan, the Republican whose race for the Senate in Illinois was derailed by allegations of sexual indiscretions in divorce papers filed by his ex-wife, the actress Jeri Ryan.

Marriage is a completely different world. Forget that men are from Mars and women are from Venus. When it comes to marriage, humans become Klingons and strange aliens dominate the roost. The minute you say, "I do," all the rules change. Even if you have been living together for years and everything is peaceful, once you marry you unknowingly cross over into a completely new territory—*the twilight zone*. Because the consequences are different, the commitment level has changed, and the legal obligations and ramifications are most assuredly different, and many times unexpected. No matter how happy and loving you were before the nuptials were exchanged, when you get married, the handcuffs have been locked—on both of you. Only the judge has the key to set you free.

If there really was such a document you had to sign in order to get married, would so many people still want to do it? Would you? Of more concern, *did you?*

A second possible solution to the marriage/divorce explosion would be legislation amending the marital statutes to provide that no marriage license could be granted until each of the applicants had attained the minimum age of 25. Those who could not resist the urge to plunge into the marital pool could do so earlier, but only after completing a rigorous course in the realities of marriage. Remember when you were taking your driver's education class in high school? The culmination of the class was usually an appearance at the courthouse or before a grim representative of the Division of Motor Vehicles. There, the judge or DMV guru would extol the virtues of safe driving and grimly outline the dangers of your failure to do so. It usually ended with a gruesome video depicting rescue workers extracting victims from a car crash with the Jaws of Life. The heroic rescue professionals would tear off the roof or door of the mangled car and lifeless bodies would be extracted from the terrible situation that they themselves had caused. The theory behind the presentation and video was to shock us into compliance with the laws of safe driving. In other words, if we knew what a car crash *really* looked like, we might drive more prudently. We would avoid the hazards of the road. We would know the serious consequences of drinking and driving or of failing to pay attention while driving. Wouldn't it make sense to require the same type of warning to potential spouses?

---

ONLY ONE MARRIAGE I REGRET. I REMEMBER AFTER I GOT
THAT MARRIAGE LICENSE I WENT ACROSS FROM THE LICENSE
BUREAU TO A BAR FOR A DRINK. THE BARTENDER SAID, "WHAT
WILL YOU HAVE, SIR?" AND I SAID, "A GLASS OF HEMLOCK."
— *Ernest Hemingway*

---

Imagine the video of the young vibrant couple—happy, running through the field of daffodils. They are in love (or at least think they are), excited, without a care in the world. Their world is suffused with passion, romance and glee. Suddenly the relationship slips as it ineffectively navigates an unexpected curve on Lover's Lane. The smiling, laughing couple skids off the road of happiness and love and violently flips into the ditch of hatred, contempt and ridicule. They fall into the pit of marital discord. The rescue workers are no longer firefighters or emergency medical technicians—they are lawyers, child psychiatrists, social workers, accountants, actuaries and appraisers. Inevitably, either the driver or passenger is mutilated beyond recognition. Frequently, no one survives without serious injuries.

The rationale behind a minimum marital age is to provide a chronological checkpoint that forces everyone considering marriage to carefully examine the dramatic step being contemplated. It is hardly news that the cost of and effects of divorce on society are dramatic. Broken families and financial ruin. If checks and balances were in place, people would be less inclined to make quick and potentially costly decisions. Some states do provide for a brief waiting period between the time lapse of the application and actual issuance of the marriage license. Minnesota, Wisconsin and Ohio lead the country by making the marriage license applicants wait a whopping five days before taking the leap. Most other states have no waiting period. In Las Vegas, you do not even need to get out of your car. Just use one of their friendly drive-through chapels.

Think about it—doesn't it make perfect sense? Many marriages that deteriorate quickly do so because they occurred when both partners were very young. Certainly too young to understand the ramifications and obligations of marriage. Society has changed so dramatically in the past 50 years that you cannot compare the forties and fifties to the nineties and new millennium. In terms of family values, morals, sex—you name it, it has all changed. For better or for worse. For every couple that gets married right out of high school or college and manages to make it, another does not. Our government tolerates 50 percent failure rate in very few areas. Why should marriage be exempted?

Consider that no one in our nation can lawfully consume alcoholic beverages until they are 21 years old. The concept behind this prohibition is that young people are more likely to behave irresponsibly and may not have the maturity to handle the consequences of consuming alcohol. Notwithstanding these restrictions, some states allow marriage at incredibly early ages. You may be shocked to learn that the great state of Alabama allows marriage as early as age 14. But I am confident that you will be appalled to know that in Kansas and Massachusetts you can marry as early as age 12 with parental consent or permission of the court. Yes, marriage before you even become a teenager. Now if your parents or the court will not give you permission, you will have to wait until age 18. Unless you don't mind taking a trip down to our nation's favorite Southern state, Mississippi. There, children can marry without parental or judicial consent as early as age 15 (Sorry guys, you have to wait until age 17—only the girls can commit at age 15.)

Supporters of marriage at prepubescent ages are quick to point out that if you are old enough to serve in the military (which is highly dangerous), then

## MARRIAGE IS AN ADVENTURE, LIKE GOING TO WAR.
—*G.K. Chesteron*

you are old enough to get married (another highly dangerous activity). Let's take a young person, 18 or 19 years old, in the military, the Navy let's say. Now, I am in no way picking on the military—plenty of kids who are not in the military choose to marry young—I am just using them as an example. Young sailors, going away on military deployments for six or nine months at a time, want to preserve the girl (or boy) they may be dating, to make sure they will still be there when they get back. Marriage frequently seems like the best way to do this. Young enlisted military couples probably have one of the highest divorce rates around, because you are talking about a bunch of 18- and 19-year-olds, left to their own devices for six or eight months while their husbands or wives, who are a bunch of brave kids, are off doing their duty above the sea and below the sea. Eventually the deployed sailor discovers that there is a lot going on at home, above

## MARRIAGE IS LIKE A THREE RING CIRCUS: ENGAGEMENT RING WEDDING RING SUFFERING

and below the sheets. Consequently, these activities lead to the frequent and well-known "Dear John" letter and serious problems when they get home.

So whom do you blame for this problem? The philandering spouse at home or the kid who was merely trying to lock in the relationship because of his or her own insecurity? Perhaps we should blame our society for permitting the young couple to complicate their lives by even allowing them to make a commitment that they could not ever be reasonably expected to meet.

An age limit on marriage is not a cure-all, because although most people tend to become more mature with age, there are plenty of people who never grow up. They repeat the same pattern over and over again with multiple partners in serial marriages. Some people are total romantics and refuse to see anything negative about the person they are planning to marry. They simply will not acknowledge anything they do not want to see. You know the old saying, "Love is blind." Other masochists believe that they can change people. Take it from me, *you can rarely change anyone.* What you see is what you get. People generally are who they are. The die was cast long before you even knew your love existed. Like steel, it is cold and inflexible. It is what it is, and absent exposure to the most unusual circumstances or conditions, it will not change. There is a reason that Superman is a comic book character. In the make-believe world, you can bend steel.

Certainly, there are exceptions to this rule—people who exercise a great deal of effort and really devote themselves to change can do it over time, and someone trying their best is really about as much as you can expect in a normal situation. This type of behavioral modification usually requires a level of desire and commitment that can sometimes come from having been a party to a bad marriage. It requires an extremely mature and dedicated individual with enormous self-discipline and control. Often, it requires the participation of a mental health professional. However, if I were you, I would just head back to the Bellagio. The odds of winning there are much better.

Another possible solution lies in a concept we can call the "trial marriage." A television commercial was out recently where General Motors was advertising a 24-hour test-drive for all their cars. Would not a test-drive be an excellent idea for all marriages? If you actually drive the car for even a brief period, you certainly have more information as to whether or not the purchase makes sense or if the vehicle drives well. Shouldn't you take a test-drive before you decide on a car to drive for the rest of your life?

After representing hundreds of people who were divorcing, I advocate that people live together first. If you are living with someone, you have an enhanced appreciation of what married life may be about. It gives you a better idea of whether or not you may really want to make that commitment to that person. There is, of course, the inertia factor, where couples who are living together get married just because they are living together. That is the motivation behind the GM test-drive campaign. If you take a car home for a night, most people will purchase it. Yes, I am aware that there have been some studies that demonstrate that couples who live together before marriage are as likely, if not more likely, to be divorced. I still feel firm in my conviction.

The trial-marriage laws might work something like this: You and the one you think you love would register at the local courthouse for a marriage license. From that day forward, you would live together as husband and wife, just without any of the legal obligations or benefits. At the expiration of six months, either party would have the option to leave the relationship. On the other hand, if things are going well, the parties could reappear at court and have the license issued. After all, a *trial marriage* is better than a *divorce trial.*

The concept of a trial marriage is the kind of proposal people find controversial for religious and cultural reasons, but the world is changing. Living together without benefit of marriage may not be biblically kosher or approved by the Vatican, but let's be realistic and truthful. When you have Protestants and Episcopalians with gay priests and (in some states) the legitimization of same-sex marriages and unions, what is the fuss about living together? Whom does it harm? I have been told that some human beings actually have sex with their prospective spouse before they get married. Some people have also been rumored to have sex when they have no intention of getting married. Imagine that.

Everyone is dealt a certain hand in the marriage game, and you can choose to look at the cards however you want. Some people know how to accept the hand they are dealt, others bluff the whole game, and yet others throw the whole hand away. Some players try to turn half their cards in to get a better hand and wind up with an equally bad or worse deal. Some people have completely unrealistic expectations in the first place in terms of what they are going to be getting as part of the game.

As you can see from our discussion thus far, there are no simple answers to the quandary of protecting the rights of intelligent, informed citizens to marry versus stopping the foolhardy who clog our state judicial systems when the marital meltdown occurs. Marital preservation usually equates to marital prevention. Marriage is traditionally what we do in America, though there are those who feel that they do not need that piece of paper. Some have seen such bad marriages between their own parents that they can never bring themselves to commit to a marriage at all.

Today, more people are aware of the alarming divorce rate and what the two words "I do" can do. It is likely that at some point half the population in America will have a parent who is divorced, or was divorced. Certainly, a family member will have endured a divorce. There used to be a huge stigma about getting a divorce. Today, the successful marriage is the exception rather than the rule. Now it is all "Mom's house" and "Dad's house." I do not think children feel as much stigma or backlash about it (although it is still a traumatic experience for any child), because many of their friends' parents are divorced as well.

Of course, all of this leads us full circle. If you are going to look at divorce from a practical standpoint, how did you get into the situation of ever needing one or having to go through one? And it starts at the beginning: You cannot get divorced without having first gotten married. Why do people get divorced? Well, *they got married.*

---

I'M NOT WORRIED ABOUT TERRORISM; I WAS MARRIED
FOR TWO YEARS. WHAT ARE THEY GOING TO DO,
*SCARE ME?* [FOLLOWED BY A SCREAM...]

—*Sam Kinison*

---

# ADVICE TO REMEMBER

$ Do not marry before the age of 25. What's the rush? Meet as many people and experience as many relationships as possible before you consider making a lifelong commitment.

$ Over half of all first marriages fail—and that does include you.

$ Ask the hard questions of your potential spouse before you ask or answer any bigger questions.

$ Carefully examine the reasons why you desire to be married: getting out on your own or to have children are generally not valid reasons—and never, never marry for money.

$ Make sure that you and your potential spouse are on the same page about as many things as possible: values, interests, morals, politics, religion, sex, children, former spouses, housing, family—anything and everything should be discussed in advance.

$ Get the skeletons out of the closet—better to deal with those issues before rather than after the marriage.

$ Do yourself and your potential spouse a favor—do not try to act like someone you are not or hide something to entice them into getting married. Lay all of your cards on the table so that everyone gets a chance at a fair deal and game.

$ If you are engaged but have a feeling that the marriage may be a mistake, break it off—even if you are walking down the aisle. It is easier to break off an engagement than to dissolve a marriage.

$ If you have not experienced any difficult times with your potential spouse, you have not had the opportunity to see them at their worst—or maybe their best.

$ You must love talking and being with your prospective betrothed. If the marriage really works you are going to be with them forever—that's an awful lot of conversation and time together.

# GENE SIMMONS & SHANNON TWEED
*The Happiest Unmarried Couple in America??*

*In 1975, I was a typical 15-year-old kid living in my hometown of Virginia Beach, Virginia. One day, my brother David and I rode our bicycles to the local record store. As I thumbed through the album covers, I came across a cover with four guys in make-up with wild costumes, with explosions igniting behind them. It was on that day that I became a fan of KISS, an allegiance that continues up through this very day. Gene Simmons is the leader of the band, and is best known for his long tongue and fire-breathing antics. His sexual antics also blazed the tabloids, including his long-term relationships with two of music's leading divas, Cher and Diana Ross. When I was in college and law school, my brother and I worked part-time as drivers for a limousine company. KISS was scheduled for a concert and I thought that I would finally get a chance to meet Gene and the rest of the band. Unfortunately, the next morning, I had to take my law school Property exam, a crucial test for a first-year law student. My brother worked that night, met the band, and brought me back an autograph from Gene containing the following message: "Good luck in Law School, Mark." I framed the autograph and kept it with me throughout school and later in my office. Twenty-one years after my Property exam, I received a phone call from Gene on my birthday at the behest of my dear friend Nile Rodgers. I was later able to have dinner with Gene and introduce him at a gala for the Larry King Cardiac Foundation. However, nothing, and I mean nothing, was equal to spending three hours with Gene and Shannon Tweed (1982 Playboy Playmate of the Year and the obvious love of his life) in their palatial Beverly Hills estate, to discussing love, life and marriage. Even though they have never uttered the words "I do," there is no question in my mind that this is one of the happiest unmarried couples in America.*

*Here are some thoughts from Gene:*

I would not dream of giving anybody any tips about marriage, because even though I've never done it, observation seems to me to be a much better teacher than experience. From observing it all around me, marriage does seem to be the societal norm, but then so does divorce. A good relationship can seem as arbitrary as a roll of the dice.

I never wanted to get married. The first real relationship I ever had occurred when I was about 34 or 35, with Cher. Before that, I had never had girlfriends. It was just female companionship. I did not want anyone to tell me where to go or what to do. "Where are you going?" *Who wants to know?* I always thought the only woman who deserved an answer to that question was my mother, because she gave birth to me. Everybody else had to take their place in line, which forms to the left. Everyone wants dominion over you. Everyone wants to tell you where to go, what to do, how to think. Ultimately, they want you to answer to them.

My dad left my mother and me when I was a child. As a little boy, you do not really even know what that means until you grow up. As an adult, I thought long and hard about the nature of marriage. But at the heart of it, and I believe this is true for all men, fear of commitment has to do with the fact that we tend to wander. We make billions of sperm every day. A man cannot wake up and say, "I'm not making any sperm today." Your body does what it does.

I did not want to get married, because I did not want to become my father. I did not want to take an oath that I could not live up to. I did not want to leave, plain and simple. And I thought I would leave—anybody. During my first relationship I thought, "Hey, this is great. I can be with Cher, we can be together, she has kids, she has her own fame, she doesn't want anything from me…." It was totally comfortable. A good relationship. What more could I want?

I was very afraid of having kids. Again, what if I left? When Shannon and I were first dating, I told her, "I just want to be clear. I don't want to get married, and I don't want to have kids. If you want to get married and have kids, you should go find somebody else and we can be friends forever. If you want to have a relationship, fine, I'll be around; I'll be there, but no marriage and no kids." They call this full disclosure before the fact.

Women's magazines, especially, want to give you shortcuts to marital happiness. "10 Ways to Keep Him Interested!" "7 Dishes He'll Love!" "Why He Thinks that I Don't Know that He Forgot…." By the time you are done reading the article you want to hang yourself. Guys' magazines do not have articles like that. "10 Ways to Keep Her Interested?" We do not care if women are interested in what we are doing. *At all.* When a man goes into his garage and starts tooling around with whatever project he's in the middle of, he doesn't care if his girlfriend or wife comes with him or not.

Women, on the other hand, want you to be interested in what they are doing. They really do. Now, as a matter of fact, I want Shannon to be interested in what I'm doing—but Shannon is unlike other women. She does not play the game. From my vantage point (and I know that plenty of women will object to this), most women have a kind of cat-and-mouse mentality. Because men are stronger and bigger and seem to have more money and power, there's the chase. Even though I want him, I cannot let him get me right away. He has to really want me…that whole kind of chase-and-capture thing.

I was never really looking for a serious relationship. I had had two live-in relationships, but I was never interested in getting married. The last thing I was looking for when I went to the Playboy Mansion in 1984 was any kind of a relationship. I was dating Diana Ross, as a matter of fact. It happened to be my birthday, and I came to a party with two other girls, Miss January and Miss October let's call them, though I actually don't remember their names. Friendly girls. I was dressed in pajamas because that was theme of the party—Shakespeare's Midsummer Night's Dream. Most of the girls were lifted, separated and pointed in my general direction. Lots of butt floss, big hair, makeup, perfume…I mean, if you were blind and deaf and dumb you would still have known beautiful women surrounded you. You could smell them, feel the vibrations of their high heels. The ratio of women to men was at least 2:1, maybe 3:1.

I was just there to have a good time. I was in the middle of shooting a movie, the first one I had ever done, so I was really excited. We had a weekend off, and a couple of girls invited me to go to the Playboy Mansion. I had never been to the Mansion, so I called Diana and said, "Hey look, I'm going with some girls to the Mansion and we're going to have some fun." No big deal. It was quite a busy social evening, and then Shannon and her sister Tracy—both of whom were well over six feet in their stiletto heels— came over and were introduced to me. Both were quite devastating.

I went into that whole thing that men do, you know, it's instinct. Like a dog, when somebody comes close, you automatically go into it. Shannon was not impressed, I have to say. She was like, "Later for you," or whatever the phrase at the time was. "Groovy twenty-three skidoo" or something like that. I was not used to that reaction. Most of the time, when I went fishing, I caught one. So I went on with my evening. I started looking around the Mansion. I was in a hallway and saw a Dali painting on the wall. I bent over to take a closer look at the brushstrokes, and there were Shannon and Tracy, peering around the corner, checking me out. Shannon whistled and said something like "Nice ass!" It was charming. I did not even get a chance to reply; they just disappeared.

So I went around the corner after her and we actually sat down and started talking. In a very short time, due to my heightened state of excitement, she could actually guess my religion. Hey, they were silk pajamas! We were talking about the nature of happiness or some such thing, and Shannon naturally came up with something like "Let me show you the wine cellar." She went behind a bookcase, the wall opened up, and all of a sudden, we were going down this staircase to a little poolroom. I think she positioned herself on the pool table...or was it me? Maybe I positioned myself on the pool table. Really, whatever happened, I don't know why, but I didn't take advantage of her.

Shannon took me down into Hef's basement within an hour of meeting her! That was pretty straightforward. She was not your usual kind of woman. Before we left the room, she gave me her number, and I went home with the other girls. I didn't drive at that time; they were my ride—so I had to leave with them.

I could not wait to call the number. I called the next morning and some man answered. "Hi, I'm Gene Simmons and I'm calling for Shannon." This guy says, "You have wrong number," and hangs up. Son-of-a-bitch! I called right back. "Listen, I know she's there, she gave me this number, just put her on." "Wrong number!" He hangs up on me again. I was furious. I was staying at the Beverly Hills Hotel. I was alone in my room, watching television, thinking things over. I could not figure it out.

I had never been played like that. This girl was interested, then she walks away, then she comes back, then she gives me a number, but it's the wrong number...I had no idea what was going on. Out of the corner of my eye, I saw something sliding under the door leading to the hallway. I went over to pick it up and sure enough, it was a photo of Shannon Tweed. I looked on the back, where there was a very direct message. "I thought you were a man, if you have the balls to ask for my number you should call it..." something like that. "Next time you are in town, if you have the balls, call me." And she wrote the number down again. And I noticed that this time the number was almost the same, but off by one digit, the last number was different. So I called it up and sure enough, Shannon answered. "Hey, you gave me the wrong number!" I told her. "No I didn't!" she insisted. It took years and years before she would even admit she might possibly have given me the wrong number.

I decided I was going over to Greenblatt's to get some bagels and stuff and bring Shannon breakfast. I went into the deli and got the food but realized I had no money. I had to come back out to the limo driver and borrow some cash. It was embarrassing. Though I was having a relationship with Diana Ross back home, I was very interested in this girl. Shannon was living with her sister and another guy in an apartment. Her tall male roommate was walking out as I was walking in…I didn't know who he was; I didn't know if I was coming or going. Maybe it was some kind of a ménage? Maybe it was two sisters and one guy? I had no idea! And they were very matter-of-fact about it, nobody told me a thing.

I was really smitten. Shannon was leaving to shoot a movie that day, so it was a short visit. I went back to New York, and when she was through filming, she came to visit me in the city. I pulled out all the stops. I arranged candles around the bathtub, you name it. I have never done anything like that before or since in my life. I could not figure this girl out. I still cannot! She won't talk to me. The guy is supposed to tell the girl to be quiet! But every night she shushes me. If my hand wanders over, she smacks it. She barely wants anything to do with me! Maybe that is the secret.

What I know is that Shannon does not play the female game. I do not know if it is a school that women go to where they get together and decide, *How are we going to torture all the guys in our life?* How are we going to make sure that joke is true…. "Why do men die younger than their wives? Because they want to!" Let's torture them to the point that all they want to do is run off into the hills with their buddies, just dying to get away….

You know, that's something I'm just not interested in. I get that all the time, "Hey, let's go to Costa Rica…hang out, just the guys." I say, "OK, what will we do there?" "Oh just hang out with the guys, drink, you know…" I do not drink, and I do not want to hang out with guys. I keep asking Shannon, "Hey, want to go on a date? Why don't we go bowling?" "Naaah," she says, "I want to stay home. I'm happy here."

A man might say, "Do you love me?" A woman will say, "*How much* do you love me?" or, "When was the last time you said you loved me?" She needs to hear the words, the affirmation. I don't do it—*at least, not very often.* So many people live cartoon lives. A kind of paint-by-numbers version of happiness. It's all "sweetheart" and "honey…" I find the phrase "I love you" bizarre. I love my shoes. I love my popcorn. I love Diet Coke and I love you. How does the word even mean anything? I don't even tell my mother I love her a lot. I talk to her almost daily, yet I don't say the words. Hmmmm…why is this?

So, Shannon and I have yet to get married 21 years and two kids after we met. I still have no intention of getting married. The irony is that I never thought I wanted kids, yet when they were born, I cannot even talk about it without welling up. I cut the cord both times. I was (unfortunately for them) the first thing my son, and my daughter, saw. They are everything to me.

Now here's the strange thing. We live in Hollywood but there is no drinking, no smoking and no getting high. Nothing. We are really square. It looks wacky to everybody else, but *it works for us.*

35

# CHAPTER 2
# STAYING MARRIED

*"I'm having my wedding ring melted down into a bullet."*

All right, despite my most valiant efforts, my powers of persuasion have failed and you still want to go ahead with it. The first chapter of this book apparently did not deter you from the temptation of seeking wedded bliss. You have no doubt concluded that the 50 percent divorce rate applies to other people, not you. You have obviously surmised that you have found your soul mate and that you will love each other and live together for all your lives. You will grow old together and spend your last days in side-by-side rocking chairs surrounded by your grandchildren. Divorce will *never* touch you and your beloved.

Please—do me a favor. Finish this paragraph and then put the book down. Go directly to your bathroom, take off your clothes and take a nice cold shower, *for about fifteen minutes.* Maybe that will shock you back in to the real world.

Back from the shower already? On the other hand, maybe you are just simply too scared to face reality. Okay, let's try something else. After you are done reading this paragraph, close your eyes and imagine the most annoying habit, quality, characteristic or attribute that your prospective betrothed possesses. If you had to identify one aspect of their demeanor that you could change, this would be it. This has to be something that you really, really do not like about them. Do not try to lie to yourself about it. There is definitely something about your "soul mate" that you cannot stand. Figured it out? If not, it is for one of three reasons.

First, there may be multiple characteristics that have popped into your mind. If that is the case, do not proceed any further. You should not be considering marriage to this person. It will fail and you will be miserable. Run, and *run fast.*

The second reason that you may not have come up with that one annoying characteristic is that you are in denial. You are either so love-struck with your future other half that you cannot see the truth, or you do not want to see the truth. In either case, in the years ahead your vision will be corrected and the distinctive characteristic (or God forbid, characteristics) will become crystal clear. Then, you will wish that you had not been so blind.

The final reason that may have affected your inability to recognize this trait is that you really do not know the other person with whom you claim to be in love. Love really is not blind and it certainly is not deaf. Spend a little bit more time with them—I am sure that the trait will rear its ugly head.

If, on the other hand, you were candid in your brief reflection, if you have reached deep in your soul to extract the truth, you have identified that most distasteful trait. It may the fact that she has an annoying sneeze; he picks his nose when he thinks you aren't looking; she overzealously decorates for every holiday to the point that you think her real last name might be Griswold. For discussion purposes, let's pick another one—your potential spouse speaks loudly on the cell phone. Too loudly. And she does it everywhere. At home, in the car, in restaurants and on the plane before take-off. You have asked her repeatedly to reduce the volume of her voice to no avail, because it really irritates you—and everyone else. You do not like the looks and glares that you observe from those around you because of this noxious habit. But, hey, everything else about her is just *perfect*.

The average decibel (dBA) level of a normal conversation is about 60 dBA. Shouting in the ear is approximately 110 dBA, so we can just average out your sweetheart's cell phone voice at 85 dBA. Most otolaryngologists or

**MEDIAN DURATION OF A MARRIAGE: 7.2 YEARS**

occupational safety experts will tell you that prolonged exposure to sounds at a level of 85 dBA or more will result in some hearing loss. Exposure to sounds over 140 dBA on just one occasion can result in a complete loss of hearing. So how long do you think you will last before you stick pencils in your ears and go out of your mind? If you are an optimist, you are most likely thinking that after a while the habit will not be that bad or even bother you—that, in essence, you will become deaf to it. Well, maybe you are the type of person who likes someone screeching their nails down a chalkboard, too. In any event, my best guess is that you are mistaken, and the sound of her voice will intensify with every phone call during your marriage until the point that your brain implodes. The point of this diatribe is that if you were able to identify the annoying trait (and remember, it is not just cell phone volume—it could potentially be an innocent twitch, a strange laugh, a crazy sibling or lavish spending), do not ignore it. The annoyance you feel now will only *magnify* with the years, not *dissipate*. In some cases, it could intensify by the minute. A good rule of thumb (okay, I admit I just created this) is that with each year of marriage the conduct will become 5 percent more unbearable. Therefore, after 10 years, the problem is obviously 50 percent worse, and after 20 years, you will have probably taken your own life. After all, they do say until death do us part; unless you simply do not get married in the first place.

Some people feel that they can enjoy the benefits of marriage and still preserve a route to flee. The preferred method of choice for most to escape is a pre-nuptial agreement. A pre-nuptial agreement is a legal contract that governs the rights of the parties to a marriage in the proclaimed "unlikely event" of a separation or divorce (I always loved that recital in the opening paragraphs of the agreement). You want to marry, but are taking what you think is a wise precaution. Pre-nuptial agreements are generally enforceable if they are correctly drafted with full and complete financial disclosure and both parties are represented by independent competent legal counsel. It is my firm belief that if you are considering signing a pre-nuptial agreement, you should rethink who it is that you marrying. In fact, if you want your bride-to-be to sign a pre-nuptial agreement, you should not marry her or get married at all. The implicit message behind the request to have the agreement is the reality that you really do not think the marriage will last. Period.

> **THE SECRET TO A HAPPY MARRIAGE REMAINS A SECRET.**
>
> —*Henny Youngman*

I sometimes advised clients who wanted to sign a pre-nuptial agreement to videotape the "execution" of the agreement. In the example below, a successful Internet entrepreneur, burned by his first wife (of course not his fault), has decided to re-enter the marital pot of love, but with what I affectionately refer to as a marital prophylactic: a pre-nuptial agreement. The video would clearly depict his attorney asking questions (albeit an abbreviated version) of the young blond prospective wife:

"Why are you here today?"

"I'm here to sign my pre-nuptial agreement."

"Why are you doing this?"

"My fiancé and I have decided that we both want to do this. He had a bad experience with you-know-who."

"You mean his former wife?"

"Yeah. Her."

"Do you understand that you don't have to sign this agreement?"

"Yes, I understand that."

"Have you had the opportunity to speak to your lawyer about this agreement?"

"Yes."

"When are you getting married?"

"Next Saturday."

"Well, today is Wednesday. That means you are getting married in eleven days."

"I think. I am not very good at math."

"Do you feel that that you have had enough time to review the agreement?"

"Yes."

"Do you understand all the terms of this agreement?"

"Yes."

"Okay, let's go over one point. Do you understand that this agreement stipulates that you will not receive any alimony or support if your marriage terminates before you have been married for a period of ten years?"

"Well, that won't happen."

"I hope that it will not. But if it does, do you understand that this agreement stipulates that you will not receive any alimony or support if your marriage terminates before you have been married for a period of ten years?"

"Yes, I understand."

"Do you understand that you will receive no alimony or support if your marriage ends after nine years and fifty-one weeks and six days?"

"Yes, I do."

*"Do you think that is fair?"*

"Yes, I think it's fair that I will receive no alimony or support if my marriage ends after nine years and fifty-one weeks and six days."

If you obtain a scenario like this on videotape, it is very difficult to challenge the agreement. The key issues are the timing of the execution of the agreement, the full disclosure of all assets and liabilities and the representation of both parties by their own independent counsel. While anyone considering marital harmony should be aware of the best way to proceed with a pre-nuptial, I would again caution you that if you feel you need a pre-nuptial, you will most likely join the army of the divorced in the not-too-distant future.

Bear in mind that you cannot govern what a court will do with respect to children in a pre-nuptial agreement. It is probably a concept designed to demonstrate as early as possible that you may not be able to control your own children. You can offer to provide support or benefits in excess of what a court might order, but you cannot limit a court in terms of what they eventually will award. For instance, you cannot provide, "In the event of a divorce, we agree that I will be the primary caretaker of any children." This is impossible; you are talking about children who have yet to be born and such language attempts to remove from the court the ability to decide how the best interests of these children might be served. Such a provision would never be enforced; however, a stipulation like "I agree that if we have children, I will pay for their college education" would generally be enforceable.

---

AT A COCKTAIL PARTY, ONE WOMAN SAID TO ANOTHER,
"AREN'T YOU WEARING YOUR WEDDING RING
ON THE WRONG FINGER?"
THE OTHER REPLIED,
"YES I AM; I MARRIED THE WRONG MAN."

---

Obviously, I do not know your own personal reasons for reading this book. You may be married, single or divorced. Male, female or maybe uncertain about that. Perhaps you purchased the book yourself or received it as a gift. No matter under which category your gender or marital status is classified, most people just want to be content in their relationship. Content does not mean perfect. It does not mean bored. It means being comfortable with your partner, at ease. So what is the cure for marital "dis-ease"?

Perhaps because of all the divorce work I have done, I observe and internally critique couples all the time. It is a very bad and judgmental habit, but one you should try. Whenever I am out, I examine how couples interact with each other: in restaurants, walking down the street, at parties, on the beach, in the airport or shopping together. You can almost instantly get a sense of the happiness, stress or malaise of the relationship. You can get a feeling of the content versus discontent. I like to speculate on which couples are happily married and which are not. It is usually pretty easy to tell those who appear to be sentenced to the marital mortuary; the walking cadavers are a dead giveaway.

After reflecting upon years of practicing divorce law, I would have to conclude that it all boils down to a simple rule: you have to know when to tune in and when to tune out. Know what battles to *fight*, and when to *surrender*. You need to let some things slide. Tell yourself that some things were not meant to be interpreted the way they sounded, that your spouse or mate was just having an emotional reaction. I always told clients that during cross-examination there may come moments when they may be confronted with a tense situation, like a question that feels like someone taking and landing a punch on you. My partner, criminal defense legend Bob Shapiro, is an avid boxer. Bob agrees that if you are tense when a punch lands, it will hurt much more than if you relax and try to let it slide off of you. The same rule that boxers follow works for cross-examination. And remember, there is usually no ring in which more punches are thrown than in the arena of marriage. You have a choice in the way you choose to

A SUCCESSFUL MARRIAGE IS
AN EDIFICE THAT MUST BE
REBUILT EVERY DAY.

—*Andre Maurois*

respond to what is said. If I were cross-examining you and I thought I had hit you, but achieved no response (you just let the jab bounce off), it would just not have the same effect.

Likewise, in a relationship you need to be able to identify whether the messages are sent to hurt or to maybe help. I used to hear clients (usually from unhappy husbands) comment about the weight of their spouse. I found such comments somewhat surprising, given that the man usually offering the criticism could have skipped quite a few carbs himself. The spouse would usually have said something heartfelt like "Boy, putting on a few pounds there, aren't you?" Is a man who says that being mean or just plain stupid? He is probably not uncaring; he just lacks any common sense, a problem which I have found that most of us men suffer from. There is a big difference between "Putting on a few pounds there, aren't you?" and the more caustic "You fat slob!" The latter is when you know you have a problem—it is a long way from, "Gee, honey, you're having a little more dessert?" What is the man really trying to say? Maybe nothing, and you should ignore it, tune it out, if you will. But maybe he is really trying to say something, and you should pay attention. Have you put on a few pounds? Is your husband trying to "delicately" send you a message when he says "Shirley, let's not order dessert." Yes, it could mean on this particular evening he is full after his meal; but he could be remarking on a pattern of your constantly ingesting fattening foods as a veiled comment on your weight. It is all a matter of tuning in and tuning out what is being said to you, and interpreting it correctly. Without killing the insensitive moron.

In the best of all possible worlds, this should become a natural process. Then again, evolution took millions of years. I believe that people try to communicate concerns to their partners most of the time. Many people commence the communication in the least offensive way to hopefully avoid hurting feelings. Just because someone is phrasing something nicely does not mean that they do not want their discreet message to result in a behavioral change. Something as minor as "Honey, I really don't want to go over to their house again tonight" might be a very important statement. Maybe your wife is trying to say that she does not like the way a neighbor was talking to her or flirting with her. Knowing how to listen and responding appropriately to what you have heard is a large key to a successful marriage. However, most of us are not particularly good listeners.

I find myself asking more and more of my friends what makes their relationship work. I asked comedic great Don Rickles for the secret of his almost 50-year marriage to his wonderful wife Barbara. He told me it was very simple: *"I do whatever she tells me."* Now Don was only being facetious (or was he?), but his comment still bares truth. What works for one relationship will fail miserably for another. Recently my wife and I had dinner with our friends Rick and Amy Levy in Beverly Hills. Rick is the Chief Operating Officer of one of the largest talent and literary agencies in the world, International Creative Management (ICM). Amy is a dynamic woman, but has sacrificed her own career to raise their two handsome sons. Rick and Amy always seem so happy together. So I asked Rick, What is the secret to your successful marriage? Without even a blink of the eye, he answered: *"Prozac."* While Rick was just cracking a joke (I think), I am sure that there are numerous couples who can only stay together with medication. I actually know one woman who has been putting Prozac in her husband's orange juice every morning without his knowledge. I am not condoning her actions, but it seems to work for them—or at least for her.

One last shameless "name-drop": I was at lunch today with two other very dear friends, music impresario Nile Rodgers and his partner of nine years, Nancy Hunt. Nile was voted by *Billboard* magazine to be the best music producer of all time. His music is familiar to all of us, whether it is from his roots as the founder and brilliant guitarist of disco super-group *Chic* (*Le Freak; Good Times; Everybody Dance*) or the songs he penned like *We Are Family* or those he produced for Madonna, David Bowie, Diana Ross and countless others. Nancy works full time as the President of the We are Family Foundation, a charity they created to battle intolerance, since in essence, we are all family. In the case of Nile and Nancy, they live together in Manhattan and Connecticut, but are not married. Their relationship is mutually exclusive and from my perspective, they are extremely content. Therefore, I had to ask the question: "Why don't you guys get married?" The reaction I received from both was of perplexed disillusionment. "Married?" Nile said. "Why? We're happy." *Oh well…*

Nile and Nancy are both extremely intelligent and articulate individuals. When I pressed them for a possible reason to marry, they could only come up with two plausible scenarios: if they had children and for estate planning purposes. Moreover, as Nile pointed out, they could accomplish both of these prospective objectives without the necessity of a pronouncement from the state as to the validity of their relationship. Nile put it in perspective through analogizing it to his recording contracts. "When I write a song, or record or produce an album, I am not thinking about the responsibilities that I have under my agreement. I put myself 1000 percent into the project to make the best music possible. Not just for me, but for the artist I am working with and for all of our fans who expect nothing less." Nile then went on to compare marriage to that very concept. "If people just put their best into their relationship without worrying about the legal aspects, the music they made would certainly be much better." A point well taken.

So let's see—how is the recording session going so far? If you cannot sit and talk with your spouse or prospective lifelong mate, if you cannot carry on an enjoyable conversation now and truly enjoy their company, it is a huge sign of trouble. *Do not marry him or her.* In the early stages of any relationship, you usually have tremendous sexual attraction. As people age and the relationship matures, for many the sexual ardor fades. In addition, if you are not careful, it can disappear completely. If you did a graph of a couple's sexual activity over the years, it goes down as time passes. Naturally so, because your life changes. Your body ages, work and child care demands arise (as opposed to your libido), you grow more secure in your relationship and you do not have that need to mark your territory, if you will. Those borders have hopefully been established. I think couples can experience sustained love, but the ways in which you express it change. Hypothetically, it is certainly possible to be just as much in love 30 years later as the day you uttered your vows, but a couple may not express that love as much through sexual activity. It is not as necessary; it becomes more of a spontaneous activity. Sexual passion is not the be-all and end-all of a marriage—it cannot be. Such a foundation would be doomed to fail. What excites you evolves.

The best example of this occurred today at that same lunch with Nile and Nancy. Nile was as giddy as a teenager in love when he learned that he could access his Delta Sky Miles account over the Internet. This from a guy with over 40 platinum albums. What excites you evolves. *Sorry, Nile...*

You do not need to have constant sex to be a happily married couple. You can enjoy spending time together traveling, visiting grandchildren or playing a round of golf. Think of all the couples in America today who wake up each morning, roll over and see the person in bed next to them and feel so let down and unhappy. I honestly believe that one of the reasons for the explosion of Viagra is all of those guys looking over at their wives and realizing, This is the only way I can even get myself halfway excited about this. I am suggesting that Viagra is addressing not merely a physical problem, but an emotional problem. Men need a physical booster because they are so emotionally unattached (Ladies—don't panic—I understand similar pharmaceutical relief is on the way.) Certainly there are multiple instances where sexual dysfunction is attendant to physical problems, age or ill health, but I do believe that there is a whole segment of the male population who use Viagra or similar drugs because this is the only way they can get interested enough to do it. In the same way that some people need to have a few drinks, some men think, "I'd better take a shot before I go attempt this."

If you have your eyes even halfway open, you can see when your marriage is heading south. You do not need a psychic to predict that misfortune. So many people say everything was fine until this bombshell dropped into the middle of their perfect life and marriage. However, that is very rarely true; and as for divorce, it was my job to point out those things most certainly had not all been just fine. Didn't you notice that sexual relations were falling off? That communication between the two of you was more distant? That she was staying later and later at the office? That he seemed to spend an inordinate amount of time at the gym or health club? That she was out of town more and more often? That he would unexpectedly call and say he couldn't make it home for dinner that night? That she spent more and more time on the computer, and when you walked into the room she scrambled to hide what she was typing or looking at?

If you are not paying attention and not listening, sure, I guess it could *seem* sudden. If you are not talking to your spouse and staying emotionally engaged, saying, "Hey, how are you doing, how are you feeling, what's going on with you?" Maybe you stop saying "I love you" every day. Some people are not as expressive as others are, of course, but you cannot convince me that there are not sufficient warning signs out there. Either you do not want to see these warning signs and willfully turn away from them, or you are just completely blind to them. Because more likely than not, your spouse will give you plenty of warning signs. It can be their disposition: maybe they become angry and snap at you. Alternatively, they become depressed and withdraw from you. They might suddenly become much more interested in the children, to the point of excluding you. The signs are there, if you are willing to read them. *Do not be myopic.*

Marriage is a fragile institution. It is delicate and it needs constant attention and nurturing. If it does not get it, I know where it will end up. In a lawyer's office. What is that old saying—if you ignore your teeth, they will go away? Same with your marriage. If you are already married, then the best thing you can do is take every possible means and measure to make your marriage content and satisfying. If that does not work, then you should try to dissolve the marriage with the same care you took to create it.

In my many years of practice, numerous justifications could be found by each party for exiting the marriage. However, in my personal experience, the straw that always seemed to break the camel's back was the violation of the commandment that philanderes love to hate: *Thou shall not commit adultery.*

*A dietician was addressing a large audience in Annapolis: "The material we put into our stomach is enough to have killed most of us sitting here, years ago. Red meat is awful. Soft drinks erode your stomach lining. Chinese food is loaded with MSG. Vegetables can be disastrous to some and none of us realize the long-term harm caused by the germs in our drinking water. However, there is one thing that is the most dangerous of all, and we all have eaten or will eat it. Can anyone here tell me what food it is that causes the most grief and suffering for years after eating it?"*

*A 75-year-old man in the front row stood up and said, "Wedding cake."*

# ADVICE TO REMEMBER

$ Only marry someone you really truly know you should marry. If the advice of family and friends is not to get married, pay very close attention—if the advice is to get married, be extremely suspicious.

$ If you have present or future wealth to protect, you must raise the subject of a prenuptial agreement on your first date. Mention a friend who went through a terrible divorce and tell your date that you would never consider marriage without one—repeat this story every four dates until the agreement is signed.

$ Alternatively, if you are considering a prenuptial agreement, reconsider the marriage. Somewhere in your mind you may really believe that the marriage will not last—so why are you getting married?

$ Investigate your intended betrothed—you can do it yourself or online, or hire a private investigator to do it. Don't feel guilty about it—few people buy a house without a home inspection, and marriage is definitely an "as is" transaction. After you get back the report, share it with your beloved for a lively discussion.

$ You will almost never change the things that you do not like about your potential spouse—they will only get worse.

$ Marriage takes incredible patience and listening skills—if your partner is not listening to you now, don't expect them to later.

$ Marriage takes incredible compromise—if you like traveling on one-way streets, take a different route.

$ It is hard work being married, and as the old adage goes, you will only get out of it what you put into it.

$ If you sense trouble in your marriage, treat it like gangrene and treat it immediately—divorce is no different from an un-anaesthetized amputation.

# LEWIS BLACK
*The Black Humor of Relationships*

*My wife and I first saw Lewis Black many years ago when he performed at a charity benefit for Children's National Medical Center in Washington, DC. It was a painful experience for me as his comedy literally tested the endurance of my bladder control. In the years that followed, we got to know and love Lewis. He is a staple on Comedy Central and HBO. In my opinion, and that of many of my closest demented friends, he is the funniest man on the planet, and certainly is in the same league as Robin Williams or George Carlin with the legendary caustic undertones of the great Don Rickles. Lewis never talks about relationships in his act, and it took some coaxing to get him to open up. I started out by asking Lewis if he had ever been in a really serious relationship. His answer? "Only with you, Mark." Here is what else Lewis thinks about relationships, marriage and divorce.*

I actually got married once, but I don't talk about it, because it's not that funny. I got married in 1974, when I was 26 years old. It lasted about 15 minutes. Literally, we were married in October of 1974 and I was essentially out of there by November of 1975. My wife was a compulsive liar, which made things difficult. We lost touch after our divorce…I believe she works in PR now…she at least found a profession where she can lie during the day and get paid for it.

This youthful experience certainly affected my views on love and marriage…just ask my therapist. We seem to come back to it a lot in conversation. How people do not live together before they get married is beyond me. I do not understand it; it makes no sense to me. The concept of two virgins getting married is, I think, at this point in time—I don't even have a word for it. Ludicrous. I don't get it. Two virgins getting married—it's like the set-up to a really bad joke.

The old-fashioned idea is that you meet someone and court them, and then you finally sleep together after a long time, once you really get to know them. I did that with a woman I had met in my mid-thirties. I had decided that this time I was going to go through an actual courtship process, which I hadn't before, to see if that worked. We had sex after we had been dating for eight months or a year. And as soon as we consummated the relationship, the dark side in her came out. Now, I don't know if I destroyed her by injection or what, but this whole other side of her literally came out. This completely depressed personality arose.

When we moved in together and were spending more time with each other, this other personality became more and more shockingly obvious. Now I do not think it was me bringing this out in her; it was her condition, just the way she was. But if I had done what I was supposed to do, get married without living together, I would have been blindsided. You know, when you are dating somebody, courting time, you can keep a lot hidden. The girl I am talking about certainly came out to play courtship time. I had no idea what was lurking in the background until we lived together.

Men hide things too, of course, during courtship. Most men hide that fact that they are, in essence, not monogamous creatures. Most men do not find that certain someone who relieves them of the insatiable desire to have sex with many women. I think that's a real part of the problem with marriage—that horny little gene that all men seem to have, but women seem to be missing. It seems to be more open and loose with this latest generation, but relationships for women still always skew back to marriage, and not sex for the sake of sex.

My parents have been married forever, but that's because they're both deaf. Neither of them can hear each other—I am pretty convinced that hearing loss is the key to a long happy marriage. If your hearing starts to go around year 25, then the next 25 will be easy. Both my parents have massive hearing aids, so they can turn them on and off. I think really what they hear is just a background hum, which must be kind of soothing. They don't really hear the words. And they are quite happily married, seriously. I also have plenty of friends who are in happy marriages. But that whole statistic that half of all marriages end in divorce? That statistic is certainly borne out in the case of my friends. About half my friends who married ended up in very stable, happy marriages, the other half wound up divorcing. Some who got divorced did go on to have happy second marriages.

The institution of marriage is great...when I see a wedding, I get it on a certain level, but I think after what I have seen and experienced...so many people seem to say it worked great for two years, or four years, or seven years. If half the people are getting divorced—and it's not just due to the fact that marriage is really hard and people are lazy and all that stuff—I believe people should face the fact that many relationships have a shelf life. You get two people together, they meet at a certain point in time, it's really great for them for a while, then comes a point that they've outgrown each other and go on.

This country is so obsessed with the idea that marriage has to be between a man and a woman that the gay and lesbian community is not allowed to marry. The sanctity of marriage is so important that only a man and a woman can do it. Even though only half of us can manage to do it properly, we heterosexuals will tell you what marriage is and who can do it. There is a quality of desperation in the air when the President of the United States has to say there needs to be a constitutional amendment to define marriage. Most people know, commonsense-wise, what marriage is in essence, because most of us marry people of the opposite sex. But to make that a hard-and-fast rule? Why, because the Bible says so? Those rules were established back in the time that people were 10 years away from being baboons. They had to come up with that rule—otherwise people would have married animals. My view is that wherever you find love, go for it. There are people living with two or three large dogs in studio apartments in New York City and *nobody—NOBODY—* is asking *any* questions...

# CHAPTER 3

# ADULTERY

Adultery. The Merriam-Webster dictionary defines the act as follows: "Voluntary sexual intercourse between a married man and someone other than his wife or between a married woman and someone other than her husband." It would seem to be a pretty straightforward definition of an activity that is probably second in frequency only to the act of marriage itself—and one that leaves out all the broken hearts and financial consequences that come along with it. As an act, adultery is no laughing matter—just ask anyone who has endured his or her spouse's indiscretion. It can end a marriage in a hurry. Even if it does not, it can also cause lasting harm and have a tremendous effect on all parties associated with the act: the spouses, the third party or parties involved, and on their children.

## DIVORCE IS ALWAYS AN OPTION, *NOT* MURDER!

*—Sharon Rocha, mother of Laci Peterson*

A lack of being in love, combined with stressors in the marital union, workplace and just plain old boredom in daily life, will often precipitate the involvement of a third party in the marital relationship. In other words, people cheat on their spouses. They commit adultery. All the time. Every day. Every hour and every minute. As you read these words, there are thousands of people cheating on their spouse. Somewhere in your city or town, probably right in your very own neighborhood, a wife just had an orgasm, and her husband was not there and does not even know about it. For every dedicated wife at home making school lunches and supervising homework or dad playing T-ball with the children, there is a spouse out stealing the bases and scoring a home run of their own. Someone you know is probably cheating *right now.*

Perhaps you just shifted in your chair or shot a quick glance over at your spouse lying next to you. Quick, look away. Do not let them see the title of this chapter. Whew, they're not paying any attention—What else is new? Feeling guilty about something? If you are not, you are probably not married, are recently married, are lying, or are a true marital anomaly. On the other hand, maybe you have convinced yourself that you really did not commit adultery or cheat—the classic *"I did not have sex with that woman."*

Adultery is an unnerving concept with a variety of degrees. President Carter caused a press tornado just for admitting to having *lust* in his heart, yet President Clinton found new uses for Cuba's most famous agricultural product and managed to leave office with a majority of the population wishing he could be reelected. Societal tolerance of marital misconduct seems to remain in a state of flux, although every survey that I have ever seen seems to indicate that most citizens feel that adultery is wrong. Yet it keeps happening every minute of every day.

There have been numerous books, studies and dissertations written by individuals far more intelligent than me that attempt to espouse the reasons why adultery occurs. My own personal theory? People who commit adultery generally fall into one of two categories: first, they are not "content" and do not care if their marriage falls apart; second, they are not "content" and do care if their marriage falls apart. Of course, in both circumstances the marriage has already actually fallen apart, at least for one of the parties. "Until death do us part" has become "until caught in the act."

The marital infidelities of your spouse will help to pay for the college education of the children—the children of your lawyer, accountant, investigator and therapist, that is. The revelation or discovery that a spouse is cheating provides a bonanza for the divorce industry, and a stake through the heart of one or more individuals. As noted earlier, the degree of marital infidelity can vary based upon interpretation of the events in question. Sometimes there are no witnesses to the marital indiscretion except for the parties themselves. Other times, the parties think they are alone but are wrong. In the case of the former, proof of the adulterous conduct is obviously more difficult. In the latter case, you have a steep mountain to climb.

In most jurisdictions, you only need to establish some sign of affection between the parties in question combined with an opportunity for marital misconduct. Not to beat a dead horse, but visualize President Clinton and Monica Lewinsky. Remember the video where the president is greeting the crowd and Monica is one of the adoring admirers? When the president sees her, he gives her a great big hug. You may also remember that the brave officers of the United States Secret Service were compelled by court order to provide statements under oath as to the whereabouts of the president in the White House during certain late hours. Of course, it

> EIGHTY PERCENT OF MARRIED
> MEN CHEAT IN AMERICA.
> THE REST CHEAT IN EUROPE.
>
> —*Jackie Mason*

came as no surprise to anyone (except perhaps poor Hillary and Chelsea) that the President and the woman with the apparent aversion to dry cleaning had spent multiple sessions alone in the Oval Office. There you had it—opportunity and the signs of affection. Adultery.

In the early days of my practice, it was rare that you actually caught people *in flagrante delicto*. Those were the days before caller ID, cell phones and e-mail made catching a cheating spouse easy. I remember the first time I saw still photographs of a couple caught in the act. Our client was the husband, and he suspected his young wife, a nurse, of bringing the term "house call" to a new level with the doctor who employed her. These house calls, her husband suspected, took place at their own home. Our client lived in a luxury three-level townhouse typical of those found throughout the suburbs of Washington, DC. We told our client to tell his wife that he was going to go out of town on a specific day for a business trip. Since the husband traveled from time to time, it did not arouse any suspicion on the part of the wife. The wife was to be aroused later.

On the day of the husband's alleged trip, the wife went to work as usual. After she left, the private investigators met the husband back at the house. The hope was that the wife would come back to the house later in the day with her favorite physician and the investigators would be able to capture them on film right there in the house. Unbelievably, their hope was realized with amazing clarity. The wife and her doctor came into the house and went downstairs, just as the husband suspected she would. There, they unfolded the sofa bed and quicker than you can say "gynecologist" were passionately engaged in conducting a mutually thorough examination of the anatomy of the other.

Now, anyone who has ever seen the Alfred Hitchcock thriller *Psycho* knows that you always need to look out for who or what is behind the shower curtain. After allowing the passionate ardor to resonate to a volume clearly audible to the neighbors, the investigators made their move. They busted out from the shower in the lower level and started snapping pictures.

Imagine the type of still photographs that you see of a model walking down the fashion runway. The quick sequences. Imagine the good doctor's head buried in between the lower appendages of the nurse. As his head withdraws in the next six photographs you can see the emotions of shock, fear, embarrassment and anger–no, hatred. Yes, the case settled, but not how you may think—the couple reconciled and the photographs were destroyed. But not the negatives. (Trust only goes so far under these circumstances.)

The traditional line of thought in cases of adultery is that you never have your client admit to anything. Ever. After all, adultery is a crime in many jurisdictions. So are sodomy, buggery and fellatio. So what if the client is in the middle of fornicating with his or her friend and the spouse unexpectedly walks in and catches them red-handed? The answer— "*It wasn't me.*" "But I just saw you!" or "Look at these pictures!" "*It wasn't me.*" Little did I know that almost twenty years later hip-hop artist Shaggy would turn this credo into a huge hit (and a song that I really like — it has great rhythm). Even more ironic is the fact that I first saw this song performed on television for a tribute to Michael Jackson. Think about the title in that context as well. In January 2001, *It Wasn't Me* topped the *Billboard* Hot 100 for two weeks, the Top 40 Tracks chart for four weeks, and the Hot 100 Airplay chart for five weeks. It also hit #1 in the United Kingdom for a week and was nominated for a Grammy Award, so either the *beat* or the *lyrics* were resonating with a whole lot of people.

Though certainly emotionally devastating, if your spouse is cheating, divorce is not your only option. There are other solutions to explore. Is one lapse of judgment on the part of your husband or wife, who went out and did something stupid one night, enough of a reason to throw away 15 years? Alternatively, are you big enough to accept the fact that he or she is human, vulnerable, makes mistakes, but still loves you and wants to be with you? No question, it is an extremely bitter pill to swallow, and the side effects are devastatingly painful. Nevertheless, maybe it is an easier pill to swallow overall than destroying a long-term relationship over one incident of poor judgment. I used to tell people that it was not a decision I could make for them, but it was something they needed to come to peace with in their own mind.

Upon reflection, many people swallowed this pill, however bitter it may have been. Some even swallowed two. However, when they got to three and four pills, they tended to overdose and say, "I've had enough of this medicine…it doesn't taste very good and it's hard to keep down." At that point, I could certainly understand their desire to end the marriage. If your spouse is not willing to make certain commitments to you, then it is time to move on and find someone who is willing to play by your rules. And everybody's rules differ. *Drastically.*

People tend to stereotype the definition of a marriage and think of it in only a certain way. There are couples who are OK with their partner seeking sexual relationships with other people. Sometimes they do it together — with other married couples. On a recent trip to Las Vegas, I was lucky to get the opportunity to "ride along" with a great police officer, Scott Majewski. All I wanted to do was to watch what it was like to be a law enforcement officer up close and personal. Maybe even go fast with the lights and siren on. Well, we did that plenty, given a Friday night in Las Vegas.

---

NEVER TELL. NOT IF YOU LOVE YOUR WIFE…IN FACT,
IF YOUR LADY WALKS IN ON YOU DENY IT. YEAH.
JUST FLAT OUT AND SHE'LL BELIEVE IT: "I'M TELLIN' YA.
THIS CHICK CAME DOWNSTAIRS WITH A SIGN AROUND
HER NECK 'LAY ON TOP OF ME OR I'LL DIE.'
I DIDN'T KNOW WHAT I WAS GONNA DO."
—*Lenny Bruce*

---

What I ended up seeing that evening even shocked me. I had no idea what a swingers club was and was stunned to learn that people pay a cover charge to "come" in these places and have sex with each other, while their spouse watches or engages in sex with someone else. There was even a room where you could urinate on each other if the "urge" hit you. How about a gynecological examination table where your wife can be strapped down and all of your friends can play doctor? I saw married couples in a transvestite strip club laughing and having a great time. As much as I try, I cannot erase the image of the stripper with the large breasts and bulge in his pants to match. When we exited this establishment, Scott was nice enough to drop me back off at my hotel so I could take a shower. I almost ended up in the hospital after attempting to scrub off my entire epidermis.

Certain couples enjoy these activities, and that is perfectly fine by me. If both parties are on the same page, they probably have a great marriage, even though it may seem different to you or me. The typical idea of marriage—a man and a woman who do not engage in sex outside of their marriage—is not set in stone. What works for me might not work for you, and vice-versa. Everyone's boundaries and limitations are unique. Remember "There's an ass for every seat?"

The desire to seek sex outside of marriage has been a constant since the beginning of time. Adultery is one of the most ancient societal concepts linked to the institution of marriage itself. Americans are puritanical in their views; there are many aspects of European living that have not immigrated to our shores. The idea of siestas in the middle of the day and long vacations and four-hour lunches—none of that has made its way into our culture. Personal grooming and hygiene are very different in Europe, where women might not shave their legs, and many men do not use deodorant. The whole concept of paramours and mistresses just never caught on here, but it is alive, well, and tolerated in many other cultures.

On the other hand, numerous cultures have policies that bear no tolerance of adulterous conduct, although often these societal mores are not gender-neutral. Certainly people are less surprised when men cheat as opposed to women, and they tend to get off more lightly too. Some men and many women, even today, pay with their lives for cheating. In other cultures, women have traditionally—and recently—been stoned to death for committing adultery.

Most present-day married American couples have a zero-tolerance policy towards infidelity. (Remember Lorena Bobbitt?) Many academics have suggested that in trying to live up to the American marriage ideal we are attempting to suppress an inherent biological drive. That monogamy is unnatural. Maybe it is wrong to suppress feelings of desire for other partners during marriage. It is certainly a fact that both men and women cheat—though I believe that more women tend to feel that sex is an emotional act, whereas many men can have sex, say thank you, leave and never think about it again.

Certainly in the case of adultery, there is a difference between a one-night fling and a "relationship." Whatever the indiscretion, the perpetrator has to carry it around with him or her and live with what they have done. Moreover, for most, it is an enormous burden to carry, whether it was committed just once or multiple times. Frequently, following an extramarital encounter, the offending spouse feels remorse and is contrite. They regret that the encounter hurt their lover as well as their spouse. They really want to believe that the encounter may actually improve the marriage in the sense that he or she realizes, I have been a real ignoramus, and from today forward, I am going to appreciate what I have. For better and for worse. Much of this process of reflection takes place in internal isolation, because it cannot be shared with anyone, especially your spouse, except in the rarest of rare circumstances. Adultery, by its very essence, must be kept a secret. In my line of thinking, a secret can never be shared by more than two people. As soon as a third party knows the secret, the information is denigrated to classified information. And we all know how "unclassified" classified information is; just pick up the paper today and I am sure that someone has told a reporter about something classified on "background."

One couple I knew had a rather unique approach to handling the conundrum of adultery. The husband was an avid golfer, and was rumored to be a player of a different sort. The wife was previously married and openly discussed the possibility, if not the perceived reality, of an adulterous event during their marriage. This couple's answer? Each of them would be entitled to one "mulligan." In the game of golf, a mulligan is a free shot sometimes given a golfer in informal play when the previous shot was poorly played. In the context of this couple, each one of them would be entitled to one, let's say, bad shot. But a mulligan is not allowed according to the Professional Golf Association Rules of Golf. Then again, marriage is a game of a different sort.

A basic premise of most religions is the concept of forgiveness. The Lord's Prayer implores God to "Forgive us our trespasses, as we forgive those whose trespass against us." However, in reality, I never saw a great deal of forgiveness implemented, at least not in marriage. In all fairness, it is hard for there to ever be true forgiveness of an affair. There will always be suspicion in the other person's heart, that feeling of trepidation. There will always be to be those questions, "Where are you going?" "Who were you just talking to?" It is hard for the wronged spouse not to heave the affair in their partner's face every time something else comes up. To imagine your love having sex with another is gut-wrenching. The person who cheated and "fesses up" or got caught winds up feeling that the debt for their indiscretion can never be repaid. The cycle of remorse and recrimination never ends. Only the most unique and rare couples can survive an affair with their marriage truly intact.

I remember one very well-respected business leader who retained my services. He had been married with children for many years, but had an extramarital relationship with a secretary, who became pregnant. She eventually had triplets. By the time that his paramour ended up suing him for child support, he had exhausted every effort to resolve the matter by voluntarily being extremely generous in caring for these children. At the time the former secretary filed suit, which by then was a couple of years after the affair had started, he was still unable to bring himself to tell his wife about the whole situation. He was humiliated by his own indiscretion.

My client actually brought his wife into my office for a meeting so he could break the news to her in front of me. It was his feeling that I would be a calming presence to put her mind at ease in terms of reassuring her that her husband planned to stay committed to her and their marriage despite this terrible event. Needless to say, it was a rather stressful situation for all of us.

My client's wife courageously swallowed some very bitter and painful medicine—the marital equivalent of ipecac syrup. In fact, she wound up being supportive and accompanied her husband to the hearings as the case dragged on. This man, from the very beginning, had wanted to do the right thing as far as he was able; he was certainly willing to financially support the triplets. However, his former secretary was making such outrageous demands that we had no choice but to go to court. The court was able to sense the greed and recognize the support my client's wife had provided. The secretary ended up getting far less than what we had offered. She appealed and lost. And when everything was said and done, my client ended up giving the secretary the amount that he had offered originally, because he had the financial ability to do it and it was in the best interests of his children. He also continued the marriage with his loyal wife, with a far greater appreciation for her, I am sure. They were that rare example of a couple who survived an affair.

Do not be misled by this story. The odds are against you, so I would caution anyone thinking about having an affair that most of the time you will eventually be caught. I had the occasion to say, more than once, to men in my office: "Listen, are those fifteen minutes of bliss worth $20 million to you *and* losing your family?" Some people tend to wake up when they hear it in those terms. However, many people are just going to do what they are going to do. People can be incredibly arrogant. Just as they think they will never get divorced, they also think they will never be caught.

I once represented a woman whose husband worked in the Senior Executive Service of the federal government. He was an arrogant prick who denied to his wife repeatedly that he was having an affair. The wife had a good idea of who he was having an affair with, but he flat-out denied it, repeatedly, every time she confronted him. *"It wasn't me."*

We hired an excellent investigator (more of which we will talk about in chapter six) who followed this arrogant SOB to a campground in rural Maryland, where he met a girl wearing a Marilyn Monroe-type white halter dress. They had a romantic candlelight dinner and started making out when the meal was finished. It was really getting steamy when the woman extracted herself from my client's husband and walked away. The camera followed her every move as she went into the woods, squatted and urinated—hardly a moment anyone would want captured on film (Even I thought the investigator might have even gone too far with that. He later explained that he did not want to turn off the camera and be accused of editing the tape. Of course, he could have just kept filming the husband instead.) Every detail was captured with a night video camera. After relieving her bladder, this Marilyn Monroe-wannabe came back to the table and started doing a sensual dance…and you can use your imagination as to what happens next. The investigator got it all on tape, and then slipped away without ever being detected. We had it all, every sordid moment, every gasping breath.

Since the husband and his paramour were blissfully unaware of the surveillance, they remained as rude and arrogant as ever. I subpoenaed the girlfriend to appear at a deposition one day and conducted a rather extensive cross-examination. She denied everything. With my intelligence incapable of any further assault, I decided to turn on the television in the conference room and pop in a VCR tape. I said, "I'd like for you to describe for me what you're seeing

**THIRTY-FIVE PERCENT OF THE PEOPLE WHO USE PERSONAL ADS FOR DATING ARE ALREADY MARRIED.**

on the screen in this videotape," and proceeded to show the whole tape. Every excruciating minute. Every so often, I would stop the tape and ask a question: "Can you identify the people on this tape who are having dinner at the Happy Trails Campground?"..."It appears in this videotape that you are disrobing and placing your breast in the mouth of Mr. Rotter. Would you agree or disagree with that characterization?"... "It appears that Mr. Rotter is placing his penis in your mouth at this point. Is that an accurate statement?"

My client was crying and had to leave the room. The other attorney was absolutely going out of his mind; he could barely control himself. I have seen many pictures and many tapes, but this was just terrible. It was the cheesiest campground...you could not have scripted it better. Needless to say, they settled the case shortly thereafter. And to my knowledge, never reconciled.

Unfortunately, that was not the worst, but only one of the tackiest cases of adultery I had the fortune of experiencing. I have omitted the story of the couple who had sex against the dry dog food in the aisle at Petco; yes, while the store was open (one of the parties explained that that was part of the thrill). Also, the one about the government worker who parked his pickup truck camper at the office parking lot to meet with his co-worker at lunchtime. The investigators in that case got underneath the vehicle after the couple entered the rear of the camper and observed and recorded the "rhythmically squeaking shock absorber springs." That is right, our tax dollars hard at work.

---

HE WHO COMMITS ADULTERY HAS NO SENSE; HE WHO
DOES IT DESTROYS HIMSELF. HE WILL GET WOUNDS AND
DISHONOR, AND HIS DISGRACE WILL NOT BE WIPED AWAY.
FOR JEALOUSY AROUSES A HUSBAND'S FURY, AND HE
SHOWS NO RESTRAINT WHEN HE TAKES REVENGE.
*Proverbs 6:32-34*

---

The worst adultery case by far was one that actually occurred *at a wedding*, as opposed to *because of a wedding*. I once represented a client, who, for discussion purposes, we will refer to as Mrs. Defaris. Mrs. Defaris had been married for over 30 years and towards the latter days of her marriage came in to see me because her husband had no interest in her. Sexually, emotionally—nothing. To her it was not just the adjustment of having had their children grow, marry and move away. It was something more. She speculated that her husband was gay, but offered nothing but speculation on that point, without any concrete basis to do so. Besides, many people often think their spouse could be gay when they sexually lose interest in them. After giving the relationship more time, Mrs. Defaris decided to divorce, and did in fact do so.

Years passed by and Mrs. Defaris called me unexpectedly one morning. She explained that her daughter who had married was now experiencing problems similar to what she had gone through with the husband's disinterest in the marriage. They had separated and Mrs. Defaris seemed very anxious about her daughter's ordeal, more so than the typical parental concern. She requested an immediate appointment with me, and sensing her strained emotions, I gave her one that afternoon.

Mrs. Defaris arrived for the appointment punctually accompanied by her daughter. After exchanging pleasantries and getting into some of the basics of the daughter's marital situation, Mrs. Defaris began weeping uncontrollably. She was obviously much more agitated about the breakdown of her daughter's relationship than her daughter was. After some prodding, the following dialogue occurred. Keep in mind; it was just me, Mrs. Defaris and her daughter Debbie present in my office.

Mrs. Defaris began speaking. "I've never told this to anyone, not a soul, but I can't live with it any longer. I cannot. It's eating me up." She paused for a second, swallowed, and then continued. "'Three years ago, at yours and George's wedding, I was looking for your father. I do not remember why exactly, something to do with a last-minute detail or something. At that point, we were an hour away from your wedding. Oh, I was so nervous, more nervous than when I married your father. The church you and George were married in was so big. Do you remember? I went looking for your father and he was not there where the groomsmen were supposed to be. George wasn't there either. No one had seen them, so I went looking on my own. I scoured the whole church and for a minute I thought, well, maybe George got cold feet or something and your father was out tracking him down. I didn't know what to think, but I knew they weren't anywhere to be found."

Now at this point neither the daughter nor I had a clue what Mom was talking about, but her sobbing was intensifying. Debbie and I exchanged sort of puzzled glances. I thought the whole diatribe was, as my boys say, "completely random."

Debbie interrupted. "Mother, our wedding day was beautiful," she said, trying to force her mother's eyes to meet hers. "George didn't run off—at least not then."

Mrs. Defaris began to weep uncontrollably, but she continued to talk as if the story had to be told now, within the next few minutes, or it would never be. "And so I ended up in this funny little room. I don't know what it was. Maybe it was where the kids do their arts and crafts for Sunday school. I remember seeing some sketches hung up on the wall and then I heard noises like maybe some kids were wrestling; only it wasn't any kids."

"Mother, what are you saying?"

"It was George and your father, honey. Their pants were down to their ankles. They were having sex right there in the church."

To be honest, I cannot remember what happened next. It must have been something akin to when accident victims experience a trauma; they block out the event out to protect their own well-being—in this case, my own sanity. I still do not understand why Mrs. Defaris suppressed the information but do know that the relationship between Mrs. Defaris and Debbie remained estranged from that moment until I last heard from them. I declined to represent Debbie. And yes, I think I drank a bottle of wine when I got home that night so I could sleep. No, *two*.

---

I HAVE LOOKED ON A LOT OF WOMEN WITH LUST.
I'VE COMMITTED ADULTERY IN MY HEART MANY TIMES.
GOD RECOGNIZES I WILL DO THIS AND FORGIVES ME.

*—Jimmy Carter*

---

# ADVICE TO REMEMBER

$ The excitement of an affair is *nothing* compared to the excitement when you get caught.

$ If you are not satisfied with your sexual relationship with your prospective spouse, do not get married under any circumstances until you can resolve those issues—if you are already married talk openly about the issues with a competent therapist.

$ The grass is almost never greener on the other side.

$ The passion of sex always changes over time—what is so exciting with your lover will eventually become "the same old thing."

$ Trust is earned—keep your eyes open and use your common sense.

$ If you commit adultery, assume that you will be caught and be prepared to accept the consequences.

$ Affairs usually occur between your spouse and the last person you would expect—in addition to those that you might suspect.

$ Most affairs can never be kept secret—a secret is no longer a secret when any third party is told about the affair.

$ There is nothing worse than having a child with someone with whom you never intended to raise a child.

$ AIDS and other sexually transmitted diseases can kill you.

$ Do not use credit or debit cards to pay for expenses associated with the affair, and do not buy gifts or pay for travel for your paramour.

$ Video cameras are everywhere.

$ Cell phone records tell stories—use a landline or pay phone.

$ If you are apprehended, keep your mouth closed.

$ Remember, it wasn't me....

# G. GORDON LIDDY
## *With a Deadly Aim*

 *G. Gordon Liddy is one of the most provocative commentators and figures of the 20th century. Amongst his many accomplishments include his service as a U.S. Army artillery officer, Special Agent in the FBI, Special Assistant to the Secretary of the Treasury and then Staff Assistant to President Nixon. Liddy's role in Watergate, and his refusal to implicate others, resulted in a 20-year federal prison sentence. Liddy served close to five years, including 106 days in solitary confinement, before his release "in the interests of justice," by President Jimmy Carter. Gordon is compassionate, intelligent and not at all reluctant to express his views daily on his highly successful nationally syndicated radio program. I sincerely admire the courage and conviction of Gordon. Simply put, he is really just a great man.*

*Here are some thoughts and advice from G. Gordon Liddy:*

Having been happily married for 47 years, my best advice for anyone considering marriage is that you really get to know the person before you walk down the aisle. The biggest problem people seem to have is marrying someone too soon; by that I mean they really don't know the person. There is an old saying…"Marry in haste, repent at leisure," and it is very true. You need to know a person for a long, long time before you marry them, so that all of their efforts at putting their best foot forward have been exhausted, and you know the real, true person. The same, of course, also goes for friends.

I do not necessarily believe that couples should live together before marriage. What I do believe is they should find out if they are sexually compatible—but you do not have to live together to determine that. Sexual matters should definitely be all be worked out beforehand. You don't want any surprises on the wedding night…someone saying, *What did I get myself into? I'm not that kind of a girl!* (or guy.)

Nor should unhappily married couples stay together for the sake of the kids. If the relationship is a big mess and the two of you are constantly fighting, that is not good for the children to witness. A lot depends on why you are unhappy. If it is a frivolous reason—a selfish reason, if you will—I believe that couples with children should try to work through their problems. But if a woman is being abused, for example, I would counsel her to get out of it as fast as possible.

The temptation to cheat is very strong. The more successful and powerful a man becomes, the more typical infidelity becomes, because women are naturally attracted to wealth and power and will throw themselves at a man who has either. It takes someone with extraordinary self-control to deny them that temptation. If a man wants to cheat, I would give him the same advice I was going to give a man who was tempted to try heroin: **DON'T DO IT.** It is addictive. I would also tell that man, don't ever think you're going to get away with it. Women always know. Once you break that bond of trust, it may be forgiven, but it will never be forgotten. You will never get back what you once had. Just don't do it.

There is a place for politics in a marriage, if you can keep the politics on a kidding level. Sure a liberal and a conservative can live together happily, in an atmosphere of mutual respect.

I am absolutely an advocate of marriage—to the right person. My personal definition of love is as follows: You have thought long and hard about it, and you can honestly say I do not wish to live the rest of my life without this person. I could do so; if this person were to die in an automobile accident I could make it, but I would be miserable. Because this person makes me feel great. This person will be loyal and supportive and help me live my life the right way.

# CHAPTER 4

# ABOUT LAWYERS

"This is just like you, Beverly. We're supposed to meet alone and you bring your attorney."

The journey through a prolonged and difficult divorce is, for most people, like being forced to go to a foreign country where the language and the customs are bewildering and different. Most of us read a guidebook or two before we go abroad, something like *Denmark for Dummies.* We try to get a little background and information on where we are going and how we should behave in this foreign environment; we try to acclimate ourselves to the laws and customs of the country. The differences in cultures can be as discreet as a gesture or other body language (if you nod your head in Bulgaria it really means no) or as dramatic as markedly unusual laws. For instance, in the Barbados it is illegal for anyone, including little children, to wear camouflage clothing. Darn. What will I wear? Want 15 years in jail? Just utter some unkind words about the Royal Family of Thailand while visiting Bangkok. In Saudi Arabia women cannot drive (All right guys—no snide remarks about women drivers in general.) Many of us do try to learn a few crucial phrases of the language of the strange new land, the bare minimum to get us around ( *¿Dónde está el baño?*)

As you plan your journey to this foreign land, you will no doubt run across friends or acquaintances who have been there before. You will hear everything from "Don't go there" to "I can't believe it took you so long to get there" to "It sure took a long time to get there" to the inevitable "I'll never go back there again." Two lines you are guaranteed not to hear: "That was so much fun—you are going to love it!" or "I can't wait to go back there again!" People will attempt (but never succeed) to be helpful as you plan and proceed along your sojourn to this undiscovered territory. As with any journey to a land where your friends have been, some of the recommendations may be helpful and some will not. No, let's change that— *most* will not.

Your friend may have visited a restaurant in a foreign land years earlier. They may have been satisfied with their experience or they might advise against eating there. You might have read about the restaurant in an old review or even on the Internet. If you really think in abstract terms, restaurants are remarkably like life. The menu may change, the chef and waiters may be replaced, and the equipment may break. The food that looks appetizing may not actually taste good, and vice-versa. Moreover, we all know that fancy desserts and thick steaks are usually trouble. Fast food is ordinarily unhealthy. Worst of all, when you leave the restaurant you may get miserable heartburn. And so it is with marriage and divorce. Your individual tastes and preferences will govern the selections you make. You will either adhere to a healthy diet or succumb to unhealthy cravings.

You will find that the advice starts flowing from the time you are engaged up through the time you get divorced. It begins with whom you should date. He is a jerk. She sleeps around. He sleeps around. He is cheap. She is a gold digger. It evolves into "You are going to marry him?" or perhaps "Yes, she's great—marry her." Without a premonition of doom or a pontification of praise, everyone wants to give you the sincere benefit of his or her experience, which is fine. The problem is that their experience is not yours. Their husband or wife is not yours, their marriage is not yours, and their experiences in most cases will not translate to your experience. Their own experience has shaped the advice they are offering to you. Unless all the facts are the exact same, which is virtually impossible, the advice will be off target. However, when people are desperate and the rug has been pulled out from under them, they seek help and advice from their friends. It's human nature, but it is not particularly helpful.

Potential clients who came to consult with me invariably said, "My friend told me that I needed to...." What usually followed was the description of some vindictive, irrational or illegal course of conduct. I always had the same response: "How much did your friend charge you for that advice?" "Well, nothing." "And that's precisely what it is worth." Get advice from your attorney; get support from your friends. Your mother and your sister and your best friend will all certainly make their opinions known. Whether their opinions are helpful is a completely different issue. Take what they all say with a grain of salt—maybe a whole shaker. Because in this new and terrible place that you never wanted to visit—marital separation or divorce—your lawyer will more or less act as your tour guide. A good tour guide makes all the difference in the world. If you do not believe me, try to navigate a few days in Beijing without one. Do not get me wrong—some people do try and do it themselves, whether it be for economic reasons or just simple lack of judgment. However, they invariably get lost and the cost of the rescue mission far exceeds what the tour guide would have cost at the beginning of the trip.

Like tour books for foreign lands, there are an enormous number of books available about the nuts and bolts of relationships, marriage and divorce. Akin to most things in life, some are good, some are atrocious. I went to Amazon.com to search the key word "divorce"—it came back with 63,574 results. Punch in "marriage" and you get 130,770 hits. "Relationships"? A whopping 180,706. Punch in "How to select and deal with your lawyer" and you will get the reply "We were unable to find exact matches for your search for 'How to select and deal with your lawyer.'" It is hard to pigeonhole all divorces into a formula, because each one is absolutely different or "unique." Kind of like divorce lawyers. They are unique and come in a variety of formulas as well. Some are easily digestible; others will make you sick to your stomach.

In any divorce, the attorney you select to represent your interests is the most important decision you will make during the process of a divorce. They are making decisions and providing advice for you that is in many situations irrevocable and life changing. I cannot overemphasize how important a person's choice of a lawyer is, because the lawyer is the person who will guide you and set forth the plan and course for the rest of your life. If you are involved in a custody battle and have the wrong lawyer, you can lose your children very quickly; faster than you would ever have believed possible. However, if you have the right lawyer, the other side may not even be willing to make the opening salvo of seeking full custody. The mere presence of the right attorney is enough to warn the other side not to try something stupid.

My mentor and former partner, Mark B. Sandground, always told me that divorce law was the "proctology" of the legal world. For those of you who may not be fully conversant with the terminology of medical specialties, proctology is the branch of medicine dealing with the structure and diseases of the anus, rectum, and sigmoid colon. In many ways, Mark was right. Like the brave proctologists, divorce lawyers see you at your very worst. You have a hemorrhoid you want removed. They see parts of you that not a lot of other people want to see. Parts that may stink. And they have their hands and fingers in areas that you never imagined another human being would ever want to probe. The only difference is that there is no lubricant and it hurts. Sometimes, really bad.

So why is the proctologist you select so important? The rules of the law are the same for everybody, rich or poor. Right. And O.J. Simpson has a right to be angry with Nicole for not being there to raise their children. While the laws truly are the same for all people, how they are applied and interpreted is subject to gross disparity. That is where your attorney becomes the centerpiece of your quest for freedom and the fair and just application of the law. In today's age of media saturation, we are frequently introduced to the legal "dream team" *du jour*. While many of these lawyers are competent professionals, others are hoisted into the limelight, and really make the profession look bad. I am not going to name names here. You know who they are. Most likely, by the time that this book is published we will have been through a whole new cycle of "celebrity" or "high-profile" lawyers. What we frequently do not see are the lawyers that tirelessly work without any media attention to secure the rights of the working single mom against a deadbeat dad in Norma, New Jersey. Or the lawyer fighting to combat the scandalous allegations of sexual abuse lodged by a wife against the father of her children just because she hates her husband and really does not care about her children. Or the lawyers fighting for the rights of all people dissolving their marriages through the enactment of important legislation. Not everyone has a celebrity for a client. I am speaking of the dedicated community of family law practitioners (they prefer that to "proctologists") who extract people from situations they could have avoided by reading the first two chapters of this book.

So how does one select the best lawyer possible? This may be one of the few areas where advice from friends *is* actually helpful. If your marriage is ending, you will inevitably receive recommendations from your friends and relatives, who will have had either a positive or a negative experience with their attorney. Someone who has been through a divorce usually has rather pointed criticism or praise regarding the lawyers they have encountered during the divorce odyssey. More bluntly, people usually love or hate their lawyers. Only the truly mediocre lawyer engenders the apathetic reply from a client, "They were okay." If the lawyer did a good job, and the process has been satisfactorily completed, it will generally be a good recommendation. A person certainly has no incentive to recommend a lawyer to you unless they were happy with how their case turned out. Again, though, I must caution that every marriage and divorce is unique, and what worked in one case may not necessarily work in another. You might really dislike the lawyer your best friend thought did such a great job.

So what type of lawyer should you "engage"? (Please note the use of the word "*engage*." If you do not engage with your attorney, he or she will never fully understand or appreciate your case. There is a difference between relaying a story and actually "engaging" in a conversation.) Remarkably, the process of selecting an attorney to represent you has many of the same qualities that you would probably seek in a love partner: Can you trust them? Can you feel comfortable confiding in them? Are they gentle or rude and abrupt? Are they responsive to your concerns? Will they return your calls? Do they listen and actually hear what you are saying? Are they intelligent? Do they have the ability to calm and reassure you in stressful situations? Do they have a sense of humor? Are you confident that you are not just wasting time with them?

The most important component of your relationship with your lawyer is that you have the ability to communicate with him or her. That the two of you have a good rapport; that you aren't afraid of them or intimidated by them; and, most importantly, that you trust them and feel comfortable that what he or she is telling you is correct. Any competent lawyer is going to appreciate the fact that at the time of your "first date"— or initial consultation—you are under extraordinarily stressful circumstances. You do not have to attempt to present yourself as Mr. or Mrs. Congeniality. However, in a way, it is still a first date. Moreover, you need to be aware that sometimes the real "gold digger" is sitting across the desk from you.

Beyond these general inquiries, there are a number of important qualities to consider. First, experience. What is the actual trial experience of the lawyer you might hire? Why do I say "actual trial experience" if you really want to just settle the case and move on? Well, because it might not happen the way you have planned. After all, you may now be considering whether to marry, whether to separate, or maybe to divorce. My guess is that you were not planning to be entertaining some of the thoughts you may have considered while reading this book thus far. Why would you not want to be fully prepared with the best counsel possible if your case were to escalate to determination by a person in a black robe?

Unfortunately, experience is not just the number of years in practice. Experience needs to be delineated with respect to the practitioner's expertise in the handling of various issues, for example custody matters versus the valuation of business interests. Does the lawyer have the respect of his or her peers through a rating from Martindale-Hubbell? Yes, lawyers actually rate other lawyers and the information is available to all members of the public at no charge. I regularly get confidential surveys in the mail from other lawyers asking me to rate them in a variety of areas as either A, which is pre-eminent, B, which is very good, or C, good. There is another part where their peers also rate their ethics. All lawyers value and covet their ratings and all aspire to reach the pinnacle rating as an AV lawyer. In my experience, some lawyers who have achieved a high rating take on a sense of self-importance with clients and other members of the bar that can be somewhat offensive. So even if the lawyer has experience and the regard of other lawyers, if you or the opposing lawyer finds him or her untenable to work with constructively, the representation is most likely flawed from conception.

In judging the experience of a lawyer, you can also visit the Court of Appeals or Supreme Court website of any state. Just punch in your lawyer's name, search for a case, and easily determine if your potential lawyer has been involved in many domestic relations appeals. More importantly, how has he or she done? Certainly, written opinions may not be easy to understand. I think some appellate judges do that deliberately, just to preserve the esoteric nature of the law. However, from a review of the opinion you should be able to determine if your proposed counsel won or lost, and how their arguments were received by the court.

Just as in the possible selection of a spouse, I suggest that you take your lawyer for a test-drive. The beauty of this test-drive is that there is no salesperson to pressure you. The legal equivalent of visiting a Saturn dealership. Just come and look at the cars, drive them if they interest you, and make your decision from there. How? Most jurisdictions in larger municipalities have regular days of the week when matters on the domestic relations docket are heard by the court. Typically called "Motions Day," it is worth a morning or afternoon of your time to watch the parade of attorneys and litigants and see firsthand how "justice" is actually meted out. At the typical carnival of righteousness, you will see lawyers, parties and judges at their best and worst. If you are interested in test-driving a particular lawyer, you can consult the court docket or the clerk's office to ascertain in which courtroom that lawyer may be found. If you are just interested in walking around the lot, so to speak, you can certainly do so. You will see every type of car imaginable from sports cars, to boring domestics, dime-a-dozen imports, and an occasional SUV. Every so often, you might see a classic, and maybe a Ferrari. Sporadically, you may see an antique that should not be on the road.

If I were you, I would take a friend with you to court. By doing so you will hopefully be able to confirm with someone else that you did actually just see what you could not believe you just saw. You will also have with you a designated driver, as you will most likely visit a bar following your experience, even though it may be early in the morning and contrary to your upbringing as a devout Mormon. There are many good lawyers, but I am convinced that there are more bad ones than good. Bad has to be divided in to two separate themes, and as a category, difficult lawyers form a total group of four types.

## MY HUSBAND AND I JUST SPLIT UP.
## I FINALLY FACED THE FACT THAT WE ARE INCOMPATIBLE.
## I'M A CANCER AND HE'S AN ASSHOLE.

The first type of bad lawyer is the type that is just downright ethically and morally depraved. They are dishonest people. This type of person could just as easily be the stereotypical used-car salesperson (I do not mean to pick on used-car salespersons. There are no doubt some excellent used car salespersons, although I have yet to personally encounter them.) Let me give you an example.

I was once representing a client in the negotiation of a property settlement agreement. He had been represented by another lawyer and was feeling that perhaps some of the provisions of the agreement were adverse to his best financial interests. In fact, he was correct. When I saw the draft of the agreement, I immediately knew it was an economic time bomb waiting to explode. I became even more concerned when I reached the signature page and noticed that the agreement was signed by my client, but not by his wife. My client explained that his lawyer had requested him to sign the agreement to facilitate the settlement. I knew that we had to immediately withdraw the agreement before the wife executed it. Customarily, a proposed property settlement agreement, pre-nuptial agreement, contract for the purchase of real property, etc., is only deemed an offer until it is accepted. The general rule of law is that an offer can be withdrawn any time prior to acceptance. With the consent of my client, I immediately phoned the opposing counsel to advise him of the revocation of the offer. The client had indicated that his wife's lawyer, a sole practitioner in Maryland whom I had not met, was at best a bit of a sleaze.

I would typically hear those types of warnings from a client about the lawyer for their spouse. People involved in a legal dispute frequently develop an intense suspicion or dislike of the other litigant's counsel, regardless of whether the suspicion or negative feelings are justified. It would sometimes unnerve clients that I was so friendly with opposing counsel. We would fight like boxers going for Olympic gold in court, then head off and have lunch together. After lunch, we could be right back in the ring again. I refused to engage in anything personal with the other lawyer. If they were dishonest or unethical, I would not have anything to do with them. But a good lawyer? I would be seeing him or her repeatedly, and they were people that I knew and trusted. A client looking for me to be an enemy of opposing counsel? It was never going to happen.

Here is something else to keep in mind when thinking about hiring a lawyer: Divorce attorneys are going to be appearing in the same courtrooms repeatedly throughout their careers, trying cases before the same judges. My parents used to say "You can only lose your reputation and integrity once," and it was something I always kept in mind as I practiced law. Once you or your lawyer is known as someone who is dishonest, you are dead. Nine times out of ten, you are going to lose your case. The judge will not believe what your lawyer is saying, and will wonder why you are being represented by that lawyer. Your credibility is attached to that of your lawyer.

Anyway, when I phoned this lawyer in Maryland, I planned to simply revoke the pending agreement and then work towards a resolution that would have some basic modicum of fairness. I was relieved when the lawyer told me "You can't do that," thereby indicating implicitly that the agreement had not been signed by his own client. If she had signed it, the agreement would have been a formal contract and my client would have been presented with an entirely different set of burdens and proof to escape its contractual clutches. It would be the difference between the intensive care unit and simple outpatient surgery. When the lawyer continuously did not want to accept what I was advising him in a clearly more agitated tone, I decided to end the conversation with the intent of sending a fax to confirm the withdrawal of the offer. That is when I realized that my client's perception about the "sleaze factor" of his wife's lawyer was as accurate as his intuition that told him he should not sign the proposed agreement.

The lawyer for the wife realized that he had made an error in not having his client sign the agreement that was already executed by my client. There was no possibility whatsoever that the wife would ever achieve the provisions made in the agreement if the matter were ever litigated. In a last-ditch effort to save the agreement, the wife's lawyer advised me that he did not care what I did because he had a solution. He was going to lie. Yes, he actually told me that. He said he was going to say that the agreement had been signed even though it had not. A deliberate lie. Unfortunately, for him, he was unaware that I had placed him on the speakerphone during his tirade and that I had motioned for two secretaries to listen to the call along with my client. When he finished, I had them introduce themselves on the phone and then we politely said goodbye. To say the least he was dumfounded. I refused to communicate with the lawyer again except in writing. The offer for the agreement was revoked and an agreement later signed that was skewed now in my client's favor. I also called the Maryland Attorney Grievance Commission when the case was finished. I hope that he crawled back under the rock from whence he came. That is a *bad* lawyer.

Luckily, this type of lawyer is rare, but there has certainly been a dramatic emergence of this species during the last 20 years. There actually was a time when not every communication with counsel had to be followed by a fax or e-mail "confirming" the conversation. Those types of relationships do still exist, though they are probably as far and few between as the lawyers who caused the e-mails and faxes to be sent in the first place. Unfortunately, the second group of bad lawyers is available in abundance.

## LAWYERS, I SUPPOSE, WERE CHILDREN ONCE.

*—Charles Lamb*

The second type of bad lawyer is the type that is bad because they do not have a clue about how to effectively represent their client or even worse, they think that they know how but really do not. These lawyers are young and old, black and white. They are women and men, and form the substance about what no one likes about lawyers. It absolutely pains me to see how some lawyers "represent" their clients. I have seen so much in my tenure as a lawyer that my male-pattern baldness becomes easily understandable. I thought my hair was genetically destined to fall out, but with what I have seen, I would pull it out, sometimes in clumps at a time. You may wonder, how can there be so many "bad lawyers?" It is easiest to explain by referencing the old joke circulated mostly amongst medical malpractice lawyers: "Do you know what they say each year to the guy who graduates last in his class in medical school?" Think about it for a second. "*Congratulations, Doctor.*"

Same for lawyers. There are a lot of great law schools and some really bad ones. And the ones that are of your mail-order variety produce graduates that can and do call themselves lawyers. And even those schools have fifty percent of the people graduating in the bottom half of their class. Now the bar examinations are supposed to filter out some of those who have slipped through their law school experience without flunking out. Depending on the state administering the examination, the bar exam can be quite a horrific ordeal. I will never forget the Chief Justice of the Virginia Supreme Court stating at my swearing-in ceremony words to the effect, "Isn't funny how just a few weeks ago you thought the bar exam was a barbaric process; but now, you consider it an appropriate method to sort out those who are fit to practice law from those who are not?"

# A WARNING TO CLIENTS
## *The Difficult Attorney*

Two decades ago, I was forewarned about several attorneys that were not to be trusted. Their names were (now, you did not really think I was going to name them did you?) known about the legal community. Other attorneys were regarded as "bull-dogs" or "bombers." I quickly learned that many attorneys given that label were merely misunderstood. When they took the medication that their psychiatrists had prescribed, they were actually very nice folks. It is my belief that there are four types of difficult attorneys:

### 1. *The liar*

This is by far the worst type. This snake in the grass preys not only on the opposing counsel, but usually on their own client as well. The liar has no hesitancy in lying to you or the Court. He or she will misrepresent your position, cite unsupported legal authorities, and smile the whole time. This cretin agrees to the extension on discovery and then suddenly has amnesia after filing a Motion to Compel. This is a lawyer who intentionally runs up a legal bill. This is the attorney who has given all lawyers a bad rap.

### 2. *The emotional lawyer*

This lawyer actually believes everything that his or her client tells him. He or she has no cognizance that there is potentially another side to the story. Compounding this ignorance is the emotional lawyer's temperament: "Your client is a lying s*&t!" is usually the opening banter when this lawyer representing the husband in a divorce case hears that I am going to deny his claims of adultery. The emotional lawyer cannot accept that a man and a woman can have drinks at The Peninsula Hotel, caress each other gently in an affectionate manner and then retire to room 402 and watch C-Span for a few hours in a purely platonic relationship. The emotional lawyer thinks their client is always right. Despite the valiant efforts of the pharmaceutical industry, they need medication that has not yet to be developed. *(As a footnote here, I must state that no doubt some fanatical mental health care advocate will criticize me for making what will be construed as an insult to families facing mental health issues. Mental health professionals are invaluable and often unrecognized for the miraculous care they provide. I wholeheartedly believe in psychotropic medications; I would even be crazier if I did not take mine every day. So to my critics, get over it and please go see your own doctor about increasing your dosage.)*

### 3. *The scarecrow lawyer*

This type of lawyer is premised upon the Scarecrow from *The Wizard of Oz*. Their mantra should be "If I only had a brain." This type of difficult lawyer is especially frustrating to deal with, especially when dealing with a case that a lawyer directly out of law school would be able to handle without any difficulty. The scarecrow lawyer may be one that should have retired long ago, or a new lawyer with a "know-it-all" attitude. The Scarecrow lawyer does not appreciate his or her intellectual shortcomings. In fact, he or she actually thinks that they are doing a good job. That is, until the judge advises them otherwise.

## 4. *The asshole lawyer*

You may encounter this type of lawyer. He's the one that you look at after a six-hour deposition of mundane questioning and you think to yourself as you sit there, "Boy, this guy—what an asshole!" Regretfully, this type of lawyer frequently is a combination of the first three categories of difficult lawyers. After all, that is what earns him the reeking distinction of being an asshole! This is the type of lawyer who makes you actually ponder the question, *"If I leapt across the table and strangled this person, would the time in prison really be worse than the agony to which he is presently subjecting me?"* I can distinctly remember two occasions when I almost came to the conclusion that the time in jail would not really be that bad…(I am not even thinking about the one attorney who consumed a tuna fish sandwich during a deposition and then proceeded with her questioning of my client with chunks of Star-Kist's best filling the crevices between her teeth. I still have nightmares about it.)

How do you and your counsel handle the difficult lawyer? Obviously, the answer to this question depends on the variety of lawyer with which you are faced. With respect to The Liar, you need to take all precautions. Avoid phone conversations with The Liar. If you do have to speak with him or her, do it in the presence of a third party. Keep a record of all phone conversations. Try to restrict all of your communications to writing or-email only. Most importantly, do not hesitate to report the conduct of the lawyer to the Court or to the Bar Counsel. Think *Nike*. Do not threaten to do it, "just do it." This type of lawyer hurts all of us and should be censured at every opportunity.

The other three categories are dealt with in the exact same manner. They do not have the intellectual capacity to understand the degree of their stupidity. The worst mistake that you can make with these lawyers is to engage in a confrontation with them. If you do, they feel that they have won. When possible (provided it does not in any manner prejudice your interests) ignore their antics or stupidity. Avoid the urge to suggest therapeutic intervention with a mental health therapist. Most judges know who the lawyers are that fit into these categories. If you become reactive to them, you might end up in one of the categories yourself. I have found that simple preparation and documentation of the antics of these categories usually results in a handsome award of fees at the conclusion of the case (and in one case, over $50,000 in *temporary* fees). Remember, *keep your perspective and maintain self-control.*

The following excerpts were taken from the Internet and are actual accounts of memorable conduct on the part of lawyers. The stories are not told in my words. See if you can guess in what category they belong. Enjoy!

**A stinking accusation.**

*The Wall Street Journal* recently profiled husband-and-wife litigators Stanley and Susan Rosenblatt, currently angling for punitive damages in a much-publicized tobacco trial in which they purportedly represent the class of all sick Florida smokers, and before that best-known for settling a class action against tobacco companies on behalf of flight attendants in a deal that "has yet to yield any tangible benefits for the Rosenblatt's' clients, while netting the Rosenblatts $49 million in fees and expenses." After the fee was received, one associate who had worked for the Rosenblatts for 13 years asked for a bonus. She was abruptly terminated and has hired a lawyer to sue the Rosenblatts, who have been quietly negotiating a severance package while preparing for the punitive phase of their tobacco case. A prominent figure in pro-litigation circles, Alan Morrison of Public Citizen Litigation Center, intervened trying to block the settlement of the flight attendant case. "*You are scum. You are absolute scum. You are dreck,*' Mr. Rosenblatt told Mr. Morrison before the start of a court hearing over the deal's fairness, according to Mr. Morrison." Mr. Morrison now forgivingly calls Rosenblatt "a fabulous thorn in the side of the tobacco industry" and says "His methods are different from mine, but I probably wouldn't have gotten anywhere near as [far as] he's gotten." (Milo Geyelin, "Suing Tobacco, Florida Firm Takes Own Path," *Wall Street Journal*, May 15.)

**From the incivility frontier.**

Richard F. Ziegler, writing in the *National Law Journal*: "Until recently, the classic example of incivility in litigation was famed Texas lawyer Joe Jamail's defense of a deposition witness in the 1993 Paramount-QVC Network-Viacom takeover battle. According to the excerpts of the deposition transcript included in an addendum to an opinion by the Delaware Supreme Court, Jamail told the examining lawyer that he could '*gag a maggot off a meat wagon*' and made other vituperative remarks that the Delaware court labeled 'extraordinarily rude, uncivil and vulgar.' ...Mr. Jamail's 'maggot' rhetoric has now been displaced by a new classic in incivility: a pre-suit letter sent by a New York litigator that threatened the prospective defendant with the '*legal equivalent of a proctology exam*' if the plaintiff's claim weren't satisfied without litigation. That wording, plus some other aggressive tactics by the same lawyer, ended up costing the would-be proctologist a $50,000 sanction (now on appeal)." The sanctions were handed down last November by federal judge Denny Chin against litigator Judd Burstein, in a case called Revson v. Cinque & Cinque P.C. However, prospective targets of legal intimidation should not get their hopes up too high: a few years ago the Second Circuit, which includes New York, "sustained as proper a pre-suit letter that sought to encourage settlement by threatening the opposing party with harmful publicity." (Richard F. Ziegler, "Litigation: The Price of Incivility," *National Law Journal*)

### The threat of life.

"Attorney Marvin Barish could be hit with harsh sanctions by a federal judge for threatening to kill an Amtrak defense lawyer and calling him a *'fat pig'* during a trial recess," Shannon Duffy reports in Philadelphia's *Legal Intelligencer*. U.S. District Judge Herbert J. Hutton declared a mistrial upon learning that Barish had allegedly told defense attorney Paul F.X. Gallagher, fist cocked, *"I will kill you with my bare hands."* "You threatened his life in the presence of witnesses, sir," said the indignant judge, after hearing an account of the incident from his courtroom deputy. "*Not in the presence of the jury,*" Barish replied; then, perhaps as it dawned that this was not an entirely satisfactory response, he added a more general denial: "I didn't threaten his life or anybody." At a later sanctions hearing, Barish said that he was "not condoning my conduct. It was really bad" but that "I didn't mean that I would kill him" and that Gallagher "wasn't in obvious fear of his life." Barish's attorney, James E. Beasley, said that his client was the real victim in the situation, having been provoked by unfair legal tactics on the part of Amtrak: "I think that having Mr. Barish go through this has been a sufficient sanction in and of itself." (Shannon Duffy, "An Angry Lawyer?," *The Legal Intelligencer*).

### Lawyers, clients, sex and...death?

It seems that sometimes lawyers have a problem keeping a line between legal duties and romance. Both the lawyer and the client may pay a high price. In the midst of all the other high-profile stories of misconduct involving sex, one involving a lawyer and the death penalty almost escapes notice. The state of Missouri is looking at executing Reginald Powell on February 25, following his conviction for a 1986 murder and the imposition of the death penalty. He was represented by an attorney who was having a sexual relationship with him. According to news reports on the case, the attorney's judgment appears to have been clouded by the romance when she advised her client to decline a plea bargain that would have *avoided the death penalty* and allowed the possibility of parole. The Missouri Supreme Court has declined his appeal.

Talk about getting screwed...

The problem with that is that, as most of us know, life requires a reasonable exercise of common sense. The bar examination is not designed to test common sense. Accordingly, people without common sense can pass a bar examination and become lawyers—and usually do so twice a year. I have seen lawyers cite statutes to a court that were abolished ten years earlier. I have seen a lawyer fail to ask essential questions that caused a woman married to a successful physician for 20-plus years to lose her claim to spousal support because of that error alone. I have seen lawyers miss crucial filing deadlines that prevented valuable expert or lay witness testimony from ever being heard by the court. I have seen lawyers quote Jewish folk songs in legal pleadings where it was not relevant or even remotely appropriate. I saw a lawyer tell the husband of a wife I was representing

## MARRIAGE IS GRAND AND DIVORCE IS ABOUT FIFTY GRAND

that it was "really not a bad result" that the court awarded a temporary support obligation of $38,000 per month, even though it was a horrific result for him (it was the highest support award ever granted by that court at that time.) I have seen attorneys make arguments to courts that even my 14- and 16-year-old sons would reject as ridiculous. I have sat in depositions listening to lawyers rambling *ad nauseum* about points that were *not* points. I remember listening to one woman lawyer drone on for almost six hours with the most inane and inarticulate examination imaginable. It was not a deposition—it was an endurance test—for both my client and me. I honestly believe that if you played a tape of this "cross-examination" in the mountains of Afghanistan, Osama Bin Laden would come running out of his little caves just to make it stop. As for me, I think I had a brain aneurism midway through the deposition. And what makes all of this worse is that innocent clients are paying for this advice and counsel. By the hour. And incompetence adds up.

I also observed something else interesting as the years went on: so-called "regular," that is, the ordinary day-to-day clients, actually benefited from a certain lack of legal knowledge. Many rich, famous and powerful clients were usually fairly accustomed to dealing with teams of lawyers and hammering out sophisticated business deals. They knew how the game was played, so they were not nervous about being deposed. They were far more relaxed but less likely to listen to their attorney—me—telling them, "I want you to do this and this and this." They really believed that they knew what they were doing. These clients tended to approach their divorce as just another business deal. And it is not. They did not take into consideration that a divorce is not just another deal strictly in and of itself. It is an extremely emotional business deal with extremely quirky rules.

The only people who even came close to understanding what was potentially ahead were businesspeople or professional practitioners who had been through a "business divorce;" perhaps a split-up of a medical or law practice partnership or some family business. If they had endured that type of an emotional experience, they had some understanding and appreciation of what was to come. The rules of divorce are different, and emotions come into play in a manner that most people would never envision. You discover that people you thought you really knew, you never actually knew at all.

All of that being said, let me assure you that other lawyers are traditionally the worst client to represent. I represented many over the years – in fact, I represented a judge once in his divorce and the Dean of a law school in a non-domestic civil matter — and boy, can they be difficult (I remember the Dean, who was a lovely older gentlemen, used to pace around my office as I sat at my desk. He would thrust hypothetical questions at me as though he was Professor Kingsfield from *The Paper Chase*. As an added measure of reminding me that I was the "student" and he was the "Dean," he would always call me "Mr. Barondess" despite the fact that I repeatedly asked him to call me "Mark.") Lawyers are so sure that they know best, that this is *their* arena. If you are a lawyer or judge, it is tough to put your own ego aside and take advice from another, which is usually the wisest course of action. However, just because your lawyer or any other professional tells you do to something does not mean that you should abandon your own common sense. I used to tell people that buying advice from a lawyer was akin to buying fish at the local fish market. When you go to the fish market, you are never going to buy a fish that smells "fishy." The same with legal advice. If the advice smells fishy, don't buy it. There are plenty of fish in the sea. Maybe it is an indication that you should try a different market. Bad fish can make you very sick.

**ESTIMATED AVERAGE LENGTH OF DIVORCE PROCEEDINGS: 1 YEAR**

Theoretically, you are paying your lawyer to represent you, so you should heed their advice. In the real world, that does not always happen. In one case, I found my opponent was a very well-known lawyer who insisted on acting as his own lawyer in his own divorce. He had originally hired another very prominent lawyer to handle the matter, but when it came time for trial, he decided he could do a better job. Wrong. I tried the case against him, and he was so emotionally involved that he could not see the forest for the trees. It was brutal. He wound up losing so much; it was a far worse result than if he would have just listened to his original lawyer. But he knew it all. *A classic example.*

An even better one is myself. I got divorced and I had a dear friend and great domestic relations lawyer, Glenn C. Lewis, representing me. He is one of the best trial lawyers in the country and always offered me sound intelligent advice. Did I take it? *Of course not.*

As you select a lawyer, you must remember the high degree of finality to divorce judgments. Of course, people can appeal the court's decision, but the rules vary based upon where you live. You may reside in an area with an absolute right of appeal or no guaranteed right of appeal. You may live in an area where you have to petition the court, say the Supreme Court, and ask, "This is what my gripe is, will you review it?" If the court says no, then you are finished. Accordingly, the selection of your lawyer is extremely important. You cannot be thinking you will fix his or her errors on appeal. It is kind of like marriage in the first place. If you are going to do it, you need to try to get it right, *the first time.*

---

DON'T RELY ON LAWYERS. THEY CAN'T REMEMBER
TO TELL YOU EVERYTHING. THEY'RE ONLY HUMAN,
AND MOST OF THEM ARE BELOW HUMAN.
—*Roxanne Pulitzer*

---

# ADVICE TO REMEMBER

$ The lawyer you select will have the single biggest effect on every aspect of your case—besides your decision to marry or divorce, there is no greater decision that you will make that will have as significant an impact in the event things don't work out.

$ Research the background of your prospective lawyer extensively and check their disciplinary record before you schedule your first meeting.

$ The credibility that your lawyer enjoys or lacks will be the credibility that your case automatically enjoys or lacks.

$ While the facts of every case mandate different results, it is almost always best to have multiple recommendations from friends and/or family about their particular experience with the lawyer you may be considering retaining.

$ Contrary to popular belief, lawyers are people too—we make mistakes. If advice from your lawyer is offensive to your own common sense, it may not be correct. Make certain that you are satisfied and comfortable with the advice you receive before you follow it.

$ As best as you are able, try and limit repetitive emotional out-cries about your life in your lawyer's office. These matters are best handled by a mental health professional in a better and more cost-effective atmosphere.

$ Remember that your lawyer is supposed to be on your side—try not to be confrontational with him or her.

$ It is far more advantageous to you to have your lawyer enjoy a good relationship with the other lawyer personally.

$ Address any concerns about your lawyer's representation of your interests as soon as they arise in a friendly manner—do not let your concerns fester.

# SHERRY & SKIP MILLER
# LINELL & BOB SHAPIRO
## *LA Lawyers in Love*

*Last fall we experienced one of the most heated Presidential elections in the history of United States. On an evening in late October 2004 we went to the magnificent home on top of Mulholland Drive in Beverly Hills of my partner and close friend, legal legend Robert Shapiro and his incredible wife Linell to have dinner and watch the Vice-Presidential debates. Joining us was another one of my favorite couples – our partner, Skip Miller, and his wife of 35 years, Sherry.*

*Skip Miller is a nationally regarded, Ferrari-driving powerhouse litigator (I'm better than he is, but he will not admit it) who married his beautiful childhood sweetheart. After over thirty years of law practice and many trials, Skip has the reputation as a top trial lawyer in the Los Angeles legal community, particularly in difficult, high-profile cases. Skip defended the City of Los Angeles in a series of cases arising from the operations of the LAPD including the Rodney King civil rights action. Clients from all walks regularly seek out Skip's services including artists and actors such as Rod Stewart, Elton John, Nick Nolte and Bob Dylan. Skip recently received accolades for winning a $7 million judgment against musician Michael Jackson in a four-month jury trial. It was during Skip's cross-examination at that trial that the public got a glimpse of that horrifying picture of Jackson with the Band-aid apparently holding his nose on his face.*

*Bob Shapiro is a household name, the man behind the original legal "dream team" that successfully defended O.J. Simpson in the most celebrated criminal trial of all time. Bob was recently profiled in the New York Times as one of the nation's most prominent attorneys. Bob has a long list of high-profile cases which includes the defense of Christian Brando and super producer*

*Robert Evans. He also successfully represented the President of Mobil Oil Company charged with manslaughter resulting from a tank explosion. Less known but equally important is Bob's expertise in international law. He has written and lectured extensively on legal issues and procedures and is the author of the New York Times bestseller* The Search for Justice. *His novel* Misconception *is currently being adapted for a major motion picture.*

## SKIP

Sherry and I both grew up in Chicago and have known each other since junior high school days. I knew very early and definitively that Sherry was the girl for me. Sherry took a little longer to come around. Nevertheless, her parents liked me, and I knew I had found the right girl, so I just hung in there. Sherry was the sweetest, smartest, sexiest girl I had ever seen. All I ever wanted was just to be with her. To this day, I can't wait until we are at home alone together so I can chase her around. I love everything about her except her politics. One of my favorite rules for love? Persistence—hang in there. It certainly has worked for me. Of course, it's all about finding the right person, which I certainly did. Don't take a stand on unimportant issues and refuse to back down. Let the little things go. Weaknesses? Jealousy. To this day, you can piss me off just by mentioning the name of some guy who took Sherry to a high school dance more than thirty-five years ago.

## SHERRY

He can't wait to get home so he can chase me around? Please! He can't wait to get home so he can watch The History Channel! I cannot believe I am married to a die-hard Republican! What was *I* thinking?? Even though we both stick to our guns in terms of our politics, it does not stop us from acting like teenagers. We still love kissing and holding hands after thirty-five years and two grown kids. Skip always makes me feel good. It is so funny to see my husband, this fearsome attorney, acting like a kid on a date with the prom queen who cannot quite believe his luck.

## BOB

I met Linell during the sixties. She was the most beautiful girl I had ever seen. I bought Linell and her roommate some drinks one night at a private club called Arthur's and asked her out, but she told me flat-out she had a serious boyfriend. Still, I started hanging around on the fringes of her crowd of friends, hoping to get closer to her. Linell was busy with her modeling career and happy with her boyfriend, so she refused to give me any encouragement. Still, I was not about to give up...I was sure she was the one for me. I stayed around for a year and a half...I even went on a double date with Linell and her boyfriend, though it was clear to everyone on the date who I was interested in dating.

Finally, one day on the state beach in Santa Monica, which was the "in" beach at the time, I saw Linell with a friend and another guy, who I didn't realize was just a casual friend. I suddenly realized that the situation was hopeless and I had to give up pursuing her. I told her that it was clear I had no chance and would not be bothering her in the future.

Linell let me start to walk away, and then called out my name. It was like a scene from a bad B-rate romance movie. Linell had a modeling shoot that night on the Sunset Strip, and I had an apartment right there, so I asked her to stop by after work. That was it...Linell had to call her boyfriend the next day and tell him it was all over. Three days later, I asked Linell to marry me. It is now 36 happy years later.

I am not quite sure that I could pinpoint a secret for a successful marriage. Timing is certainly important—get married only after you have experienced the life of a single person—it is always a mistake to be tied down too soon. If you plan to experience the single life after you are married, you will most likely divorce. Pick someone with whom you are intellectually compatible, because this is the person you will spend the most time talking with for the rest of your life. And it goes without saying that you should marry someone with whom you have a strong sexual compatibility. Linell had everything—looks, wit, style, charisma...we had similar interests socially, athletically and morally. She was well worth waiting for.

## LINELL

Bob and I have a great deal of mutual respect for each other. We understand how the other person is feeling without even having to speak. Many of my friends have the attitude, *A man is just a man*...they seem resigned, like this is just a fact of life. They never set any standard of conduct for their mate, though they are always disappointed when their mate cheats, for example. I think that is a very poor attitude to have.

Bob and I both have similar high standards. We share the same morals and core values. The year and a half I knew him, before he made his stand, I was always impressed with his integrity, honesty and character. I knew I could trust him. However, I did have a serious boyfriend, and I am not a believer in cheating. Nevertheless, he certainly got my attention that day at the beach – I suddenly realized that I liked having him around. I did not want him to disappear from my life. After just one date, we knew it was true love. Bob was just graduating from law school and we probably had $600 to our names. We had a very small wedding in Palm Desert just three months after our first date.

Two sons and 36 years later, we still have fun today. We both enjoy the same kinds of things: food, wine, sports, people, exercise, our boys and our five dogs and cat. We are just as happy at home having a simple chicken dinner with our boys as we are going out at night, though we have a good time when we do that too. All these years later, I still love to be around Bob. We are truly a part of each other. Sincerely, I believe that feeling is what every married couple should strive to achieve. It is wonderful.

# CHAPTER 5

# MORE ON YOUR LAWYER

*"Just another of our many disagreements. He wants a no-fault divorce, whereas I would prefer to have the bastard crucified."*

People contemplating marriage or divorce are frequently scared. As a lawyer, it was often difficult to provide a client with reassurance about our planned course of action, other than to assure them that, in essence, "everything will be fine." Over the years, I developed an analogy to help clients identify divorce in a unique light.

All of you who travel frequently have most likely endured a rather stressful experience involving air travel. I am not speaking of the terrifying part—the horrific lines at airport security checkpoints, the rude airline representatives who treat you as though you are a sub-human species or even the extraordinarily inflated prices for "food" while you are stranded because of "air traffic control" delays. The nerve-rattling experience I am referring to usually occurs on the taxiway on your ride to the runway for takeoff. Over the intercom, you hear the steady voice of the captain of the plane, who proceeds to advise you that the weather and prior reports of aircraft ahead indicate that there are numerous "vectors" along the planned flight path, which will require maneuvering. You are advised to expect "moderate to severe chop" and as such, you will need to keep your seat belts "securely fastened" (it is at this point that they usually throw in that condescending line, "just like we do in the cockpit," which always irritates me for some reason.) You have just been cautioned by the person who is about to control your destiny—your very life—to expect a rough ride. Despite the anxiety and apprehension, you logically understand that the odds are that you will safely arrive at your chosen destination. You will have to ride it out. You do not have a choice.

Such is the case with divorce. Strange terms, concepts, anxiety, fear and apprehension—and most of all, the uneasy knowledge that your life is in the control of someone else. Nevertheless, think for a moment. When you take an airplane trip, you rarely have the opportunity to meet or speak with the pilot before the flight. For that matter, the pilot does not get a chance to know you either. It does not matter the slightest bit if the pilot likes you or not. You are just a name on a flight manifest, an individual to be counted to calculate the fuel necessary to be loaded on the plane. However, even if you did get to meet the pilot beforehand, would it really make any difference? What would it get you, anyway—an extra bag of peanuts and a free cocktail? What really matters is that you and the pilot share something crucial: a stake in your safety. If the pilot does not do his job correctly, it is more than likely that neither one of you will arrive at your destination in one piece. So what about your flight on *Air Divorce*? Does it make a difference if you get to know the pilot and if they actually like you? Yes, absolutely it does.

When the lawyer you select really admires and respects you as a person, not just a client, he or she wants to do their very best for you. The lawyer will exceed his or her professional obligation to zealously represent your interests. And when your lawyer does not admire or respect you, the results may reflect those negative feelings. Despite rumors to the contrary, lawyers are people too. Their feelings factor into their work just like that of every other professional. Remember, although your heart may be broken, a lawyer is not like a skilled cardiac surgeon operating on you while you are lying motionless and under anesthesia on the operating room table. Your lawyer registers every cry of pain and anguish that you convey, spoken and unspoken. They also hear every complaint, whine, gripe, criticism, moan and grumble. Moreover, they hear your praise and appreciation. Loud and clear.

From a lawyer's perspective, there are some substantial advantages and disadvantages to developing a strong positive relationship with your client. On the plus side, over the years of my practice I developed many friendships that continue up through the present day. I even met my wife—but that is a completely different chapter.

I always told potential clients to ask me as many questions as they liked. Though preferably, not the same one over and over. If I could not provide the client with what they thought was an intelligent answer to their question, then I was probably off base somewhere. There would certainly be times when I did not know the answer to a client's question. Intelligent counsel readily admits to the lack of knowledge and finds the answer to the best of his or her ability. I also always encouraged potential clients to get a second opinion. When the client would express reservation at really wanting to do so (some people do not want to hurt the feelings of the professional) I would tell them, "Absolutely—get a third and a fourth opinion too while you're at it."

Can you imagine going to see a doctor for, say, a hysterectomy or removal of your prostate gland? Understandably, you might express reservations to your doctor about undergoing such a drastic surgical remedy. You might ask him or her, "Should I get a second opinion?" Imagine your doctor saying, "No, I wouldn't bother getting a second opinion. It's not necessary. You need this procedure and I am more than qualified to do it. Seeing someone else would just be a waste of your time and money." Now, would you even consider allowing this physician to place you under anesthesia? You should *always* feel free to get a second opinion, because, not to belabor the point, your lawyer has the ability to determine the destiny of your case, and that decision deserves plenty of research. If you get a lawyer who is incompetent, unprofessional or unethical, your life can become even more miserable than it may already be.

# A WARNING FOR LAWYERS
## *The Nightmare Client*

*Who is the nightmare client?* As you might have guessed, this interesting breed of humanity is not necessarily discernable upon the initial consultation. The nightmare client may first be viewed as a pleasant, but troubled, individual. Unfortunately, for the unsuspecting lawyer, the nightmare client is able to convince you to assume their representation. It is after the representation has begun that you discover the dreadful mistake that you have made. What makes a nightmare client so horrific? There are many reasons.

Generally, the nightmare client is just a miserable person. They may be angry, greedy or malicious. The nightmare client is someone you would never invite to dinner. In fact, this type of person makes you question whether or not you should assist them in obtaining a divorce; after all, they might go out and marry someone else and ruin their lives too. Sometimes the nightmare clients who are the worst suffer from terrible personality or character flaws. The nightmare client is often a "know-it-all." The nightmare client can't make up their mind, and when they do, they usually make a very poor choice initially, followed by an even worse decision thereafter. Despite any advice that you may have given the client, he or she will eventually blame you or others when things go wrong. After you have remedied the dilemma that was unnecessarily created by the client, the client will attribute the problem to something you did, or will credit the resolution to his or her own imagined actions. The nightmare client is almost always unappreciative. Here's a typical dialogue between an attorney and a typical nightmare client after leaving the courtroom following a wonderful victory:

*Attorney:* I just got you an award of $24,000 per month in lifetime alimony and a monetary award of $8.9 million. This is the part where you say *"Thank you."*

*Nightmare client:* I don't have to say thank you. That's what you were paid to do...

The nightmare client makes you crazy. No matter how large the retainer you will have received, the money you collect will not even come close to compensating you for the loss of your time and energy. This person has a way of becoming your most draining client, if not in terms of workload, then certainly in terms of taking away years from your life. Others have described the nightmare client as "narcissistic and self-absorbed, paranoid and passive-aggressive, relentless and cruel." The nightmare client doesn't care that you have other clients. As far as they are concerned, you don't. They will call you frequently, often, recurrently and regularly (I think you get the point) such when your receptionist announces the call that you get the feeling that your teeth have turned around and begun eating your brain. You may be in a crucial meeting with your most important client. Somehow, the nightmare client will interrupt with an "emergency." The sun rises and sets at their whim.

There are many reasons why attorneys frequently get involved in cases involving nightmare clients. Some include helping a friend of the family; a referral from an appreciative but unknowing client; or the desire to be involved in a case that might be perceived as "high-profile" or otherwise lucrative. The frequent excuse of needing to generate income to meet payroll and other expenses is a much-cited reason for bad decision-making on the part of the attorney. Trust me, it is better to be evicted and live in a halfway house with diseased lepers than to deal with the nightmare client.

When you are interviewing new clients, be sure to have a criterion that they must meet. They need to be cooperative and to follow your instructions. In the end, you'll be glad that you did. If they are unwilling to agree to follow your instructions, be like Nancy Reagan and "Just say NO!" By not agreeing to represent this type of client you will not only add three years to your life (and probably avoid possible in-patient hospitalization in a psychiatric ward), you will create a reputation as being a lawyer who does not take every case that walks in the door. Remember, after the nightmare client is long gone, you will have to appear in front of those same judges that your nightmare client embarrassed you in front of. It's just not worth it.

Look for the warning signs of the difficult client:

1. Represented by prior counsel?
2. First, second or third marriage?
3. Overly concerned about legal fees?

4. Uncontrollably angry with their spouse?

5. History of psychiatric problems?

6. Body language?

7. Argumentative?

8. Prior counsel fully paid?

The biggest mistake made with the nightmare client is not getting out of the case when the warning signs appear and remain uncorrected. The closer you are to trial, the less likely you will be able to successfully withdraw. I recommend that all lawyers properly document in their file and directly to the client all areas in which you feel that your client has failed to comply with your advice or with the underlying engagement letter with your law firm. If necessary, have another lawyer, paralegal or secretary sit in on conferences or listen on the speaker phones to phone calls with the client. If necessary, this may be of help in corroborating your difficult circumstances. Do not be afraid to terminate the relationship at the first sign of trouble. If problems with the client have begun, they will only be compounded over time. The nightmare client is a parasite that will drain you of your sanity and very existence.

People have different objectives when they seek a consultation—advice, comfort, and sometimes guarantees. I always advised clients that I could never give odds on any matter of better than 50-50. Not because I did not feel that I could do better, but because it was preferable for the client to have their expectations set lower and maybe, be happily surprised. If you are looking for a lawyer to tell you that they will absolutely get you this or guarantee you that, it is not going to happen; not that you might not be able to obtain the guarantee from some unscrupulous practitioner that ultimately fails to deliver on their promise.

Most competent practitioners do not make guarantees. Not lawyers, doctors or accountants, and especially stockbrokers. The problem with making a guarantee is that in the law, as in medicine, certain aspects of the care are outside the control of the care provider. No lawyer knows (or ethically should know) how a judge will feel the day that you appear in court. Maybe he will have gotten laid the night before and he will be happy; or maybe he will have had a huge fight with his wife before he comes to court that morning and be in a terrible mood. Some judges are mean, miserable people. Others are even-tempered, compassionate, caring people. There is no way to guarantee anything.

---

A MIDDLE-AGED GUY IS OUT TO DINNER
WITH HIS WIFE TO CELEBRATE HER FORTIETH BIRTHDAY.
HE SAYS, "SO WHAT WOULD YOU LIKE, HOLLY?
A JAGUAR? A SABLE COAT? A DIAMOND NECKLACE?"
SHE SAYS, "CLARK, I WANT A DIVORCE."
"OH," HE SAYS,
"I WASN'T PLANNING ON SPENDING *THAT* MUCH."

---

It frequently happened that when clients consulted with me it would take only moments to become aware that they had ridiculous expectations, as to both the legal process and anticipated results that any lawyer could provide. Quite often, those expectations were put into place by a "friend"—one who had thrown emotional fuel on the fire that precipitated the visit to my office in the first place. People going through the breakdown of a marriage have already encountered one of the most brutal forms of dashed expectations. In some instances, the disappointment is with their spouse, sometimes, in themselves. Regardless of the etiology of the disappointment, divorce for some reason (I bet Dr. Phil can explain) engenders expectations from a process that is not designed to render everyone happy. Excuse me, anyone happy.

A good example was the woman who had triplets by her former employer. Her expectations were composed completely of emotional dreams, not legal reality. Had her initial legal counsel recognized the elevated level of hemoglobin in her ocular region, they might have told her, "I cannot get that for you; that is an unrealistic expectation." Unfortunately, for her, and my client, her expectations were not properly adjusted at the commencement of her introduction to the legal process. She was the type that needed a judicial adjustment of reality.

A divorce lawyer's job is to zealously represent their client within established boundaries, generally known as rules of professional conduct. Should a lawyer try to get as much as they can possibly get for their client? No question. Does there come a point where a lawyer might be able to get more, but if he or she docs, there will be a compromise in other areas—whether it be increased acrimony, hatred between the spouses, or harm to the children? Absolutely. The lawyer must assist the client in that sometimes delicate balancing act. Is that extra million dollars really worth what it is going to cost in terms of fees and acrimony and other post-marital bliss? Is the extra day that the father has requested for visitation really worth a custody battle? Those are decisions that ultimately the client has to make. Moreover, the counsel your lawyer provides regarding those decisions will probably influence not only where you live, but also how well you live there.

Many times, people involved in divorce cases retain then subsequently terminate their legal counsel. Sometimes the client is dissatisfied with the services they have received from their lawyer. Many times, they leave because their lawyer will not provide them with the advice that they *want* to hear. Sometimes the lawyer is fed up with a client who is used to having everything their way and refuses to heed their advice. At a certain point the lawyer may just say, "I'm not going to do it this way, and if you want somebody to do it that way, go find another lawyer." Lawyers can and do terminate clients—especially good lawyers. It is certainly a red flag to a prospective lawyer when a potential client seeking services had been represented by two or more prior lawyers. When I found myself in this situation, and I knew the lawyer who had previously represented them, I sometimes easily understood—their first lawyers were incompetent or dishonest, and I could understand them seeking other counsel.

However, if their former lawyer was competent, someone who I respected, I would call him or her to see what their relationship was with the client. Certainly that sort of information might be considered privileged, but when the other lawyer said something like, "I'd rather not talk about it," that was all I needed to know. I would most likely not be representing that person. Therefore, while it is important that you are satisfied with the performance of your lawyer, you must remember that you should not change lawyers with the same frequency that you change underwear. It can create an impression of instability that you never intended.

It is also important to understand that lawyers are traditionally very busy professionals, and a good lawyer is that much busier. Clients need to understand that their lawyer is not a psychologist, psychiatrist, or counselor (despite the fact that some clients wrongfully treat them as such). If you need that type of support, which would be completely appropriate and well advised in most cases, you should seek that professional care through the proper channels. You need to understand that your lawyer may come across as insensitive at times and they probably are not; it is just that they have probably been through hundreds of divorces, and may forget to keep reassuring you, "I know this is really hard," or whatever you want or need to hear. I always tried to be sensitive towards the emotional vulnerabilities of my clients, but at times, failed to do so.

---

A LAWYER IS NEVER ENTIRELY COMFORTABLE WITH
A FRIENDLY DIVORCE, ANYMORE THAN A GOOD
MORTICIAN WANTS TO FINISH HIS JOB AND THEN
HAVE THE PATIENT SIT UP ON THE TABLE.

—*Jean Kerr*

---

Sometimes I had clients come in to my office nearly in tears, wringing their hands and saying, "My husband hired Jim Kottrel!" They would be referring to another very competent, well-respected and typically feared divorce attorney.

"That's great news!" I would say. The client would always appear bewildered.

"What do you mean? He's supposed to be a son of a bitch. He represented the husband of my best friend. He *destroyed* her. He's going to do this and this and he's going to do that..."

"He's perfect! He's a great lawyer, just a bit misunderstood – I'll call him." Here is the side of the conversation my client would typically hear:

"Hey, Jimmy, it's Mark. Yeah, I'm good, just a little tired. What about you? Really? South Beach? Wow. Who knew? Listen, I'm representing Mrs. Ramsey. Yes, the wife of the famous investment banker. No, she seems to be quite nice. What's he like? Sure, just like all of your clients, a real angel. Can we get it resolved? Yes, she wants to. Perfect. I will call you when I know more. Thanks, and don't forget to use your lotion."

The moral of this story is that you should never fear another lawyer based upon his or her reputation. You *want* your spouse to engage competent counsel. It certainly makes sense to be prepared for any case by hiring the best lawyer possible, especially when your spouse has engaged well-respected (or feared) counsel. After all, you would not want to bring a dagger to a gunfight. You will lose. On the other hand, a fistfight does not require the use of a nuclear weapon. It is a question of degree, and the proper estimation of your potential risks and vulnerabilities is crucial to your success. A good lawyer knows how to measure both and will draw upon his or her arsenal accordingly. The incompetent lawyer will not....

COMBINED AGE OF
THE WORLD'S OLDEST
COUPLE TO GET
A DIVORCE: 188

So let's assume that you have engaged a real barracuda of a lawyer to take on the formidable task of doing battle with your spouse. If he or she wants to fight, you are ready. But should you? If I had to speculate, I would say that 95 percent of my cases were resolved by virtue of a settlement. I do not offer this statistic as a pat on my own back. Settlement requires willingness and effort on the part of four individuals: the two lawyers and both parties. I must attribute most of my settlements to a byproduct of the cold war, the concept of mutually assured destruction. MAD is the theory that any use of nuclear weapons by either of two superpowers would result in the destruction of both the attacker and the defender. The doctrine assumes that each side has enough weaponry to destroy the other side and that either side, if attacked for any reason by the other, would retaliate with equal or greater force. The expected result is that the battle would escalate to the point where each side brought about the other's total and assured destruction. Under MAD, neither side would be so illogical as to risk its own annihilation. Accordingly, neither side would gamble to launch a first strike. The payoff of this doctrine was peace, albeit a "maddening" one.

And so it is in divorce litigation. When the stakes are high and both parties have the weaponry, both parties are facing what might be termed "Marital Armageddon." When I opposed competent counsel, they understood this concept with crystal clarity. Both of us knew what was going to happen—mutual destruction—so why go through the whole *mishegoss*? Other lawyers (and sometimes clients) did not understand this simple concept. Unfortunately, for them, they would launch the first missile, only to realize that their perceived warhead was only a sparkler. When the returning warhead impacted, it was too late. The war was on.

A number of clients want their counsel to be as aggressive as humanly possible. When requested to do so, I would oblige within the ethical confines of the law. After all, that is why many lawyers are hired. However, once we reached the point where I concluded that the client had received a fair offer that I felt should have been accepted, I would expend as much effort as possible to try to help the client understand why he or she should accept the settlement. I would listen to their concerns, and if their rationale for proceeding made any sense, I would honor their wishes. I would try my hardest to understand the client's perspective. If the client could not articulate any legitimate or even logical reason for the proposed missile launch or was obviously just acting out of vengeance, my efforts would be unsuccessful. At that juncture, I would refuse to take their case any further. If the client wanted more, they needed to find a new lawyer.

Why? Because I would continue to spin in the revolving door of the divorce world that they would soon exit. In other words, I had to appear before the same judges again in the same court, and I had no desire of being remembered by a judge as being unreasonable in any case. Unreasonableness typically is the result of a lack of judgment. A lack of judgment calls into question one's competence. And most (but apparently not all) lawyers prefer to avoid that label. The bottom line is that when and if you divorce, or happen to be negotiating your pre-nuptial agreement, you must secure skilled and ethical representation—it makes everything so much easier and keeps the missiles where they belong—in the silos.

When your lawyer is a sincere professional, they really are genuinely on your side. If you wind up with a lawyer who is perhaps not quite so professional you will need to be constantly on guard making sure that he or she is not deliberately escalating fees and costs, trying to extend the proceedings, discouraging settlements and sordid actions of that nature. Good, successful lawyers do not need to do that (though I recently encountered some lawyers who were financially successful but still did exactly that). There is plenty of divorce work available because plenty of us get married; no truly competent lawyer needs to continue to toil over and over the misfortunes of an existing client. A good divorce lawyer just wants your matter solved to your satisfaction.

---

## AN INCOMPETENT ATTORNEY CAN DELAY A TRIAL FOR YEARS OR MONTHS. A COMPETENT ATTORNEY CAN DELAY ONE EVEN LONGER.

—*Evelle J. Younger, Former Attorney General of California*

---

You can foster a strong relationship with your lawyer by being honest with him or her and communicating openly with them. You need to let your lawyer know what you expect from him or her at the commencement of your case; and you also need to ascertain what your lawyer expects from you to avoid any potential disconnect. It is your job to fully understand how the billing practices of the firm work and do not work, and to understand the general strategies lawyers use to settle versus try cases. How do you do that? Simply ask. If you do not understand what you are being told, have your lawyer explain it differently. Do not act as if you understand what you are being told if you actually do not. It will only lead to problems and misunderstandings later.

All states have regulatory authorities that govern the conduct of lawyers. In some jurisdictions, this duty is implemented by the administrative offices of the highest court of the state, and in others by state agencies. If there is one thing that most lawyers fear, it is a letter from the state bar marked in red "Personal & Confidential." The process to discipline lawyers varies widely from state to state. Most of the time the proceedings are open to the public, and in all states you can ascertain whether your lawyer has a disciplinary history. Today, you can even check the disciplinary record of your proposed lawyer online in most states, and you should not feel bad at all about doing that. The initial perception that the court has of you is usually inextricably intertwined with that of your lawyer. Most likely, the court knows your lawyer, but not you. And after all, what can it harm to ascertain that your lawyer has a perfectly unblemished disciplinary record? Nothing at all.

The bar complaint most frequently filed against lawyers arises from the failure to return the phone calls of clients. You have to understand that your lawyer may not be as responsive as you would like. That is why it is so important to establish from the commencement of your representation how, exactly, you plan to communicate with your lawyer. Will you do it all by e-mail? That does not mean sending a seven-page dissertation – but just a quick question where you will get a quick response. If you can ask for a yes or no answer, that is best. Will all communications be by phone? If so, are you consolidating the information that you want to get to or receive from your lawyer, so that you receive the full value of the incremental billing you will be charged, despite the brevity of your call? Lawyers typically bill in increments of 15 minutes. I used to advise my clients, "Save up, save up!" so they could properly utilize all of their time, because as clients they would be charged for it anyway. Every once in awhile a client would call and say, "Mark, I've just got a really quick question – don't charge me!" And if it really was just a quick, one-minute query, I did not charge them. However, they had to keep it to one quick question. Maybe two or three if I really liked them.

Lawyers usually do not return calls when a client has literally inundated them with the same questions repeatedly, creating the equivalent of a legal factitious disorder. Every minor problem to this type of client is a catastrophe. There were clients that would call me so frequently and annoyed me so much that when my secretary would announce that they were calling for the fifth time that morning I would swear that blood was about to spurt out of the veins in my head. I still wanted to help the client; I just did not want them to monopolize me from serving everyone fairly. Save yourself some money and your lawyer his or her sanity—try to limit your calls to those times when they are necessary and consolidate your questions. Be con-

**LARGEST DIVORCE SETTLEMENT: $1.7 BILLION**

cise. Be specific. And give them time to return your call. It is extremely aggravating to get a call from a client every hour. Your lawyer has other clients. They have conferences with other clients, just like they have with you. They have court appearances. They also probably have a life of their own. The signals that you send to your lawyer are important in terms of how your lawyer will perceive and represent you.

The signals that you as a client send to your spouse's lawyer are just as critical, if not more so. The last message that you ever want to send to the counsel of your spouse is that you are weak, unintelligent, insecure or unreasonable. In other words, unless instructed otherwise by your own lawyer to do so (for example, a spouse playing the victim role), you should never let the other lawyer know that he or she has affected you or gotten under your skin. The other lawyer very well may have, but when you show them that they have aggravated you, you empower them and your spouse. It is akin to the advice that most park rangers would give you on encountering, let's say, a wolf: never make a sudden movement or show the wolf that you are scared. If you do, you will probably be attacked as opposed to just being growled at. Besides, as the old saying goes, it is more fun to get even than to get mad.

---

## WE WERE VERY HAPPILY MARRIED FOR EIGHT MONTHS. UNFORTUNATELY, WE WERE MARRIED FOR TEN YEARS...

---

Let me try to demonstrate for you how *not* to communicate with opposing counsel. The courtroom was beautiful. High ceilings, large brass chandeliers circa 1895, like something you would see in a movie. I was cross-examining a famous athlete on the witness stand in a highly contested divorce trial. During the course of the contentious cross-examination, his attorney voiced a very technical objection that required careful consideration by the court prior to issuing a ruling. The judge decided to remain on the bench while he reviewed the cases provided to the court for consideration by counsel. I stood behind a simple wooden lectern conducting my examination, looking down at the case the judge was reviewing in anticipation of answering any questions he might have. I looked over the courtroom audience, and then glanced up at the witness stand where the sports legend was seated. He was glaring at me; and then he silently mouthed the words "*F%^# you*" to me.

I had a decision to quickly make: either I could tell the judge, or I could do what I chose to do instead: *smile at him.* Because I knew at that very moment that he was, all mine. I had totally gotten under his skin. So much so that years later, when my wife and I were on vacation on Hawaii, I ran into him at the swimming pool. He was swimming, but the minute he saw me I think his tan turned white and he promptly exited the pool and surrounding area. Not being a sports fan, I had no idea that the Pro Bowl was that week. The quarterback had had a very good lawyer, but Mr. Joe Theismann was not used to playing a game on this field—and he sent the wrong call from the huddle to the opposing team. Then again, I'm sure he did not appreciate my opening statement in the case, when I said words to the effect, "This man committed adultery, and the evidence will show you that the reason he articulated to his wife for committing adultery was as follows: *"God wants Joe Theismann to be happy."* He had actually articulated divine absolution for adultery! As the case was tried in a conservative county outside Washington, DC, it was in *The Washington Post* the next day. *"God wants Joe Theismann to be happy!"* I think, was the headline of the article. He denied saying it, of course.

---

MY HUSBAND AND I DIVORCED
OVER RELIGIOUS DIFFERENCES.
HE THOUGHT HE WAS GOD,
AND I DID NOT.

---

# ADVICE TO REMEMBER
*Cross-examination, speaking with your spouse and carving a turkey*

In lieu of my typical "advice to remember" section, I wanted to give you a few pointers about the best way to handle yourself during the lovely legal process called cross-examination. That is the part of the case that most litigants look forward to with dread. The way you view it depends upon how confident and truthful you are, who your lawyer is, and who the other lawyer is.

As I pondered the advice I wished to convey here, it occurred to me that cross-examination has much in common with carving the holiday turkey. Think about it. Who wants to carve a turkey with a dull knife? No one. It makes the whole process more difficult. Instead of swift clean slices, you end up with a real mess on your hands. It takes longer. You end up tearing off the legs and wings. It lacks precision.

Same with cross-examination. There is nothing like a good lawyer employing the crafts of his trade to methodically dissect a witness. Hollywood and television thrive on these types of reenactments, from Raymond Burr in *Perry Mason* to Tom Cruise in *A Few Good Men*. Remember the scene in that movie where Jack Nicholson crumbles on the witness stand yelling, "You can't handle the truth!"? Everybody loves a good cross-examination, except for the person on the cutting board. The skilled lawyer utilitizes sharp inquiries designed to obtain a result with the least possible resistance. Think of it as the difference between using a machete to carve a turkey versus a surgical scalpel. The latter may get it done, but it will make a mess. It is difficult to maneuver or handle. It is imprecise.

There is an old adage amongst trial lawyers that on cross-examination you never pose a question to which you do not know the answer. If you do so, there is a substantial risk that you will hear an answer that is unfavorable to your case. Lawyers frequently have difficulty knowing when to stop— we like to hear ourselves talk. The end result is usually asking that one question too many, giving the witness the chance to take the carving knife right out of your hand into theirs. The next thing you know the lawyer has a machete stabbed through the heart of their case.

You will note at this point I have not stated how all of this ties in to communicating with your spouse. Now I am sure I will make some folks angry here, but speaking with your spouse can sometimes feel like cross-examination (and I swear Rose, I am not talking about you). "Where have you been?" "Who were you with?" "Was he there?" "Was she there?" Did you go there with her?" "Did you ever tell another guy that?" I think you get the gist. How you answer these questions can be your salvation or damnation. It is like being on the witness stand right in your very own home, with no judge present to control the hostile advances of your examiner.

The following are a series of six rules and some examples that you should always use during a cross-examination—be it in a courtroom, in a deposition, or during some of those "tense" conversations with your spouse:

### Rule #1    Tell the truth

As we will discuss in the chapter on Human Nature, lying in court (and for that matter anywhere) is just not a good idea. Once you utter the first lie, more will follow and eventually you will be caught. I just read in a great novel by Nelson DeMille titled *Night Fall* words to the effect that lies are like cockroaches. Where there is one, there are others. And nobody likes cockroaches.

## Rule #2    Tell the truth only in response to the question posed

Just as lawyers like to hear themselves speak, so do many witnesses. Listen to the question that has been posed on cross-examination. Repeat the question to yourself before forming your answer. I always recommended to clients that they practice and start this process from the very beginning of the examination. When you are asked the question "Please state your name," repeat to yourself, "Please state your name." It gets you in the habit of making sure that you understand the question being posed. It gives you a moment to form the correct and truthful answer in your mind. It slows you down. Things done more carefully and slowly are oftentimes done more correctly than those that are rushed. Then, and only then, answer just that question. Nothing else.

Because I believe this to be so crucial in the success of your cross-examination, I will give you a few examples. If on Tuesday, March 4, 2005 the opposing lawyer asks you on cross-examination, "Can you please tell me what today is?" what would you say? Tuesday? March 4? Both are wrong answers. The lawyer has asked you a yes or no question. Either you know what today is or you do not. Make your adversary work. Do not volunteer information.

Most questions on cross-examination are capable of yes or no answers. Your basic inventory of answers during cross-examination should be composed of the following: yes, no, I do not know, I do not understand the question and the perennial favorite, I do not recall. Learn and remember these. If you think about it, in response to the question "Now, can you please tell me what today is?" could be answered correctly by saying any of the following: yes, no, I do not know, I do not understand the question and, of course, I do not recall.

## Rule #3   Preparation is best through practice

Whenever you are going to be subject to possible cross-examination, you must practice. Most litigants are not accustomed to cross-examination, the process whereby someone subjects everything you say to intensive scrutiny with no desire to help you. It takes getting used to. You want to be cooperative, but not evasive. You have your emotions to control in a tense and difficult environment.

If you have retained competent counsel, they will hopefully devote substantial time towards getting you ready for this age-old dance of words. If your counsel has not done so, get them to do it. At least on two separate occasions. Do not accept "You'll do fine" as an answer from your lawyer unless he or she has first tested your ability to cope with this aspect of your case.

This is one aspect of the process that you can also practice at home with your friends or unknowing participants. How many times has someone walked up to you and asked you "Do you know what time it is?" Next time, look at your watch, repeat the question to yourself, and then answer "Yes." After all, that is the correct answer. You know what time it is, the person asking does not. I like it on the telephone when I am leaving a message and the person on the other end of the call asks me "Can you spell your last name?" I usually just answer yes, and enjoy the awkward moment of silence. They just did not ask the right question.

## Rule #4   Speculation is fun for gamblers, not cross-examination

This rule actually embodies the concepts of the first three rules. The witness stand is no place to guess. If you know the answer, see if it fits one of your inventory answers, or is susceptible to some other response you know to be true. If you really do not know the answer or do not understand the question, do not answer the question until you do know. Do not be pressured to give an answer or an estimate with which you are uncomfortable. It is an exaggerated example, but I used to try to emphasize to my clients this point by asking the following question: "Am I a male or a female?" Most would answer that I was male. However, the real answer is unless they peeked at me in the bathroom, they did not know. They were guessing. Try it with your ordinary conversation with friends. It is amazing to actually see how much we volunteer information as opposed to simply answering the question posed.

### Rule #5   Don't forget to leave the door open

Most of us have heard at some point during our lives words to the effect, "Make sure the door is closed." The rule for cross-examination is the exact opposite if you are the person being cross-examined. The lawyer asking you the questions wants to close the door on you, to prevent your escape. You on the other hand, always want a way out. The best way to keep the door open is to indicate (when you cannot use any of the inventory answers) something along the following lines: "Sitting here right now, I am not sure that I can remember everything that might be responsive to your question. I will attempt to answer the question to the best of my ability, but I may recall additional facts later." By doing this you usually will avoid be impeached or contradicted at a later date or even later in your cross-examination. You can most likely supplement or clarify your testimony. You have left the door open.

### Rule #6   Keep calm

Emotions have no place during cross-examination unless your legal counsel has advised you otherwise. Take a deep breath and relax if you need to. Pay attention to your body language. Ask to use the restroom or take a break. Cross-examination is not torture unless you make it such. It actually can be kind of fun.

# FRED GRANDY
## *Cruising The Love Boat of Life*

---

*Fred Grandy is an amazing man. Most of us were introduced to Fred when he portrayed the beloved ship's purser "Gopher" on television's The Love Boat, a major hit from 1977 to 1986. What most of us did not know was that Fred had graduated magna cum laude from Harvard University in 1970 with a degree in English. That same year he was married, later had two children, and then went through a painful divorce that ended in 1982. In 1987 he married Catherine, and later became the father to another daughter, and he remains happily married. From 1987 until 1995, he was a Republican member of the United States Congress (Iowa-5th District). In 1995 he became the President and CEO of Goodwill Industries, one of the largest non-profit organizations in the country, and received numerous accolades for his leadership and work. Today, Fred gets the morning going for me and thousands of other Washingtonians on 630 WMAL as the host of a four-hour daily radio show with topical guests, interviews and the people of ABC News. I think that you will be surprised by Fred's experience, candor, advice and keen insight on cruising the real "Love Boat" of life.*

*Here are some poignant thoughts from Fred:*

**THE LOVE BOAT** probably did for love and marriage what Godiva chocolates do for dieting. It tastes great, but it's not good for you. The show was pure escapist romance. To its credit, it did wind up becoming what you would now kind of call a "family show" with solid values—commitment is important, love is not to be trifled with, and so on. The whole idea of being on a cruise is that you have escaped from everything. What happens on the Lido deck *stays* on the Lido deck kind of thing. I do not know if it really influenced anyone in their real-life relationship – what

I know is that it profoundly influenced the cruise industry. The whole industry was moribund when the show started, and was very robust by the time the show ended, and remains so to this day.

*The Love Boat* took its effect on my own marriage. While I was busy sailing, I actually got divorced. *The Love Boat* was the first real success I had in my show business career. All of a sudden, my wife and I had the means that we didn't have when I was starting out as an actor. We found ourselves with the luxury of incompatibility. We didn't *have* to stay together anymore, because we had enough resources to dissolve the marriage. Rightly or wrongly, my success allowed us to separate and set up two households, which we did. We arranged a very carefully constructed joint custody relationship with our two kids, who were both under 10 years old at the time. We were scrupulous about making sure that we both saw the kids on a regular basis, and that they didn't feel estranged or disrupted anymore than they had to be. That happened anyway, of course, and I think that is a reason why they both waited so long to get married themselves. I think they both thought, "I'm not putting my kids through *that.*"

My son and daughter both waited until they were 30 to say "I do." I certainly believe that it is a wise idea to wait until age 30 to marry. If there was any dividend out of that divorce, it was that my son and daughter became very close as siblings and remain very close friends as adults. If one of my children came to me right now saying they were unhappy and thinking about divorce after a few years of marriage, I would tell them they didn't know what unhappiness is. If you want to know what *real* unhappiness is, start the whole process of divorce. To me, three years is like quitting a round of golf after the third hole. Sure, you can do it and walk off the course, but you've left most of your game undiscovered. I would certainly discourage quitting easily. But I would be stunned if either my daughter or my son said that—because of what they saw, both waited until they could really zero in on their prospective mate and agree to the contract. I don't think divorce will ever happen to them. They are a lot smarter than I was in figuring out what marriage entails before signing on the dotted line.

Looking back, I think I got married prematurely. I did it for all the right reasons at the time, but the problem *was* the time. I was just not ready for the demands that kind of relationship made, and I wasn't old enough to understand what they were. Naturally, when you are in your twenties and early thirties you are more career-focused and ambitious and I would even say more rapacious in those years when you're trying to lay down the foundation of whatever career you are seeking. You are obliged to be a little more selfish about going out and doing what it takes to build a career to provide for yourself and your family. Ironically, though, that's going to pull you away from a relationship, unless you have a very strong foundation. This is why I think waiting until you have a little bit more perspective on your life and your career to get married is important.

I had wanted to be an actor when I got out of school, and I plunged into it. My first wife and I moved to New York where I was a struggling but working actor, and then to Hollywood. Whenever there was a possibility for a job, I was on it. My first wife understood that, and we both accepted it as a consequence of our relationship. I do think in our particular case there was another factor that led to our split. Because we had children fairly early on-by choice, not by accident—my wife had decided to put her career on hold. I think to some degree that suppressed career ambition on her part, probably festered and produced some tension and ill feeling that eventually bubbled over and caused the separation.

I left *The Love Boat* in 1985 to go back home to Iowa to run for Congress. I wasn't elected until 1986 – *it was the longest audition of my life.* I served for four terms – eight years. After I was elected, I remarried in 1987. What I can tell you about being married to a politician as opposed to an actor is this: the demands on a legislator are inhuman, particularly someone who serves in Washington. You literally have to be in two places at once. You've got to be at home, and you've got to be in Washington. We tried every variation on that theme. We lived in Washington. My present wife and I have a daughter together who has just turned sixteen; she was just a little kid when I first got elected. We did everything we could to stay together as much as we could. If that meant living in Washington when I was first elected, then moving everyone back out to Iowa, that's what we did. The professional demands on someone who serves in Congress can really take their toll. There's a very high divorce rate in Congress, just as there is in Hollywood; but I think because I'd already weathered that storm once, and of course my wife was older and she had been married before, we were perhaps a little more focused on the work that went into this relationship and less inclined to sacrifice everything for my career.

*Divorce is dying without death.* At least when you are going through the process of watching a relative or close friend die, you know there is going to be an end to it. With divorce, you're never quite sure of it. Even though you have signed the papers and you are legally unconnected, there are all those kind of lingering feelings of recrimination and doubt and bitterness, which is terribly hard on kids, and you as well of course. The hardest thing to learn about divorce is how to know when it's over and how to begin again. My first wife and I are quite friendly now, as a matter of fact she lives in the Boston area and sees my daughter from my second marriage regularly. She's a great comfort to my daughter who is far away from home at boarding school. My daughter sees my first wife probably more than she sees us at this point! But that's something that finally evolved over twenty years. To some degree, you have to accept that a divorce is an organic relationship just the way a marriage is, and it takes some effort to make it work. You don't just kind of de-couple, you have to kind of refine the uncoupling as well, or you're going to be at one another's throats forever. Or avoid each other entirely, which of course is terrible for your children.

The best way to keep a relationship afloat? One of things you have to acknowledge about marriage is that this kind of accommodation is always a work in progress. It is kind of like democracy – you never quite get it right. It always needs a little bit of tinkering, but the process, perhaps, is more important than the product. You need tremendous amounts of patience to get through a marriage, which is yet another good argument for waiting, because obviously when you're in your twenties and even early thirties you tend to be a little more impetuous and a little less tolerant of letting things settle in and mature. One of my rules would be, DON'T JUST DO SOMETHING—STAND THERE. Unlike the rest of life, where the argument is always "Don't just stand there, do something," in marriage, it should be "Don't just do something; stand there." It is hard to do; because of course when you are courting the opposite is true. Any kind of romantic notion you have is impulsive and sometimes you have to lead with that impulse. Romance at some point certainly reaches another level, particularly after you have had children and watched those kids grow.

I would define love the same way John Lennon used to define life. He said, "Life's what happens while you're busy making other plans." To me, love is what happens while you are planning other engagements – your work, your career, and other personal relationships. To me love is what distills down and holds two people together. Love is one of those few things that allows two people to be together for a long time and remain close, even if they're not terribly compatible. If you're thinking seriously about marrying someone, rather than necessarily living together or acting out the marriage, go right to the trial separation first. See what your life is like without one another after you have a close bond. See if you can survive that and then perhaps if that becomes unbearable, you have learned something about what your commitment toward one another might be.

# CHAPTER 6

# DETECTIVES, DOCTORS
# AND EXPERTS

Your lawyer, in his or her role as your captain of the plane ride through the turbulence of divorce, may suggest that you hire a private investigator or perhaps other experts or forensic witnesses to investigate and support your case.

Forensic witnesses were traditionally witnesses that related to or dealt with the application of *scientific* knowledge to legal problems. Today, that definition has expanded to include *any* expert that specializes in testifying in court. Often, the retention of these individuals is critical to obtaining a successful result on a variety of issues. Other times, it is an utter waste of time and money. Why is there such a dramatic difference in the decision as to the necessity to employ these individuals? When we look at who these forensic specialists are, the rationale behind their retention should become rather apparent. However, before we do so, you must first appreciate one very basic theory that many lawyers and litigants ever fail to grasp.

It is my firm belief that expert witnesses and investigators should not be engaged unless there will be an equivalent or greater economic or non-economic return on your investment by retaining their services. In other words, why spend tens of thousands of dollars on a business valuation expert unless there is substantial reason to believe that his or her involvement will increase the marital or community property by an amount equal to or greater than that which you have spent or their services? Very few intelligent people will enter into a transaction where you will not receive something of equal or greater value in exchange for what you are paying. It simply does not make sense to do so. That being the case, why would you consider doing so during a time that you will most likely be encountering some amount of economic turbulence?

Most litigants rely upon their legal counsel when it comes to making the decision to retain these professionals. However, many times, lawyers will employ a formulaic response to a given set of facts instead of tailoring the response to the specific set of circumstances presented in your case. Remember Pavlov and his dog? It is what psychiatrists call classical conditioning. A dog believing that he is about to be fed "yum-yums" will start whining or salivating, regardless of whether or not you actually give them the treat. Lawyers can react the same way. Almost an unconscious, involuntary response: Oh, your husband is a having an affair? Let's hire the detectives. Nevertheless, what about the jurisdictions (and there are many of them) that are strictly "no-fault"? What is the perceived advantage in expending the money and proving facts that may not even be admissible in Court?

Many times the motivation behind the retention of investigators is the emotional disposition of the litigant at the time the issue is considered. If you have just learned that your spouse is having an extra-marital relationship, you are no doubt hurt and angry. You are out for blood and want to hire an investigator, *immediately.* But why? So you can show the video from the investigators to your friends? So that you will have a morbid souvenir of their marital indiscretion? Again, you must ask yourself, will there be an equivalent or greater economic or non-economic return on your investment in retaining their services, or is it just emotion usurping your otherwise good judgment?

I do not want to be misunderstood on this point—there are plenty of occasions when an experienced investigator does add legitimate value to your marital war chest. For instance, if marital misconduct such as adultery is a relevant factor to be considered by the court in allocating property, it may be important to be able to independently corroborate the misconduct. This will also be true if your spouse has been squandering monies accumulated during the marriage on substantial gifts for or travel with their lover. If custody is a potential issue, it may be necessary to explore the extra-marital conduct of your spouse in more detail. Is he or she engaging in the indiscretions in the presence of the children? Was he at the Happy Trails campground banging a bimbo, instead of being home with the children he professes now to love, care for and nurture?

Many times, the need for the investigator may not be present at the inception of your case, and instead may arise thereafter. In contested custody litigation, many times a spouse wants proof of what the other spouse is or is not doing while the child is in their care over the course of visitation. Is the husband actually taking care of the child, or is a nanny really doing it? Has the wife actually stopped her drinking as promised, or is she still frequenting her favorite watering hole? Does the husband actually use the car seat for the toddler, or does he disregard the safety of the child for his own convenience? These may actually be very relevant considerations for a court. Let's look at an example where hiring a private investigator was a gross waste of time and money:

I had a case where a private investigator actually followed my client, the mother, from the United States all the way to Greece. My client was the wonderful caring parent of a beautiful 10-year-old daughter. I had known her for some time, having handled her divorce from her husband maybe five years earlier. The husband never seemed to have gotten over his former wife. Her parents resided in Europe where she was raised, and my client enjoyed what might be described as an affluent "cosmopolitan" lifestyle. Each summer the parties would vacation at her parents' summer home on the Greek isle of Mykonos. Now I have never been to Mykonos, but I have heard many wonderful things about this paradise. The beautiful beaches, wonderful food, friendly people and idyllic scenery. I had also heard about the wild nightlife, partially nude beaches, fully nude beaches, and gay beaches. And by the time that the case was over, I had seen so many pictures of the island that I actually felt like I had been there.

From the evidence I was able to collect, my client and her family had visited the same beaches for many years, season after season, and knew many of the people that frequented the beaches they visited. One of these beaches was a family beach where some of the swimmers would elect not to wear all of their swimwear—and in some cases, none at all. As you may know, in Europe (as opposed to in most areas of our conservative great land) people frequently go topless on beaches. Nobody there thinks anything of it—it is a perfectly natural and culturally accepted practice.

So on a particular summer sunny day on Mykonos, my client, her 10-year-old daughter, her sister, her sister's 6-year-old daughter and her father all went to the beach, unaware that they were being videotaped the entire time by a private investigator from Washington, D.C. My client, on this particular day, elected to wear her entire swimsuit. Her father wore his and her sister went topless. So did the two little girls. But for the fact that some of the people in the videotape are wearing absolutely no clothes (including a completely naked male friend of the family who came up to

132

the family to visit with them) it would have seemed like a typical boring summer vacation video. In the video you could clearly see the children playing, even talking with the family's male friend, as they went about playing in the sand and frolicking on the beach, as other unclothed bathers strolled by. They completely failed to react to the naked male in any abnormal manner. They were used to it. When in Greece, *do as the Grecians do.* And that is exactly what they did. The little girls, as well as the adults, clearly understood that the rules were different in Mykonos as opposed to say, Bethany Beach, Delaware. Nonetheless, the father attempted to utilize these actions to cause a change in the custody arrangements and to preclude any future visits to Mykonos by the child. He cited that he was religiously and morally opposed to such behavior.

The father lost. The court, after viewing the videotape, ruled that it was perfectly within the mother's rights to act as she did, as nude beaches were a part of Greece's culture and customs, and there was no inkling of evidence or any danger of harm to the child. The father was the only one who had a problem with it. Not only that, we had in our possession (which we were kind enough to share with the Court) videotapes that the father had previously taken years earlier on this same nude beach, zooming in on nude girls and narrating about them with great relish in the background. So much for morals and religion. He had totally forgotten about those old videos. We refreshed his memory. Moreover, in the process of doing so proved that it does not always pay to hire an investigator.

---

## IT CANNOT BE SAID THAT NUDE SUNBATHING ON A BEACH IS A FORM OF EXPRESSION LIKELY TO BE UNDERSTOOD BY THE VIEWER AS AN ATTEMPT TO CONVEY A PARTICULAR POINT OF VIEW.

*—Vito J. Titone, Judge, NY State Court of Appeals. Unanimous opinion that nude sunbathing is not a constitutionally protected form of expression.*

---

Private investigators are just like lawyers in the sense that many are competent, principled professionals. They take their job extremely seriously, and many times, have some unusual experiences in doing so. Others are just downright sleazy, like the kind you see on TV or read about in cheap mystery novels. Private investigators merely document someone's behavior. The evidence they obtain does not ruin someone's fate; what that person has done has ruined their own fate. They are merely reporting and documenting the conduct of someone else; or rather their misconduct. Again, the central question you have to ask yourself and answer is *why* are you hiring the private investigator?

Clients often asked me for the recommendation of investigators, and I certainly steered them to detectives who I believed would competently complete the designated assignment. As an attorney you have to be careful, because if the same lawyer arrives in court every single time with the same investigator it starts to look like the investigator is just on retainer for this law firm and whatever the lawyer wants, this P.I. will find for him. The only thing that saves you from this kind of appearance is your own credibility; but it is wise to spread the wealth around a little bit, to avoid any potential appearance of impropriety.

In addition, different investigators have different surveillance styles and capabilities, as well as how they present their final report, all of which you and your lawyer must consider in making the final selection of the investigator to utilize. As with the process of selecting a lawyer, I have found that people will generally honestly convey their positive or negative experiences with an investigator previously engaged by them, so feel free to ask around, discreetly.

The most frequent complaint I heard about investigators usually occurred at the end of their surveillance. And almost always, it was not related to disappointment with the investigative results—it related to the amount of the investigator's bills. It is extremely important to set financial limits on your private investigators, and you should advise your lawyer, "I will spend $5,000 on a private investigator and I'm not willing to spend a dime more. Whatever we need to do, we have to get it done within that framework." The bills for an investigator can quickly mount to unexpected levels. Do the math—two investigators at $100 per hour each waiting all night for your spouse to emerge from his all-night "marathon business meeting." It adds up fast. Once again, you must keep in mind: what is the potential for an economic return? The bottom line that matters is how much are you going to benefit from catching someone doing something—how much is it worth in dollars or actual benefit to you?

---

**AN OLD MAN GOES TO THE WIZARD TO ASK HIM IF HE CAN REMOVE A CURSE HE HAS BEEN LIVING WITH FOR THE LAST 40 YEARS. THE WIZARD SAYS, "MAYBE, BUT YOU MUST TELL ME THE EXACT WORDS THAT WERE USED TO PUT THE CURSE ON YOU." THE OLD MAN SAYS WITHOUT HESITATION, "I NOW PRONOUNCE YOU MAN AND WIFE."**

---

I am embarrassed to admit it, but when I practiced family law, I would be more inclined to tell a male client who suspected his wife of cheating to hire an investigator than a woman client who believed her husband was cheating. I believe that, like it or not, for whatever stereotypical reason, no one is ever surprised when a man cheats on his wife. If a husband cheats on his wife, to many, including judges, he is just being a guy. When a woman is having an affair, it just looks worse. She is a slut. There is still the perception that men can have affairs and women cannot, unfair as it may be. Moreover, with a predominately-male bench, I believe that view will prevail. In addition, female judges do not like women who cheat either. It is as if they are protecting their own turf. Life is not fair. I especially used to tell my female clients that they had to be careful in their behavior. They would get angry and say, "My husband's doing it, why can't I?" Well, unfortunately, that is just the way it is. Our society does not accept female adulterers as readily as it does with males. For the female readers, you should note that recent studies have shown that the gap between the number of men who have affairs and the number of women who have affairs is rapidly closing. Nevertheless, if a man came to me suspecting that his wife was doing the pool boy, even if the economic value was not immediately clear and understandable, I would encourage him to get the proof and keep it his marital armory.

Remember: it is a myth that the law mandates a "fair result." Divorce is a vehicle of statutes; in other words, the statutes set forth the rules and regulations utilized by a judge. The judge cannot "bend" the rules. You need to know in advance that the laws in a divorce are designed to deliver a result that is "equitable," if you will. That does not always happen. I was on my share of cases that did not turn out the way I wanted them to. Any lawyer who says he or she has not been has not tried many cases. There are definitely cases where you get an adverse result, and as a lawyer, you ask yourself: Did I do the best I possibly could?

In addition to private investigators, your lawyer may suggest that you hire other experts including accountants and physicians. Now you are probably asking yourself, why a physician? You mean a psychiatrist or psychologist, right? Well, yes and no. Out of any group of healthcare providers, in most family law matters, the mental health specialists play the greatest role. Especially in cases where custody of the children may be an issue. Most courts can require a parent seeking custody to proceed with a complete battery of psychological testing if requested by one of the parties, or it may be independently ordered by the court. The children may have to see an "independent custody evaluator," but we will talk more about that in Chapter 11. Other times, physicians may be utilized for reasons that are more isolated: to prove injuries as the result of spousal abuse or pediatricians used to establish child sexual abuse. I have used occupational health experts to establish the inability of a spouse to work and thus contribute to their own support, particularly if the underlying condition was precipitated by the actions of their spouse. However, for me, probably the most unusual example of utilizing the services of a physician in a divorce case occurred rather unexpectedly.

The case in which I was representing the wife was contested vigorously. And when I say vigorous, I mean that these people *despised* each other. One of the issues in this multi-million dollar divorce was the fidelity of the husband and the ramifications of the same. It appears that sometime after the time of the parties' separation that my client was diagnosed with a sexually transmitted disease, which was a pre-cursor to cervical cancer. She had advised me that she had not had intimate relations with anyone other than her husband; it could have only come from him as the result of some extra-marital encounter he had had. However, how do you prove it?

We retained an infectious disease physician from a prestigious hospital who was a specialist in sexually transmitted diseases. Armed with affidavits in hand, we presented the court with a compelling case that the husband had not only harmed his wife emotionally, but that he had physically endangered her as well. It would have a dramatic effect on the entire case. The only problem was the nature of the test that had to be administered to the husband to prove that he was carrier of the disease. Courts do have the authority to have physicians perform medical examinations on parties when those issues would be relevant considerations for the court. Anyone who has been involved in an auto accident case with any potential for a large recovery has encountered such an expert. And had this just been a simple physical exam, x-ray or blood test, it would have been a "*no-brainer.*" The difficulty here was that the only way to test for this disease was for the husband to go to the physician's office, where his penis would be wrapped in a piece of cheesecloth that had been dipped in an acidic solution. By doing so, the physicians would then be able to ascertain the presence of the microscopic presence of the disease. Apparently, the skin of the penis would "whiten" if the bacterium were present—kind of like when you put hydrogen peroxide on a cut and it gets all fizzy. Not only was the whole experience as a bit of a humiliating event, it was also described by our own expert as being rather "uncomfortable." I would imagine so—acidic solution on the penis strikes me as something that would never make my top ten list of fun things in life. Now all of the women reading this are probably saying, "Go get him" or "Serves the bastard right" while the men are thinking this is barbaric as they cross their legs and wince. After all, if my physician refers to a procedure as "uncomfortable," I generally try to avoid it.

Unfortunately for the husband, the court ruled that he had to undergo the painful testing. Unfortunately for the wife, the husband was found *not* to be a carrier of the disease with which she had been diagnosed, meaning that she derived it by some other means. Sometimes, things do not go as planned. Employing the physician was intellectually the right decision in this case, although it would have been much better if the results had come out differently. Sometimes clients just do not tell you everything, and then they suffer the consequences in the end. However, getting back to the point, your lawyer can creatively use physicians and other forensic experts as an effective weapon depending on the facts of your case.

So what about accountants? Like everything else in life, there are good ones and bad ones. Nevertheless, depending on the issues raised in a given case, the right forensic accountant is of critical importance. As the wealth of many families has increased, so has the role of the financial expert. Courts have come to rely upon these experts to unravel the complexities of the parties' business interests or simply just to help them understand their valuation and possible division. While similar theories may apply to, say, the valuation of a law firm or medical practice, those same principles may not work for valuing a company with tremendous capital assets like a manufacturing plant or asset-based business. The valuation principles are very different for a restaurant, as they are for a real estate conglomerate that owns numerous commercial properties, as they are for a company that owns a fleet of taxis or private sedans. If you are or will be potentially involved in a divorce, the accountant you work with to value and trace assets will be crucial to your future economic well-being.

The area of forensic accounting is one that I found was ridden with what is affectionately known in the legal community as "whores." These individuals are willing to do and say anything to obtain a particular result and can be bought and used just like a whore. These characters usually come into the mix while valuing business interests. Because of the methodology involved, and the important fact that these methodologies were not devised for use in divorce litigation, there is a wide spectrum of latitude afforded to these "experts" in reaching their opinions. In other words, if you are looking to value a business at $x$ dollars, you will usually be able to find a way to do it. The more complicated the business interests, the greater the latitude in arriving at your value of choice.

Lawyers frequently rely upon the same expert witnesses time and time again. I was guilty of doing it, not because they would tell me what I wanted to hear, but because they were the most competent to perform the assignment. If I saw an expert do a great job while representing an adverse party, I would take note and be sure to retain them in the future. Likewise, it is difficult to assail the capabilities of an opposing expert when your lawyer has previously retained the accountant to perform a valuation in another case. But that is exactly what happens.

It is important to take note that the retained expert witness must be not only able to perform their work with precision, but they also must be able to communicate their findings to and leave a perception of objectivity with the ultimate finder of fact—the court. In other words, someone who is just book smart will not be your best expert. As we all know, in life and in marriage, it sometimes is not really *what* you say, but *how* you say it that actually counts. And so it is with expert witnesses.

---

**THERE ARE AS MANY OPINIONS AS THERE ARE EXPERTS.**

—*Franklin D. Roosevelt*

---

# ADVICE TO REMEMBER

$ Only hire an expert if your lawyer can assure you with a reasonable degree of legal certainty that the economic investment in the expert's fees will yield an equal or greater return of economic or non-economic value.

$ Like the lawyer you may hire, research the background of your prospective expert extensively and ask your lawyer to provide you with recommendations from other satisfied clients about their particular experience with the expert.

$ Like the lawyer you may hire, the credibility that your expert enjoys or lacks will be the credibility that your case automatically enjoys or lacks.

$ Make sure you have a clear understanding of the costs involved with hiring the expert, as expert witness fees can equal or exceed your legal fees. You must establish in advance a budget for all forensic witness costs.

$ The perceived emotional gratification of hiring a private investigator is often outweighed by the actual results or benefits of having done so.

$ Just because your expert says something is true, does not mean that the court will ultimately agree with him or her. There are always two sides to a story, and courts frequently seek a happy median as opposed to strictly adopting the view of one expert over another.

$ Get to know the expert you actually hire. Frequently, the development of a positive relationship with an expert handling intricate financial issues can greatly increase their knowledge, understanding and appreciation of many fundamental points that may dramatically effect the overall conclusions to be reached by the expert. Do not rely upon your legal counsel to fill in all of the gaps, and insist upon the right to have unfettered access to any experts that are retained.

# P.K. SHAH, M.D. & RICHARD KATZ, M.D.
## *Heart Healthy Love*

*Prediman K. "P.K." Shah, MD, is the Director of the Division of Cardiology and the Atherosclerosis Research Center at Cedars-Sinai Medical Center, where he holds the Shapell and Webb Family Endowed Chair in Cardiology. Dr. Shah is also Professor of Medicine at the University of California, Los Angeles School of Medicine. An internationally renowned cardiologist, clinician-teacher and consultant, Dr. Shah is not only a highly innovative clinical and basic researcher, he is an extraordinarily delightful man. He is one of the greatest cardiologists of our time, a good friend, and I think you will find some of his advice remarkable and his philosophy on life an excellent guide for heart healthy love.*

*Here are the doctor's orders:*

## P.K. SHAH, M.D.

Love, marriage, divorce, breakups, emotions, social isolation, marital stress, loneliness...all of these factors, and negative emotions like depression, anger, and frustration have significant effect on the cardiovascular health of individuals. Studies have shown that, number one, if you are happily married versus living alone, you have a better chance of living longer and have less risk of having all diseases combined together – especially cardiovascular disease. That is if you are *happily* married. Number two, if you harbor negative emotions such as anger, frustration and depression, you have almost a two-fold increase in the chances of having a heart attack or sudden death compared to those who do not. Number three: if you are socially isolated versus having a supportive family around you, you also live for a shorter duration. There are many studies showing that positive emotions, and positive social interactions are actually conducive to good health overall.

Physiologically, how does all this relate to the blood vessels and to the heart? Experiments performed on dogs showed that if you made the dogs (with normal arteries, and normal hearts) angry, all of a sudden their electrocardiogram shows the pattern of a heart attack in a dog, triggering a heart attack or an arrhythmia that is fatal. Likewise, there are standardized ways of provoking mental stress in humans that psychologists and psychiatrists have developed. When you do those standardized tests, we can demonstrate that blood flow to portions of the heart is going down, as if they are having a mini-heart attack. We can demonstrate that in scans and blood work. There's no question that the mind has a tremendous impact on the heart itself, on the blood vessels that feed the heart, and on the nervous system that regulates the electrical and squeezing function of the heart.

When your spouse dies, or you get a divorce, right around that time there is an increased risk of having a heart attack. When we have an earthquake—the Northridge earthquake, for example—within two days following that there was a sudden jump in the number of heart attacks that could not be accounted for by anything other than the stress associated with the earthquake. Right after 9/11, those individuals in New York who had defibrillators in place for a previous arrhythmia showed a higher firing rate soon after 9/11. So clearly, there is evidence to implicate the emotional state, whatever the trigger for that emotion, can have a major impact on the heart and a physiological link through the nervous system.

When I take a patient's history, I ask them about their marital history. We talk about stress; we talk about all the events that are going on in their lives. Oftentimes patients are reluctant to volunteer that kind of information, and I have to probe. Why all of a sudden is my blood pressure going up when I've had normal blood pressure all my life? Then we start to figure out that something has happened in the last two weeks…a fight with a spouse, a pending divorce, or kids' problems with school, things like that. And you begin to unravel that there is this whole slew of emotional triggers that the patient doesn't initially connect until you begin to probe. "Yes, the reason your blood pressure is up is because you are having an argument with your spouse, you're going through a divorce...or you're having trouble with your kids."

*Divorce* as a cure for heart disease? If a divorce relieves you of the stress and the anxiety and pressures, then I suppose *a divorce could be good for you,* though I cannot say that for sure, but conceivably, yes. If you get out of a horrible relationship and are relieved of all the terrible stresses, then I suppose it would be good. However, I cannot prove it to you, because no one has studied it quite that much.

Who you marry has a tremendous effect on your health for the rest of your life. A positive relationship is actually conducive to better health and longevity. Social isolation is one of the worst things that can happen to people. Elderly people who live by themselves and don't have friends, neighbors, or family support, don't live as long and have a greater chance of mental and physical health deterioration. It's not simply because they don't have access to care...it's the social deprivation.

All of what I am saying applies equally to men and women. There is not necessarily a distinction. I know quite a lot of angry women. It varies. Menopause can be a pretty tricky time for men – their wife's menopause, that is. They say that if you can survive your teenage children and your menopausal wife, you've made it.

Stress will absolutely raise your blood pressure. It's the primitive fight-or-flight response...there is a tendency to have an adrenaline surge so you can move fast...run away. That very primitive response has evolved through evolution to get away from danger. And that requires your muscles to be agile and your mind to be quick, so you can run away. A secretion of adrenalin hormones causes that. Yet when that happens repeatedly, it actually takes a toll. It is damaging. That response, which is so useful to run away from danger, if it happens repeatedly, becomes a liability. Even a performer, who gets a rush from the excitement of the crowd—it may help his or her performance, but if it happens repeatedly, it is going to take a toll.

So, what advice do we have? This is a very complex issue, the issue of human emotion. There is no simple answer. Is a hundred dollars or whatever really worth fighting over? Just give up and move on. Separate. It is not worth it. Give up the money…peace of mind is not worth bickering over. A person needs their peace of mind. Two: seek some help, some professional help. Three: practice things that we know reduce stress. That's yoga, meditation…there is no question that transcendental meditation helps. Our group here is doing research on TM and they are showing that a person can drop his or her blood pressure by ten to fifteen points if you meditate regularly. That can make the difference between high blood pressure and low blood pressure.

I do not meditate, but then I don't allow stress to get to me. Every personality is different. There are people who are hot reactors, and there are people who are cool reactors. It's not how much stress you are exposed to; it's how you react to that stress. Two people who both like to argue and yell might be very happy together. People are just very different. I have colleagues who at the drop of a hat, everything bothers them. If the dog looks that way, or the sun comes out a little late, they just sit there and stew about it. Others are like Teflon, like Bill Clinton…everything just washes away.

I have to tell you something very interesting about adultery. There is a term called coital death, meaning death, which occurs during intercourse. (I hate when that happens!) The only study about coital death was actually published in a Japanese legal journal years ago. What it suggested was that if you are having sex with someone other than your spouse, you have a greater risk of having a heart attack, or sudden death. Though the overall risk of death during sex is quite low, it is relatively higher if you are having sex with someone other than your spouse. In other words, cheating is dangerous. *Cheating can literally kill you.* This is, of course, in relative terms. In absolute terms, how many people die each year from coital death? Probably a pretty trivial number. Of course except for those it happens to—to them, it's not so trivial. Adultery is not a good thing for your heart.

Male enhancement drugs, like Viagra, do not go well with nitro-glycerin, as in the recent Jack Nicholson movie where he denies taking Viagra until the doctor says, "Good, otherwise this could kill you," and then Nicholson yanks the IV out of his arm and leaps out of bed. Overall, the use of Viagra has only led to problems in people who have severe underlying heart disease, severe heart failure, low blood pressure and those who are taking medications that lower blood pressure, or who took nitro-glycerin either before or after taking Viagra. Those are the settings where the use of Viagra could be dangerous. What Viagra does is dilate the blood vessels. You want to dilate them only in one critical area, but the drug is not that specific, so it dilates blood vessels in not only the genital area, but elsewhere in the body. Excessive dilation of blood vessels can lower blood pressure. If you are already taking medications for high blood pressure, which are also lowering blood pressure, you have the potential that the other one may abruptly drop the blood pressure to the point that you would faint or even have a heart attack. Fortunately, I think in the average Joe Blow, with stable heart disease and well-controlled blood pressure, there is no particular excessive risk associated with the use of Viagra.

I have been practicing for 28 years right here at Cedars-Sinai. Of my patients, I would say at least 30 to 40 percent are divorced. I usually spend an hour with a new patient, and in an hour, I can learn a lot about what kind of person they are and how they react to things. I can also tell when their spouse is in the room with them how they relate to the spouse while we are talking…there's a whole dynamic that goes on that you can immediately tell, if these two individuals have respect for each other. You can gauge a lot just on that. I can easily see when I ask the patient a question and the spouse jumps in and contradicts or corrects or interferes…I can immediately see what's going on. Just watching them. Some of the people actually tell their spouses to leave the room, and we go from there. That is another way I immediately know there is a problem…either they don't want their spouse to hear what I'm saying, or want it discussed in front of them, or they don't want their spouse to interrupt or interfere with what's going on. Yes, there are plenty of people like that.

I think a happy relationship generally comes from respect for each other. Once you have respect for each other as spouses, you can work most things out. The relationship starts to deteriorate when you lose respect for one reason or another. I think understanding and having respect for each other makes you tolerate each other's quirks better, and you become more tolerant to their idiosyncrasies, because God knows we all have our little idiosyncrasies. Respect and love are two things you have to have in a relationship. Of course just talking, communication is very important… extremely important.

My definition of love? Love is when somebody hurts and you feel hurt too. When they have a pain, you feel that pain too. When somebody else's heart hurts, you feel it too. That's love!

I have been married to my wife for 18 years. We met right here at Cedars, through friends. We have known each other for 20 years. My wife was in the fashion business, but since our kids have arrived, she is the domestic engineer par excellence. We have a wonderful marriage, and it is based on trust and understanding and love and respect for each other. Certain things she certainly does better than I do, and certain things I do better than she does. We both understand our own and each other's limitations, and accept them. My wife and I dated for six years…we had a long escrow before we closed! (You know California.)

Can a broken heart be mended? Of course, we can physically do all kinds of things to fix the actual structure of the human heart. Mending an emotionally broken heart is more difficult, though I suppose you can if you reverse the triggers that actually started it all. Time, of course, is an excellent healer. I have had several patients who when soon after their spouse died the other spouse also died. Usually heart-related. *People can literally die of a broken heart.* But people are also resilient. Many people can come through that trauma with the passage of time, and if they have a supportive family or friends, that can make a huge difference in their recovery. That social connection is very important for healing.

Negative emotions—which would certainly include an unhappy marriage or divorce—are a powerful trigger for cardiovascular complications. Anger and hostility are two of the worst things for cardiac patients. Anger and hostility are deadly. That whole traditional concept of Type A and a Type B person is not as powerful as the concept of negative emotions: anger, hostility, and depression.

## RICHARD KATZ, M.D.

*I mentioned earlier in the book that I would never undergo an operation without getting a second opinion. So to be consistent, I decided to ask another good friend, Richard M. Katz, M.D. some of the same questions that I had posed to Dr. Shah. Dr. Katz is another one of our nation's finest cardiologists, and amongst other titles is the Chairman of the Department of Cardiology at George Washington University Medical Center in Washington, DC. He is a member of the Board of Directors of the Larry King Cardiac Foundation, the only recipient of its physician's laureate award and the Chairman of the foundation's medical advisory board. Dr. Katz certainly knows a thing or two about love and broken hearts.*

My wife's grandparents were married for more than 70 years. When her grandmother passed away at age 97, her grandfather died two weeks later. It was almost a blessing; he could not have gone on without her. I do not even think they informed him of her death. Nevertheless, it stands out in my mind as a perfect example of something I have seen many times, as every doctor has: how after years and years of attachment and being together, when one partner goes the other one just calls it quits. There is clearly a very strong connection between relationships and how they affect the health of the heart and survival.

I have known many people whose spouses either suffered a serious cardiac problem, or even worse, died after being admitted to the hospital. Either that day or the next day that person's spouse is in the emergency room with chest pain. Maybe a real heart problem was brought about by that emotional stress. There is really something that can literally break your heart.

A well-described medical study some years ago followed men whose wives had passed away and what happened to their health in the ensuing years. Compared to men of the same age and health, the widowers died sooner. There was something about that loss, and subsequently being alone without that loving relationship, that actually affected their health and mortality. Or we can look at people who have had heart surgery, for example, and see a big difference in how they fare afterwards depending on whether or not they going home alone versus with a supportive spouse and family.

On the plus side, with relationships I also often see the importance of how people help each other through things. When they have a partner who helps them physically and emotionally, it makes a substantial positive difference.

To some degree, stress can aggravate heart problems. For the sake of your heart, it's generally good to decompress. The "Type A" personality that we used to talk so much about did not actually pan out as being a strong risk for being heart attacks. I used to say that if being Type A was a major cause of heart attacks, everyone in Washington DC would be clutching their chests and falling over right now. There are different people who may be vulnerable, and people have different or greater stresses at different times in their life.

However, having said that, I had one patient who was a classic New Yorker; one day somebody took a parking space he'd been waiting for. He got so furious that he collapsed and died on the spot. It seems ridiculous, but he just got his adrenaline so churned up that it literally killed him. Now as his doctor, I have to say, that really was not necessary. However, this kind of personality is beyond help. Sometimes a medical scare can cause people to change. I see people who have had serious medical problems stand back and reassess life and say, "Hmmm, maybe I need to take some of these extremes of stress out of my life." Life in general is stressful, and it is not as if all stress is bad; we can't all be laid back all the time and living in California. *But to die over a parking space?*

Divorce, I suppose, could be good for the heart—in certain cases. We know that if we give medications that are adrenaline blockers—so-called beta-blockers – to prevent the surges of adrenaline, people have fewer heart attacks. That is the drug equivalent of a life change. Reduce stress. Take vacations. I suppose some people might need to take a permanent vacation from their bad spouse.

I have been happily married for 34 years…and my secret for a successful marriage is cooking together. In that situation we can plan, divide tasks, work in the same small space and have small successes and failures together. It is very Zen-like, but it works well for us. *To each their own…*

# CHAPTER 7

# HIGH-TECH LOVE

*"And just what was that little window you clicked off when I came in?"*

As discussed throughout this book, divorce (and for that matter, marriage) surely test the limits of human nature. It is almost a cliché that there is a very thin line between love and hate or even pleasure and pain. None of us ever imagine as we avow our undying love and fidelity on our wedding day, that we might one day be frantically snooping around and doing anything and everything to dig up filth on our beloved. It is hard for most people to imagine that one day their cherished love will turn to bitter hatred. As you have probably gathered from reading so far, a divorce can unhinge a person to the point where they will behave in ways they previously never even dreamt they could. But what about you? Let's try a little experiment.

If you are reading this book and you are still living with your spouse or perhaps a lover, put down this book and make up some reason to go and speak to them for a minute. When you do, look them right in the eyes and just engage in a brief, but non-threatening conversation. While you are looking at them, think about the last time that you shared a passionate feast of love with them. If, perhaps, you have not had a good meal together in quite some time, try to think of another experience the two of you shared that you felt was especially intimate—something that filled you with joy, love, and happiness that this person was in your life. Go ahead and do it now. What I am trying to accomplish will not work without you doing this, so as Nike touts, "Just do it." I will wait right here. Go ahead—see you back here in a minute.

Did you really do it? Okay, if you did, now I want you to do it again. Come on, a little exercise and honing of communication skills never hurt anyone. Except this time, as you look into their eyes, I want you to imagine your spouse or lover engaging in an act of oral sex with your very best friend. That's right—lewd and lascivious oral sex. With your *very* best friend. Their lips and tongue, you know where. Go ahead—do it. They will have no idea what you are imagining. We will discuss how you feel as soon as you get back. If you need to stop by the bathroom and vomit before you resume reading, that is permitted, but wash your hands so the pages do not get sticky.

All right, how was it? Clean up okay? Did you actually visualize in vivid and painful detail the oral sex I asked you imagine? By chance, did you kiss your mate on their tender lips at the end of your second brief chat? Didn't think so. I am speculating that, like most people, the thought of such a betrayal may have revolted you somewhat. Probably to the point that you start to understand what causes people to do everything in their power to garner as much information as possible when their loved one has allegedly done them wrong. However, should you ever find yourself in such a position you need not fret about your potential to access information. Because marriage is the epitome of the abandonment of all personal privacy, and it is all-too-easy to collect muck on your spouse. Let's discuss how.

There has been such a proliferation of the accessibility of various kinds of audio recording devices in recent years that most courts will no longer allow people to use those recorded conversations in domestic judicial proceedings. In fact, there are strict federal laws that preclude the recording or interception of interstate conversations (calls between parties in two different states) unless both parties are aware that recording is taking place. (That is the reason why you always get the recorded warning when you call basically any business, advising you that your call may be recorded or monitored for "quality control or training purposes." Actually, it is recorded so that it can be used against you in a court of law if necessary.) State laws control the recording of intrastate phone conversations (that means both parties to the call are located in the same state) and determine whether such conversations may be used in court. Some states allow the recording of phone conversations if the consent of one party to the call is present. In other words, if you record one of your intra-state phone calls, then you may be permitted to record the call without the consent or knowledge of the other party. By the way, if you do not believe that you can be prosecuted for recording phone calls without disclosure, ask Linda Tripp. While all of her phone calls with Monica Lewinsky were interesting, they were also illegal, resulting in criminal charges being brought against her by the State's Attorney in Maryland. Before you start recording any conversation, be sure to clear it first with your lawyer. It makes no sense to attempt to procure evidence that may not only be inadmissible in your divorce case, but which may be admissible in your own criminal prosecution. However, in this day and age, recorded phone calls are not very valuable. The real treasure trove is a combination of processors, hard drives and chips.

Statistically speaking, considering the large number of people that own computers, very few people are actually very savvy about the information that is on their own computer at any given point in time. In fact, most people are extremely naïve. Sure, most of us may have an anti-virus or firewall program installed, but that is probably as far as it goes security-wise. And what about the information you send or that is received by you at your computer?

First, you must know that your government is allegedly looking out *for* you by looking *at* you. It started with a program developed for the FBI called Carnivore. The program was designed to gain access to the new hotbed of crime, the Internet. In 1997, the FBI began using Omnivore. According to information that actually was released by the FBI, Omnivore was designed to sort through and examine e-mail traffic traveling over a specific internet service provider (AOL, EarthLink, MSN, etc.) and capture the e-mail from a designated source, saving it to a storage drive or actually printing it in real time. Apparently, Omnivore was retired in late 1999 in favor of a more intrusive system, the DragonWare Suite, which affords the FBI the opportunity to read your e-mail messages or view downloaded files or web pages. Keep all of this mind when you are considering cheating on your taxes. We are well past *1984,* and Big Brother *is* watching us.

More action in this area by the government is ongoing. The ominous federal law entitled *Uniting and Strengthening America by Providing Appropriate Tools Required to Intercept and Obstruct Terrorism Act of 2001,* also known as the *USAPA* or the *USA PATRIOT Act,* introduced numerous legislative changes that expanded the surveillance and investigative powers of law enforcement agencies in the United States. Many critics of the law argue that the Act did not provide for an adequate system of checks and balances that traditionally safeguards civil liberties in the face of such laws, and that is probably true. However, for your purposes, civil liberties are of no concern.

It is important to be mindful that as more and more computers become a mainstay in our world, that the state of "cyber-law" will remains in flux. As a general rule, the interception of your spouse's communications might violate both state and federal laws. It is important that your legal counsel advise you as to be the specific laws that may be applicable to any action you may be considering including the options presented in this chapter.

By way of example, later in this chapter I will explain the benefits of installing spyware on your spouse's computer; but if you happen to live in Florida, be careful. Just as this book went to print, the Florida Court of Appeals in the case of *O'Brien v. O'Brien* ruled that a wife who had installed spyware on her husband's computer during their divorce (the program recorded her husband's e-mails and instant messages as well as websites visited by him) had commited a criminal act in violation of the Florida wiretapping statute. While the intercepted communications were not oral or wire communications, the court held that the purpose or the statute was "to protect every person's right to privacy and to prevent the pernicious effect on all citizens who would otherwise feel insecure from intrusion into their private conservations and communications." The point I am attempting to emphasize is that before you try some of these nifty tricks, make sure your lawyer validates them as legal in your jurisdiction. And yes, in the Florida case just referenced, the wife did discover the husband's relationship with another woman.

Everything that you have done, seen, visited and emailed over the Internet can probably be found and retrieved. If you do not have adequate firewall protection, or you have an Internet connection that is always on (Cable, DSL, ISDN), you are just asking for trouble. Every hour you leave that computer on you are dramatically increasing the odds of someone getting into your computer, unless you have taken steps to preclude them from doing so. If you have had the same home computer or laptop for several years, or transferred over information from prior computers to the new hard drive, your entire electronic life can be tracked. You can bet that someone out there in cyberspace has already tried to look through your computer at some point, especially if they have your usernames and passwords. People like your spouse.

It appears today that fewer people actually sit down and write letters. At least, I am not sending that many, and I certainly do not receive too many either. Letters have been replaced by e-mail, and I receive and send plenty of those. In some ways, it is a blessing—in others, it is a curse. The volume of communication has increased—which can be good and bad. E-mail has created an expectancy of immediacy. You shoot someone a quick e-mail, you expect a quick reply. And PDA devices are an "always with you" means of communication. But the problem with this technological wonder is that most people do not think things through and consider the overall ramifications before they enter data through a few simple keyboard strokes and hit the *Send* button. That is one of the valid criticisms people have about email in general: that people do not take enough time to thoughtfully respond, but just shoot off a reply. A little later you tend to look back and think, *Hmm, I should not have said that. Or at least I should not have put it in writing quite that way.* And everyone has had the experience of meaning to send a private email to someone but hitting the wrong button and sending it to everybody. It happens everywhere, all the time—just ask the girl who accused Kobe Bryant of rape in Colorado and whose confidential sexual history was accidentally leaked by the court through e-mails. The other problem, of course, is that when you send someone an ill-advised e-mail, they immediately forward it to twenty others.

Your e-mail is a message from you. It bears your digital signature. It says what you are thinking and what you may be doing. It indicates to whom you are sending it, from where, at what time and on what date. Moreover, if you are not careful, it provides a plethora of information and evidence that can be potentially utilized against you.

There can be multiple uses for tracking a spouse's e-mail. It may relate to financial or custody matters. Nevertheless, as you already know, the single greatest reason to track those tiny bits of information streamed through cyberspace relates to spousal infidelity. See, people generally feel secure about their e-mail privacy—rightfully or wrongfully. They sign onto their computer with a password, and as Emeril would say *"Bam!"*—

they are connected to the one they think they want to be with. However, in the personal domestic arena, e-mails in particular are just so dangerous. If you are going to carry on a relationship through emails, which many people do, you are truly living life on the edge—of divorce. Besides having a video from the Happy Trails Campground, it is the most traceable, concrete way of obtaining proof of an extra-marital relationship. It is all right there in black and white. Simple text files, and if you are lucky (or stupid enough) maybe some digital pictures too—remember Scott Peterson at the Christmas party with Amber?—What can you possibly say to deny such stark proof? E-mails are like photographs—people do not think about the consequences of clicking the shutter—or the mouse. E-mails are certainly admissible in court, as long as they are not intercepted in a manner prohibited by state or federal law. You are not tapping someone illegally if you read your husband's e-mails and find passionate messages from or to someone and then print them out and bring them to your divorce lawyer. You have done nothing wrong. You are well within your rights to merely have gone into your home computer and printed out a few files—albeit good ones.

So what are the warning signs? If you are walking into your spouse's office and he or she is jumping up and hiding the screen at your approach, you can be pretty sure that they are not browsing the web for a recipe for *angel hair pasta with smoky mushrooms and tasso*. I cannot tell you how many times I heard that scenario—someone would innocently ask their spouse what they were typing and their husband or wife would quickly reply "Nothing!" and leap up from the desk. Some sneaky people try to get around this by downloading a patch where you only have to hit one button to kill the screen instantly when you see your spouse approaching. When a husband or wife came to see me with a story like this, I would tell them not to behave suspiciously in any way. Just play dumb and be non-confrontational because it will pay off in the end, as you will see. Other warning signs may include an eagerness to check e-mail without any obvious sign of an external business purpose, and the disposition of the spouse after having done so—are they happy, sad, uptight, agitated or anxious? Keep in mind that e-mail is a legitimate manner for millions to communicate and one that many people become addicted to. How many times have you seen executives on a plane quickly "thumbing" out their Blackberry (or as it has affectionately become known to the real addicts, "Crackberry") messages before their cherished devices must be powered down? It really can become an obsession (I am a personal testament to that fact).

So let's assume that you have some time alone with your spouse's computer. The first thing you need to get past on the computer is any password protection. I have found that people are remarkably uncreative when it comes to passwords. They need to use something they can remember, so it is usually birthdays, children's birthdays, pet's names, graduation years, etc. Some are really creative and type words like "secret" or "password." You can certainly try the guessing game, and it very well may work. But what if it does not?

I am not a computer expert, an assertion you would readily agree with if you saw the amount of money I am forced to spend annually on computer hardware and software support. So to elicit some of the best information on how to spy on your loving mate, I spent a great deal of time with computer security specialist John L. Crawford of e Computer Labs, Inc., located in exciting little Millersville, Maryland. And you might ask, what is so exciting about living in Millersville, Maryland? Well, let's just say it is a stone's throw from a campus of government buildings that all computer wizards either love or hate: Fort Meade, the home of the National Security Agency, the people who really use the Patriot Act.

Apparently, you can get passwords through one of two principal means: either social engineering or physical engineering. Social engineering is really quite easy and at times deceptive. It is taking advantage of access to information through other people or information. People write down passwords on scraps in their wallets so they will not forget them; some even put them on those little yellow post-it notes. And remember, it is always easy to inconspicuously try to observe the password or phrase being entered—you just need to be very discreet. Some folks sometimes obtain their spouse's password another old-fashioned way—they call and ask for it. All they need to do is call the Internet Service Provider and tell them they forgot the password, identify the billing person on the account, which you and/or your husband or wife normally is. They will ask for your address and the last five digits of the credit card used for billing, which you can easily provide. Okay, at AOL we are about customer service—we are going to resend to your computer the new password. And they will email you a new password. There, *"You've got mail"*—let your fun begin.

Sometimes you get that annoying little prompt from Microsoft when you log onto your computer that prompts you for a password. Most people do not install one when the machine is set up or enter something that is usually very obvious. Try the guessing game here, and if that does not work, try to log in to the computer as the "administrator." You can find it on the user name drop-down menu. There is usually no password associated with that, and unless your spouse has really thought this through or read this book before you, you will probably be able to get in that way by just leaving the password blank and hitting enter. Also, if your spouse uses a third party ISP mail account, they probably will not care about giving you the log-in code for the basic use of the computer (unless they are really dumb and used the same one twice—look for the warning sign). Just find a reason to use the computer and ask for the password. They will think that they are still protected and are actually pulling one over on you.

Let's suppose that you are not up to the challenges of taking the time to figure out the password. You want access to your beloved's computer and you want it now. Believe it or not, you can actually purchase software that has as its only mission in life the recovery of forgotten passwords. That's right, you purchase the software, install it on the computer at issue and it tests every possible combination of letters and numbers until it finds the hidden password. Simply amazing, like something out of the movies where the thief needs to break into the vault. I am not going to directly advertise these programs, but will advise you that a simple Internet search of password recovery software will put you well on your way to cracking open the safe, so to speak. There is also software available that allows you to create a new log-in password if you have forgotten your old one. Effectively, this new password allows you to bypass the old password so that you can access all of the information on the computer. Keep in mind, these tools were created for people who forgot their passwords. They were not created for any other purpose, and I should really be ashamed of myself for mentioning these potentially devious tools to you—but then again, isn't that why you bought the book?

Crawford says that the easiest way to track almost everything that is done on your spouse's computer is to install a "key-logging" program. A key-logging program literally tracks every key that you press on your keyboard, and then neatly stores all of that information in a log right on the same computer for your future enjoyment. These programs are available for purchase over the Internet, are available in many languages, and are easy to install in a matter of a few moments. The more sophisticated programs that can be purchased actually log the date and time of the entry of the data. Others will take a virtual "snapshot" of the information being viewed on the computer. This is ideal for those married to porn-addicted spouses seeking custody of children. You can also obtain programs that will look for specific code words—such as a specific name or "love" or maybe some other four-letter word. The better key-logging programs are invisible to the user. There is no desktop icon for them and no, they are not listed in any of your program files. What about in the control panel section where you add and remove programs, where the whole list is populated? Nope, it is not in there either. Instead, the program is kept in a system operating file that would literally take months to try to find. You know where it is, but nobody else does.

As the key-logger harvest log grows, so does your knowledge about why your betrothed is actually spending all those long hours on the computer. And if required, you are stocking your marital war chest with some of the best high-tech offensive weapon systems available.

Let us now say that, for some reason that I cannot comprehend, you are not really up for being quite that sneaky. You have not been pushed that far—at least, not yet. What else can you do? This part gets really technical according to Crawford, so I will not even try to explain what it means; I will just explain how you can get it and how it can help. Apparently, all information, text files and images are copied onto the hard drive of your computer and stored as "cache." Therefore, even if you think you have erased something you were looking at on your computer, you can still find it in your cache files. How do you do it? (Sorry MAC users; only Internet Explorer instructions here.)

---

OPEN THE *INTERNET EXPLORER* PAGE
CLICK ON THE HEADING AT THE TOP LABELED TOOLS
CLICK ON THE TAB, INTERNET *OPTIONS*
CLICK ON THE TAB, *GENERAL*
CLICK ON *SETTINGS*
CLICK ON *VIEW* FILES

---

You should now be able to see all the Web pages viewed over the Internet, incriminating or not. Some files may provide links to specific internet addresses that you will need to examine independently.

Here is a real simple way to check and see if your betrothed is looking at pictures other than the ones of the last summer's family vacation at Disneyworld:

CLICK ON *START*
CLICK ON *SEARCH*
CLICK ON *PICTURES* AND *PHOTOS*
CLICK ON *ADVANCED SEARCH*
ENTER *\*JPG* IN THE AREA LABELED
*"ALL OR PART OF THE FILE NAME"*
CLICK ON *SEARCH*

Faster than you can say "caught you" almost all photo images ever viewed should magically appear. Of course, there is an exception to every rule; some photos or files that were not created in the jpeg format may not appear. In that case, you can simply expand your search to not specify *\*jpg* in the section *"all or part of the file name."* The same method also works for "gif" and "psd" files, as well as any other popular photo formats.

A super-simplistic tool to check is the internet history file. How this appears on your screen will vary according the version of Windows on your computer. It may be as easy as clicking the history icon at the top of the Internet Explorer page, but can alternatively be accessed by taking the following steps:

OPEN THE *INTERNET EXPLORER* PAGE
CLICK ON THE HEADING AT THE TOP LABELED VIEW
CLICK ON *EXPLORER* BAR
CLICK ON *HISTORY*

On the left hand side of the screen, you can now see all of the sites visited on the computer. For your viewing pleasure, you can search and view the sites by several different features, including the most visited sites. This simple step known by every seventh-grader may be all you need to do. Remember, most people are not very computer-savvy.

If your loved one uses the popular Microsoft Office suite of tools, their e-mail and scheduling program is Outlook. When e-mail messages are received, they are placed in a folder called the Inbox. When they are sent, they are placed in the Sent Items folder. And when they are deleted they are placed in, you guessed it, the Deleted Items folder. Now you may luck out and find what you are seeking to ascertain regarding your spouse's misconduct there, but more likely than not, they deleted the message and then emptied the Deleted Items folder. Out of luck, right? Wrong.

Without getting technical, all of these tasty morsels of information are still on the computer and are found in the Personal Folder or .pst files. How do you find them?

---

CLICK ON *START*
CLICK ON *SEARCH*
ENTER *PST* IN THE AREA LABELED
*"ALL OR PART OF THE FILE NAME"*
CLICK ON *SEARCH*

---

Your efforts will reward you with a treasure trove of information in the large file you now see present on the screen. Eat away.

Pick a password that would be difficult for anyone to figure out. Even if it is just your birth date, change it by a few days. If you cannot remember that, then you are really too dumb to even try cheating, so just stay home and behave. Change your passwords frequently. If for some reason your pass phrase has been compromised, you can limit future security breaches by taking this simplistic step.

If you are concerned that a password does not afford you satisfactory protection you can always buy a fingerprint access pad. This inexpensive nifty little device will not allow access to your computer unless your fingerprint is placed on the little pad each time you wish access to the computer. IBM now even offers a laptop with this nifty device already built in. Those who have any concern about mutilation by your spouse should avoid this option; it is not worth a severed finger.

If you do not want to leave a trail of your sojourns into the darkest crevices of the web, try the following steps. It will do as much as you can to destroy the internet cache files that we learned how to trace earlier:

---

OPEN THE *INTERNET EXPLORER* PAGE
CLICK ON THE HEADING AT THE TOP LABELED *TOOLS*
CLICK ON THE TAB, *INTERNET OPTIONS*
CLICK ON THE TAB, *DELETE FILES*
CLICK ON THE BOX *DELETE ALL OFFLINE CONTENT*
CLICK *OK*
CLICK *SETTINGS*
ENTER *0* ON THE LINE *AMOUNT OF DISK SPACE TO USE*
CLICK *OK*
CLICK *OK*

---

What about all the people using their Crackberries? Can you get that information too? Sure, that is why it is important to delete all of the messages that are stored on the website serving your individual Blackberry service provider. And do not forget to empty the Deleted Items folder associated with that as well. We should also not forget about that stealthy demon, key-logging software. Since I advised you that you could not see or easily detect it, how can you protect yourself from this type of spousal surveillance? According to Crawford, some commercially available spyware programs may detect the existence of the key-logging software, but only the high-quality versions. Instead, you can discover the existence of such a program by taking the following steps: Create a new word document or other text file, and in that document just type something that might be unique—how about the word *"supercalifragilisticexpialidocious"*? Save the document under a name, maybe Mary Poppins. Now you are ready to check for the key-logging software. Just take the following steps, which may now be familiar to you:

CLICK ON *START*
CLICK ON *SEARCH*
ENTER *.* IN THE AREA LABELED
*"ALL OR PART OF THE FILE NAME"*
ENTER *SUPERCALIFRAGILISTICEXPIALIDOCIOUS*
IN THE AREA LABELED
*"A WORD OR PHRASE IN THE FILE"*
CLICK ON *SEARCH*

The results of your search can be viewed with several different features, all of which can limit your search after the initial search has been performed. The bottom line is that if your search reveals more than just the text file (and its backup file) you have just created containing the word "supercalifragilisticexpialidocious," you either have an extraordinary vocabulary or you have key-logging software on your computer. Getting rid of this type of software is still difficult and may require a company like Crawford's to help you. At least you know it is there, so stop typing.

We are almost done with all this technical babble, so just be patient. There are a few more details that we need to cover to facilitate your marital infidelity; I meant computer security. Remember the search for the deleted e-mails in Outlook and those little pesky *.pst* files? Get rid of them by doing the following:

OPEN *OUTLOOK*
RIGHT CLICK *PERSONAL FOLDERS*
CLICK ON *PROPERTIES* FOR *"PERSONAL FOLDERS"*
CLICK *ADVANCED*
CLICK ON *COMPACT NOW*
CLICK *OK*

While you are in this section, you should also enter a different password to make access to your *.pst* files restricted. It can save you aggravation in the future about your past.

There are some other simple things you can do to enhance misconduct on line. I am not going to explore them all except to mention computer encryption software and virtual PC software. Neither of these software applications were designed to hide what you may be doing, but they have the effect of helping you to get there—under a much greater umbrella of secrecy. If you cannot suppress the urge to communicate electronically, use public access internet terminals, (like those at the local library, hotel business centers, *FedEx Kinko's* or an internet coffee shop). If there is a charge, pay by cash. You also need to know that the hard drive of most computers can be easily removed and copied by a professional computer technician without anyone knowing. That method, while more expensive and inconvenient, will give you plenty of time to research what is transpiring in a completely different detail, and atmosphere.

Okay, no more computer talk. Let's just spend a minute talking about video cameras. Completely aside from the Internet, which is fraught with danger, people in general have little appreciation or even idea of what kind of video surveillance they are constantly under. Everywhere you go, there are cameras around. Just think about it—at the mall, in the bank, in 7-11, at traffic lights—almost everywhere you go in public you are being monitored and recorded. It can come back to haunt you if you are somewhere you should not be. Videotapes can be subpoenaed. Remember that.

Same thing goes for voicemail. Do not leave stupid messages or have them left for you. You must assume someone that you do not want to hear the message will in fact hear the message. In addition, if you access your office voicemail from home, remember that the pass code you enter is stored on the phone. If your phone has an LCD display, you can easily ascertain your spouses voicemail pass code. You can then check your spouse's messages and mark all the ones you listen to as new. They will never know that you heard them first. Pretty sleazy, huh?

I do not have the time, energy or expertise to make but a cursory mention of DNA evidence. You can pull just one piece of hair from a hairbrush in your bathroom and prove that this is not your hair and not your husband's hair — so whose is it? How did it get here? Same with stains on bed sheets. Because look, people are bold, they cheat right in their own homes. They do not necessarily take it to the Happy Trails Campground. If there is one thing I have learned, it is that people do it anywhere and everywhere.

It is also quite easy to track somebody's movements via a global positioning device (GPS). The police used this device to keep track of Scott Peterson's movements before he was arrested. Police put a monitoring device right on his car. Now there is a direct way to find out where someone is going; put a device right on his or her car and you can follow every move someone makes. Many private detective services use them. You can even plant a GPS device right on someone! Drop a little tracking device right into the bottom of somebody's purse or pants cuff; they would never know it was there.

The digital world has left an indelible imprint on the world of marriage and divorce. And as technology develops, the chances are that the risk of you being caught will increase as well.

---

PEOPLE GO, "MAN, AREN'T YOU AFRAID TO TELL JOKES
LIKE THAT? DON'T YOU THINK YOU MIGHT GO TO HELL?"
HELL? I WAS MARRIED FOR TWO YEARS.
HELL WOULD BE LIKE *CLUB MED.*

—*Sam Kinison*

---

# ADVICE TO REMEMBER

$ Computers are as wonderful as they are dangerous.

$ If you are considering an illicit relationship, the computer is the wrong means by which to pursue it.

$ If you do not wish to have someone else read or see what you are doing, don't do it on a computer at work or one at home. There are plenty of public access terminals available through libraries, airports or hotel business centers.

$ Store-bought calling cards are far more preferable to cell phone or land line calls that are traceable. Phone records are easily obtainable.

$ Files on computers are harder to erase than you think.

$ Copying the entire hard drive through a professional vendor is the best way to obtain the most information—be it about finances, infidelity or anything else done on the computer in question.

$ Learn the simple little tools identified in this chapter.

$ Thinking about doing something? Smile, you may be on some investigator's candid camera.

$ Viewing internet pornography and seeking child custody is like having a drink before you go to your AA meeting—you may get away with it temporarily, but it will come back to haunt you.

$ Instant messaging is preferable to e-mail.

$ Voicemail is a voluntary recordation of your voice—imagine your message played in court; then begin speaking.

# DR. PHIL MCGRAW
## *Getting real on marriage & the "D" word*

*Many of us first met Dr. Phil McGraw when he began his broadcasting career as Oprah's resident expert on human behavior. Dr. Phil has earned a reputation as the doctor to see for his "tell-it-like-it-is" advice, instructing his millions of viewers to "get real" about their own behavior to create positive lives for themselves. Since 2002, his nationally syndicated daily one-hour series, Dr. Phil, has been a television blockbuster. Dr. Phil is also the author of an unbelievable five #1 New York Times bestsellers, most recently with his book, Family First: Your Step-by-Step Plan for Creating a Phenomenal Family. With over 19 million copies in print, his books have been published in 37 different languages. Dr. Phil draws on his 30 years of experience in psychology and human functioning. He earned his B.S, M.A. and Ph.D. in clinical psychology from North Texas State University with a dual area of emphasis in clinical and behavioral medicine and has been a board-certified and licensed clinical psychologist since 1978. In conjunction with his books and television empire, he is the go-to source for millions of Americans looking for answers to the questions that arise in our daily lives. Dr. Phil is an absolutely delightful man to chat with, and I was struck by his sincerity, cordiality and his simple brilliance during our meetings. I have repeatedly read this essay as I feel that it is such an honest recitation about marriage and the unfortunate realities of divorce. I know that you will enjoy it, and I urge you to follow his sage advice and example.*

Erroneously, most people think that they did not manage things very well when their marriage ran into trouble. I believe that the outcome of most marriages is determined well before you walk down the aisle. The key word is *PREPARATION*. Having spent the last fifteen years as a litigation consultant, I have learned that the outcomes of most cases are determined before you ever walk up the courthouse steps. It is much the same with marriage. It is the preparation and the presentation that leads to success. Merging two lives is always going to be a painful adjustment; I don't care how much in love you are, how long your engagement was, or if it is your first, second or third marriage—it *will* be a painful adjustment. Any time you merge two lives, you have to start making sacrifices and accommodations; and that exacts a toll. You are going to have to understand accountability, the division of labor and resources; you literally must start sharing your money, space and time. However, if you have negotiated and worked out as many of these matters as you possibly can in advance, your chances of success are that much better. You will have much less stress since you have already contemplated and resolved the major issues. As an added advantage, you may even identify incompatibilities that may cause you not to go forward with marriage, if the differences cannot be resolved.

It is essential to engage in pre-marital preparation, whether it's counseling, reading relationship books, making lists and checking them twice, talking with couples who have been married for many years and finding out about their pitfalls—do everything you can to think about potential differences *ahead of time*. What types of topics absolutely need to be considered? Your expectations concerning sex, money, geography, division of labor, children, in-laws, and religion are a good start. These are the issues that people have to live with every day—they need to analyze these to arrive at an arrangement that both people are excited about—or at a minimum, can live with.

I have said it a million times: People spend more time planning their wedding than they do their marriage. A wedding is a one-day event, albeit a significant rite of passage. Nevertheless, to spend more time on bridesmaids' dresses than on what the couple are going to do in terms of their children or in-laws is just a foolhardy lack of preparation.

What really upsets people—whether it is in their career, their marriage, or something as simple as their vacation—is not what actually happens, but when there is a violation of their *expectations* as to what they believe should have happened. If you sail into marriage expecting that it's all going to be hunky-dory wonderful, and then get in there and undergo this period of adjustment I'm describing, you might panic and start to think you've made a big mistake. On the other hand, if you go into it knowing, "Hey, I've been single for a long while now and I'm used to doing things my own way. This is not going to be easy, and I am going to have to be patient. It's all right for me to be irritated; it's all right for her to be upset. I expect it; I know it is coming; we'll get through it." It is not the fact that you have friction that is the obstacle—it is the fact that it seems to come out of nowhere.

*Marriage is not an extended date;* unfortunately, we tend to be attracted to and marry those people who are the most fun on a date. Before you begin to consider marriage, you need to make sure that your relationship has matured to the point that you truly know each other and that your feelings have survived that examination and maturation process. You need to have visited all those topics listed above, and be confident that your feelings have survived that examination as well. If you've got a money plan, a plan on how to practice religious faith, on how to spend time with in-laws, where to live, how many kids to have, who's going to work—if you can get through all these real-world challenges (not very romantic, but real) and your feelings are still intact, I'd say that's a pretty good sign. It may be somewhat facetious, but I have said many times that you should never marry anybody until you have nursed him or her through the flu. If you have done that, you have seen your potential spouse without their best foot forward; they are not courting you or for that matter even paying any attention to you. They are just trying to survive. That will give you a much more realistic look at marriage.

When I got married, Robin and I were very young. We did not have two dimes to rub together. I certainly did not have a prenuptial agreement—we could not have afforded the paper to write it on, so what would have been the point? In advising other couples, I do believe that if one partner is disparately wealthier than the other is, on a second marriage or someone who is older and might have a difficult time starting over in the face of financial setback, then I think prenuptial agreements are appropriate. Prenuptials do not have to be one-way. They can certainly protect separate assets, but they can make clear provisions for the less economically advantaged partner if there is a dissolution of the marriage. Again, this is not a very romantic topic, but the truth is that we have a 50% divorce rate in America. You have a one in two chance that you will be divorced. People always assume it is going to happen to the person next to them, but the truth is, everybody is vulnerable.

Just as I believe many people get married too quickly without doing their homework, I think many tend to divorce too quickly, without doing their homework. You do not just get a divorce because you are not having fun anymore, or you have suffered for however long. I think *you have to earn your way out of a marriage.* You do this by asking yourself some hard questions: *What am I doing to contribute to the problems in this marriage? What did I do to try to heal this relationship and fix the problems, instead of taking my partner's inventory and criticizing their faults?* Own your situation; look at what you can do to improve the situation. Turn over every stone; investigate every potential avenue of rehabilitation. Go to counseling, go see your pastor or Rabbi, talk with your parents—look high and low for any potential avenue of rehabilitation that you can find. Only when you can look yourself in the mirror and honestly say "I have done everything I can do to turn this marriage around, but I'm out of options," should you seek a divorce? You never want to be in the position where your child comes to you and says, "Why did I have go grow up without my mom, or dad?" If your only answer is, "We just weren't having fun anymore," that isn't a very good answer. Your answer should be, "We did everything we could to make the relationship work; we did it all. But we concluded that it would be a happier life for you and the family if we lived separately and loved you as much as we always did from different locations and perspectives." Only when you can make such statements are you truly ready to entertain the idea of divorce.

Even adultery does not have to spell the end of a marriage. While it is one of the biggest and most painful challenges a marriage can ever face, you can survive it. To do so requires an honest exchange and a willingness of the part of both partners to heal the wounds—both the ones that made the marriage vulnerable, and the wounds caused by infidelity itself.

I have certainly grown into and matured into my own marriage. When we first married, I was an absolute workaholic. I was a young doctor starting a practice, and it was not uncommon for me to work 14-16 hours a day, six and seven days a week. Obviously, that was not good for our marriage, but Robin had an ingenious strategy. She never complained. She never nagged. She just made being home so warm and pleasant and inviting that soon enough, I didn't want to go to work! I did not want to be gone for long periods, because I enjoyed being home with her so much.

As I grew older, my priorities shifted. As a young lion, I had the feeling that "the one with the most toys wins." Make all the money you can, get all the stuff you can, provide for your family financially as best you can. However, as I matured, I realized that there are many other kinds of assets and income. There is monetary income, which certainly important. However, there is also psychological income, emotional income, spiritual income, social income, familial income. Once I recognized that I had to look at all the balances in *all* my accounts, I began to invest in these other areas. You might stack up a lot of money in the bank one year, but if you really have not been a participating partner in your relationship, you get a zero balance there. 100% here and 0% there averages out to 50%, and that is an F. I began to realize that I needed to have that balance, and I was blessed that Robin took the strategy of *inspiring* me, not *requiring* of me.

Robin and I have now been married for 29 years, and the "D" word has never been spoken in our home or about our relationship. From the start, we always had the mindset that the marriage itself transcends any daily turmoil. I think one of the biggest mistakes so many couples make is to throw the D word around carelessly. They put the marriage on the line through emotional hurt and pain. They'll say things like, "We might as well just get a divorce," or "I'm leaving you because you won't stop spending so much money," or "you don't help with the kids," or "you're always rude to me," or whatever. *Do not put your marriage on the line.* It takes so much pressure off the relationship when you do not. Robin and I both know that if we have a disagreement (which is rare, because although we're both very expressive we don't argue much) it's not the end of the world. I can get frustrated with her; she can get frustrated with me; and we will deal with that. It has nothing to do with the marriage. The marriage is always there, as a basic tenet of or lives. It is never on the table. We would *never* play for such high stakes; nor should you.

# CHAPTER 8

# THE JUDGE

I can appreciate that many people are cynical about our entire legal system and lawyers in general. There have been, and will no doubt continue to be, a number of cases where bad behavior is rewarded and honesty does not seem to pay; but overall, the system does work. A few bad apples are sincerely not representative of the whole judicial system. And that holds true, not only for lawyers, but for judges too. Most judges are fine public servants that I believe are insufficiently compensated to listen to intolerable sagas that most of us could never even imagine. Most judges serve their prestigious role because they care about other people and believe in the system. Nevertheless, just like lawyers, there is no shortage of bad judges—and I have had the displeasure of appearing before some of them.

The worst kind of judge, in my view, is the one that seems to have forgotten what it was like to be a lawyer. It is as if once they were elevated to the bench, amnesia immediately set in. Some have forgotten the pressures imposed upon most lawyers in busy litigation practices. Others have forgotten their humility. A number of them forgot their manners. A few of them seemed to have forgotten to take their psychotropic medications. I had the feeling sometimes that judges were so impressed with their own importance that they had forgotten that it was Jesus who allegedly walked on water, not them. And the worst part is that their arrogance was not predicated upon their legal accomplishments, but merely upon the office that they now held. Overnight, from being Joe Blow, Esq. they became The Honorable Joe Blow. Lawyers, who knew Joe Blow for years as "Joe," now must refer to him as "Your Honor." Moreover, many times these judges forget that they are just a "Joe Blow" like you and me. In forgetting their roots, these judges display an attitude that lacks compassion or patience for either counsel or litigants.

I have encountered other judges who are downright mean and nasty. The recipient of their anger is usually an unknowing lawyer or his or her client. I can only surmise that these wretched cretins must really have a miserable existence at home to bring such hostility and lack of social presence into a place where the resolution of disputes is supposed to occur, as opposed to the escalation of the dispute—especially by the judicial officer presiding over the matter. Being a judge strikes me as one of those jobs where the lawyers or parties appearing before them should not have to cower at their mercy just because they are having a bad day, or life.

I once watched a judge completely humiliate a very experienced divorce lawyer over the manner in which he was presenting his evidence during the course of a trial. While many of the objections I made to the introduction of evidence were properly sustained, I did not believe it was necessary or correct that the Court, on the record and right in front of his client, eviscerated a long-standing member of the bar. The judge in this particular case told the lawyer at the end of the second day of the trial to bring his partner (a younger, well-respected lawyer) to court the next day so that the case would move forward without so many objections being sustained. And he did. For the next few days of the arduous trial, he sat not at counsel's table, but on the first row of the courtroom—and he was not a happy camper. Not with the court; not with himself; and of course, not with me.

The lawyer who had been chided, a veritable dean of the domestic relations bar, had had a bad day in court. That's all. We all do. Because the judge was unable to maintain his own composure and decorum from the bench, he intentionally (or perhaps even worse, unknowingly) humiliated a good lawyer. As a result, the lawyer who was humiliated, and with whom I had to work on any number of other cases, would not speak to me for a year. My relations with his partner were also strained to the point that he wrote me a three-page letter after the trial chastising me for embarrassing his partner in court. His point to me was that it was unfair for me to be so aggressive to a respected member of the bar. In reality, my actions did not cause the problem; it was how the judge "mishandled" the case.

Judges are appointed to the bench by our elected representatives or voted into office by the public. I must confess that I never understood how or why jurisdictions actually elect judges. Who goes out and campaigns for these judges, and isn't there an inherent conflict of interest presented by doing so? Is this really a role where we want people running for office?

While traveling I have seen billboards in some states which tout the "law and order" of judicial candidates. Usually something along the lines that they are tough on criminals, maybe a picture of handcuffs or something else to visualize the message, *"Judge Joe Blow is Hard on Crime."* I actually saw one today that advised me that a given judicial candidate was *"As tough as you are."* What in the hell does that mean? How does he know how tough I am? Moreover, what if I were a sniveling indecisive wimp? Does that mean he will be too?

Given the huge number of divorce cases in America, I am surprised that there are not any billboards that address the important role of judges in divorce cases; maybe an ad that says *"Tired of paying too much alimony? Elect Judge Joe Blow"* or *"I care about Marital Infidelity. Re-Elect Judge Joe Blow."* Better yet, how about *"I have been divorced. Elect Judge Joe Blow."* That would keep everyone guessing and elicit votes from both sides.

I remember a judge in the Superior Court of the District of Columbia actually asking me in open court if I was wearing a real Rolex watch. Really. When I told him I did not understand the question, he went on a diatribe about how the fancy PI [personal injury] lawyers wore them, but he did not know divorce lawyers did too. What in the world do you say to a comment like that?

I recall trying a terrible child abuse case once in an outlying county of the Washington, DC Metropolitan area. I was representing the mother of a child who was allegedly sexually abused and was seeking to terminate the father's right to unsupervised contact with the child. Now for most jurists, this would be a matter of tremendous concern. However, for some reason, this judge just seemed to be bored, even when the 14-year-old boy was compelled to take the witness stand in open court. Throughout the trial, the judge sat on the bench, leaning on his desk as if he was on sedatives. The only times he showed any signs of life were when he pulled up the sleeves of his robe to pick at some sores on his arms. It was disgusting—he was like a gorilla picking at himself in the zoo (and I do not mean in any way to demean our mammalian cousins by saying this).

I have tried to suppress, but cannot help but to call to mind, another judge who was presiding over a lengthy divorce trial in a location I will have to leave unnamed. For some reason he chose to wear a dark blue robe; I am assuming this was some kind of a fashion statement, because he was the only member of the bench who did so. He had big white fluffy hair—and dandruff to match. Now do not get me wrong. I have used Head & Shoulders on my remaining follicles from time to time. And you can look at the picture on the flap of this book—I am nothing special to look at. People get dandruff. I understand that. But this guy was unbelievable. Every time he would scratch his head during the trial, it would unleash a literal blizzard. It was not disgusting; it was repulsive. There would be almost drifts of dandruff piled on his blue robe. I thought the National Weather Service had issued a snow warning from the looks of his shoulders. I was ready to get out my snow tires and chains.

So what is the point I am making? I am not attempting to assault anyone for suffering from a skin disorder that may well be incurable (although I believe that there are medical treatments available for eczema and dandruff). I am assaulting members of the bench who do not hold themselves out to the public and to the members of the bar in a manner that replicates the scales of justice that they are sworn to uphold. They are people who are to exercise judgment over others. And frankly, if a judge is not intelligent or caring enough to get some shampoo to control his dandruff problem, or is so tacky as to inquire as to whether my timepiece is real, I do not want him judging anything pertaining to the rights of my client.

Frequently, bad judges are lazy. That is really the worst—having a judge who is more concerned about getting to the golf course than about adjudicating the rights of the citizens appearing before them. Or the type of judge who does not have the *cojones* to make a difficult decision. I would see this sometimes in custody cases. The children's interests would be better served by awarding custody to a father, but the judge would not have the "courage" to make the right decision, a result that could be enormously frustrating, not only to the father who deserved to win, but to counsel as well—at least one of them.

Some parties (and lawyers) are unable to distinguish between a judge that appears to be "lazy" by rushing through a case and one who is judicially expedient. I personally see no problem in a Court "moving the case" along. Lawyers should be succinct and precise in the presentation of evidence. The lawyer who enjoys his or her own perceived eloquence is a danger to your case. It is so easy to see when a judge is losing interest in any particular aspect of the lawyer or witness's presentation. Here is a valuable tip: When you see the top of the judge's eyelids for more than, let's say, a blink, you need to move on. When the conversations between the judge and his or her clerk seem to increase in duration and frequency, your points are not being made. When the other lawyer's objections of "asked and answered" are being sustained, you have already covered the subject. Just like many other aspects of life, when to stop is so very important.

Probably the most dramatic example I ever observed of a judge cutting to the essence of the case occurred in a Virginia courtroom. The judge was presiding over a custody matter involving two pre-teen children. He was a most efficient jurist, but known as a "husband's judge." Of course, on that day I represented the wife. (Yes, judges are known sometimes as "husband's" or "wife's" judges based upon their perceived historical predilection to be more receptive to a particular gender. Forget about equal protection under the law. It is important to note that male judges do not always favor the husband—nor do female judges the wife. In fact, frequently female judges are harder on women, I imagine out of some need to overcompensate for any perceived favoritism to their own gender.) My opponent was a great lawyer, who later became a respected judge in his own right. Both of us had expended considerable effort in the case to achieve a settlement, but we were simply unable to do so. I perceived that the impasse was the result of the unreasonable demands of his client, and my adversary felt the same, vice-versa. I felt that the position of my client was fair and reasonable, and my adversary felt the same. This was one of those cases that seemed destined to have to be tried.

We arrived at the courthouse, huge legal briefcases and file boxes in hand, both sides fully prepared to engage in the battle that has become the definition of custody litigation. The judge took the bench, let counsel know that he had reviewed the case file, and asked us if we wanted to make opening arguments or proceed directly to adduce evidence and testimony.

We both chose to make opening arguments, and once we had finished the judge took a most unexpected action. Usually, at the conclusion of the opening argument you expect to hear the judge say something like, "Mr. Barondess, please call your first witness." The judge in this case did not do that. Instead, he proceeded something along the following lines: "Gentlemen, thank you for your opening arguments. I appreciate the time and effort that you both have obviously spent in preparing your cases and the summary of the evidence and testimony that you hope to present. I know that this case is important to your clients and the interests of these young children. And it is important to this Court. Now, having said that, we can spend the next three or four days hearing the evidence that would be presented as you suggest. On the other hand, I think that I know enough about this situation from your arguments to just go ahead and give you my findings. None of the evidence and testimony probably is necessary. I already know what to do in this case."

If you do not happen to be a lawyer reading this book, you may not appreciate how unusual a situation this was. To be honest, I cannot even remember exactly how the judge ruled in that case, but I know that both sides agreed to forego presenting the evidence we had worked on preparing for months. Although to some, such action may have seemed arbitrary, and perhaps unable to withstand any appellate review, the lawyers understood and appreciated what the judge was doing. He was getting to the essence of the controversy, the heart of the matter. He was saving the court, the parties and counsel time and money. But in reality, he was actually saving the parties the unnecessary agony of the dissection of their lives.

There are also judges on the bench who could not make it as lawyers. They actually failed *upward* to the bench—when a judgeship became available, they campaigned to get it. As a lawyer, I used to see them and remember what their practices as lawyers were like. Non-existent. And as you might have already guessed, their performance on the bench was just about as memorable. One judge I remember vividly demonstrated such ineptitude on the bench that it was astonishing. Or maybe "terrifying" would be more accurate.

I opposed several lawyers as counsel who later became judges. I mentioned one earlier. Fortunately, none of them ever saw the need to recuse themselves, nor did I ever feel the need to ask any judge to recuse himself because of any negative history between us. The typical judicial code of ethics requires judicial officers to put aside any personal feelings toward the lawyers appearing before them. Nevertheless, you need to appreciate that judges are just like everybody else—they hear their cases in the morning, then go off and have lunch with their co-workers—other judges. They sit around and talk about the things they have seen and, most importantly, what they have heard. Divorce court is a very small stage with many of the same actors appearing in play after play. You may get divorced, and hopefully you will never need a divorce attorney or have to appear in court again. You are merely passing through…but everyone else involved will be showing back up at the same courthouse year after year—the same lawyers, expert witnesses and other characters in this never-ending drama of life.

---

WHAT'S THE DIFFERENCE BETWEEN
A GOOD LAWYER AND A GREAT LAWYER?
A GOOD LAWYER KNOWS THE LAW.
A GREAT LAWYER KNOWS THE JUDGE.

---

# ADVICE TO REMEMBER

⚖ Lawyers have very little latitude (if any) in the selection of the judge that may preside over any aspect of your case.

⚖ Most judges are ordinary people with common sense.

⚖ Don't think that you will fool the court—most experienced judges have seen and heard it all.

⚖ Once your credibility with the judge is lost, it is almost impossible to regain it; stay safe by not losing it in the first place.

⚖ Judges loathe witnesses who do not directly answer questions—do not argue your own case—that is your lawyer's job.

⚖ Be aware of your body language and what you say and do from the moment you enter the courthouse until the moment you leave—you never know which judge or judge's clerk may be right around the corner.

⚖ Be especially aware of your body language in the courtroom—never react while someone else is speaking or testifying, and do not be a hyperactive note scribbler—it makes you look unprepared, defensive and somewhat neurotic.

⚖ Always be respectful of the court, its rules and process.

⚖ The judge will be more likely to rule in your favor if you are truthful, acknowledge your own mistakes and are sincere.

# THE HON. JOANNE F. ALPER
## *Advice Straight from the Bench*

*Judge Joanne Alper received a Bachelor of Arts degree, magna cum laude, from Syracuse University in 1972, where she was elected to Phi Beta Kappa. She pursued her legal education at George Washington University Law School where she received her JD degree, with honors, in 1975. She began her law career as a clerk at a law firm in Arlington, VA earning a whopping $4 per hour. She ultimately became a partner in that firm and developed a niche in the field of family law and was highly regarded by her peers and the Court for her skills in that arena. She became a judge of the Juvenile and Domestic Relations District Court for the 17th Judicial District in Arlington, Virginia in July, 1991 and was elected Chief Judge of that Court in 1996. In 1998, she became a Circuit Court Judge. Throughout her career, Judge Alper has been involved in numerous professional organizations and activities, serving as the President of the Arlington County Bar Association, President of the Virginia Chapter of the American Academy of Matrimonial Lawyers, and Chair of the Family Law Section of the Virginia State Bar. She is also the President of the Syracuse University Alumni Association.*

*I have known Judge Alper since well before her elevation to the bench. It was a difficult choice for me to select a judge to convey the information you are about to read. Despite what you may have perceived as a "rant" against judges in this chapter, there are hundreds of dedicated jurists like Judge Alper throughout our judicial system (and especially in the jurisdictions where I have practiced) who selflessly resolve disputes of inconceivable magnitude. Judge Alper represents everything that a judge should be: she is intelligent, fair, compassionate, patient and just. Pay attention to her advice about marriage and what to do if you find yourself in court for a divorce trial—it is a rare opportunity to get legal advice from a sitting trial judge.*

I have been married for almost 32 years—a rarity these days. I think the secret to our marriage is that my husband and I are truly partners. He was a prosecutor in Washington, DC when we married, and he was completely committed to helping me advance my career. In the 1970's this was not nearly as fashionable as it is today. He kept regular business hours and was willing to take over a great deal of childcare and running the house to accommodate my frenetic trial and travel schedule. I say he accommodated me, but we actually accommodated each other. Thirty-two years later, we are still very happy.

A judge in our society has a great deal of power, and judges often tend to get an inflated sense of self. In our business, we call it "Robeitis." On a daily basis, everyone stands when you enter the room, you wear an impressive robe, and you always get the final word (at least until the appeals court rules, and even those decisions aren't made to your face). I have always believed that the best way for a judge to remain a regular person is to have a family. It's good for me to be a wife and mother and have a regular family life. It keeps me from becoming too full of myself. I will never forget lecturing my young son shortly after I became a judge and him telling me, "You're not the judge here!" He was right—I am Mom at home. When my kids were growing up I always just wanted their friends to call me Mrs. Alper, like they called their friends' moms Mrs. Smith. They knew what I did for a living—I didn't need to be called Judge Alper at home.

Though all judges start out as attorneys, I have to say there is a divide between the bench and the bar. Judges tend to become isolated— it's pretty much built into the job. As an attorney you can spend time hanging out with your colleagues, having lunch, or going to a bar after work. Once you become a judge, you can no longer do that – you can't have drinks with someone one day and decide their case the next. Therefore, judges tend to become isolated and interact more with each other than they do with lawyers and "regular" people.

I remember once several years ago, when I being interviewed for reelection as Juvenile Court Judge, someone asked me a very astute question: "What do you do to make sure you don't lose your perspective?" My solution is to have some good friends who are lawyers, but whose cases I don't hear. With them I can socialize comfortably, learn about what's going on, the latest trends and ideas, what's circulating around the courthouses and stay in touch with the reality of the practice of law without compromising integrity and impartiality.

The best thing about being a judge is the constant intellectual stimulation I get from a wide variety of cases. Murder one day, divorce the next, a covenant ordinance the next…. My colleagues laugh at me, but I actually love Friday Motion Days, where I get to hear an extraordinarily wide variety of cases during the course of a few hours. The hardest part of being a judge? Definitely criminal sentencing. It never gets easier. It is an awesome responsibility to deprive someone of their liberty, even for a day. On the civil side, the hardest part of being a judge is a similarly gut-wrenching type of case: termination of a mother or father's parental rights. That is never, never easy.

Over my career I have heard hundreds of divorce cases. Even though I sit on the bench in the Commonwealth of Virginia, which is a jurisdiction that has fault grounds, I do not see very many divorces go to trial on fault. One of the most consistent reasons I see for divorces is certainly money—or lack thereof. Economic problems, too much work stress, not enough money or time to go around are all underlying causes for many divorces. I also believe that the transient nature of the population in this Washington, DC metro area is another factor that contributes to separation and divorce here. There are so many people who come to Washington from all over the country for government jobs that may be short-term or long-term—who knows. They seem to leave their stability behind in Iowa or South Carolina or wherever they came from. The rushed, transient nature of life in political DC extends, I think, even to marriage.

If I were giving a friend who was getting a divorce one single piece of advice, it would be to hire the right attorney. It makes a tremendous difference in your case whether you hire lawyer A or lawyer B. Your lawyer brings his credibility and reputation to every case—it is his or her most important stock in trade, one that takes years to build and only moments to shatter. If you lose it for just one case, you have lost it, perhaps forever.

Remember what I said about judges becoming isolated? Since we really do not generally socialize with the lawyers who appear before us, guess who we talk to? Each other. And can you guess what our favorite topic of conversation is? That's right, lawyers. Lawyers talk about us, we talk about them. We tell each other about the good lawyers and definitely about the bad ones.

It is frustrating to me when I see a client who has unknowingly associated with one of the bad lawyers. I cannot do anything about their selection. I cannot overemphasize the importance of interviewing lawyers before hiring them, and getting referrals from clients that are satisfied. Ask other lawyers about the lawyer you are considering hiring. You can usually get a good feel about what you are in for by their reaction.

On the other hand, when a lawyer whom I have known over the years to have an outstanding reputation for honesty and fairness appears before me and says, "I have tried everything to settle this case, but it's going to have to go to trial," then I believe him or her. I know that it is true and that lawyer has done his or her professional and personal best to keep the client from going through a long, expensive and draining trial. Divorce trials are absolutely brutal. Divorce in and of itself is gut-wrenching, but it gets ratcheted up to another level if you cannot settle and must endure a trial.

From the cases I have seen, the biggest mistake divorce attorneys and their clients make is to oversell themselves and try to malign their former spouse. Remember that the judge is listening, and thinking that these are two people who once loved each other, lived together, had children together and shared life's most intimate moments together. Now all of a sudden she's a drunk who won't get out of bed and never took care of the children? Any judge who is human knows that nothing and no one is 100% black or white.

A compelling witness will grant some dignity to the other spouse. When they say something like, "Look, we had a lot of fun together, and he did some great things with the kids, but this is why I feel I should have permanent custody…" most judges will be much more likely to listen to them than if someone is throwing everything they've got at their former spouse in a blind rage.

Children need two parents, whether they are living together or not. Real and lasting harm is done to children when they become estranged from one or the other parent during a divorce. What kind of relationship with the other parent will each foster with the children? Will they ensure that the other parent has a real relationship with the child or children, including meaningful involvement in all aspects of the child's life? This is a very important consideration in custody trials. I have seen what people can do when they put their kids first in very difficult circumstances—infidelity, let's say—and I've seen what happens when they don't. Judges make custody decisions based on the best interests of the child; these are among the most important, and difficult, decisions we have to make and they carry lifetime ramifications. Parents should consider the long-term consequences and effects of prolonged hatred and battle on their children.

Not only is it important what you say and how you act when you are on the witness stand, it is also important to be mindful of your conduct while sitting at counsel table. Whenever a witness is testifying, I am cognizant of how the adverse party is reacting to what is being said on the stand. Heavy sighs, anger, head-shaking, tugging on the arm of your lawyer, or fanatic scribbling in response to testimony does nothing to help your case, and may aggravate the court. If something said from the stand is untruthful or against your interests do not react. You should remain stoic and calmly pass a note to your attorney. Be respectful of the process.

Maintaining a marriage is hard work, and it goes without saying that a couple should try to weather the storms of marriage and stick together, if possible. It's so easy, when you're unhappy, to blame everything on your marriage or your partner. Many times, I believe, the true source of unhappiness is not really the marriage but something else—career, children, health – but the marriage is the first to take the hit. If your marriage cannot be saved and divorce is inevitable, try to walk away with your dignity and some of your estate in your hands—and not give it all to the lawyers. Life can and will be good again.

# CHAPTER 9

# HUMAN NATURE

"I know I'm perjuring myself, but I'm trying to make a point!"

The laws of human nature are much more complex, misunderstood and misapplied than even the most convoluted divorce statutes; and there are plenty of them. Nonetheless, the laws of human nature are present in almost every aspect of dating, marriage and divorce. These laws govern how we think and don't think. They dictate our emotional drives that may have landed us in both the marriage or the divorce. In many situations and circumstances, the application of the laws of human nature can be unfair. Human nature is described as the psychological and social qualities that characterize humankind, especially in contrast with other living creatures. As best as I can understand such a concept, it is how we think, live, and act. It is what makes us tick. It defines how we interact with each other. How can we love, and then hate, the very same person? How can we marry, and then divorce?

I have often watched animals interact with each other and pondered whether their social dynamic is better than that which humankind has created. For instance, today I saw some squirrels playing in my yard. Now I do not want you to think that I am a complete idiot, but do you think that squirrels have the equivalent of marriage? And if they do, can a squirrel commit adultery with another squirrel, because a lot of them seem awful friendly with each other. Moreover, if the male squirrel does cheat, what are the consequences? Does the female squirrel take away his nuts? (That, incidentally, is the warning I get from *my* wife.) These questions really are not as ridiculous as they might appear on first blush. When we were younger, we all probably read a story or saw a movie with animals portrayed as a family. *Bambi. The Jungle Book.* If you are really young, *The Lion King.* It is just how we think. Animals do socialize in "family" roles, so is it unreasonable to think that within their own societies, animals have developed their own rules to govern their relationships? Keep in mind that we live in a country where a television series based on a talking horse, a dog or a porpoise can be broadcast for years (and then reruns). The bottom line is that we do not know, nor will we ever know, if a squirrel can be unfaithful or not. Logically, the laws of human nature are what separate us from the laws of nature. Yet if we are so civilized, so socially advanced, why do the laws of human nature seem to facilitate such unpredictable, bizarre and often painful consequences?

I remember when I was a young lawyer, having practiced for only a few years. Remember the type of client I referenced in Chapter 5 who calls incessantly? Well, I had one of those. My client was a man going through a "normal" divorce. By normal I mean that there was nothing extraordinary

---

SIR, IF YOU WERE MY HUSBAND, I WOULD POISON YOUR DRINK. —MADAM, IF YOU WERE MY WIFE, I WOULD DRINK IT.
—*A conversation between Lady Astor and Winston Churchill*

---

about it—just the usual issues. There was nothing particularly noteworthy about the facts in his underlying case either, although he just was a bit of a needy "worry-wart." I came into the office early one morning and my boss, and later partner, Mark Sandground asked, "Did you return Mr. Gelber's call last night?" He was referring to the man I just mentioned.

"No, there was nothing new to tell him." I was actually somewhat annoyed. I was thinking to myself that the client must have called Mark to complain that I had not called him back. Not only was he a nudge, now he was a troublemaker.

"Well, *he killed himself last night.*"

I was shocked. I felt confused. I felt guilty. I felt a complete lack of comprehension. It slowed me down for a few months. I suddenly learned that the painful despair of divorce could also be deadly. One of the basic laws of human nature is self-preservation. In this instance, the agony of the divorce was so severe that the client in essence disregarded the law and took his own life.

Several months later, the anguish of divorce would irrevocably affect one of Mark's own clients. Mark was representing a man in a custody dispute regarding a young child. As we will discuss later, all custody cases are generally laden with mistrust and anger. Moreover, those emotions manifest themselves in different ways. In the case of Mark's client, the outcry of agony came in the form of a knife. The client decided one day that the best way to win the case and obtain custody of his daughter was to pin his wife to their hardwood kitchen floor with a machete—and he killed her. Working in the proctology of law can be dirty and ugly—and it certainly provides a front row seat to the worst side of human nature.

> LYING
> IS LIKE
> ALCOHOLISM.
> YOU ARE ALWAYS
> RECOVERING.
> —*Steven Soderbergh*

More often than not, human behavior follows a pattern. Does someone go out and murder someone with no warning? Perhaps, in a fit of rage. But does someone cheat on his tax return once? What about cheating on their spouse? Does a person who writes a bad check do it only one time? Does somebody who tells a lie only do it only once, or are they somewhat of a habitual liar? If someone gets into a drunken rage and strikes their spouse, will it be just one isolated occurrence? After many years of observation, I have to say no—these types of behavior tend to become ingrained and follow a pattern. They are deep character flaws. Unless the perpetrator of the conduct receives professional care such as psychotherapy, their behavior will perpetuate itself and the patterns repeat themselves. Unless a person has a sincere awakening of some variety and truly wants to effect change, I genuinely believe that behavioral modification is very difficult. I think it is far more likely that most people do not want to change, or are simply too lazy to do so—and so they just do not. It would appear that is another example of the law of human nature.

---

**THE PURE AND SIMPLE TRUTH IS RARELY PURE AND NEVER SIMPLE.**
—*Oscar Wilde*

---

In love and in life, most people are aware that the concept of the "truth" is subject to an apparently great degree of latitude. The definition of truth has been the subject of religious and philosophical discussions since the beginning of the recordation of the history of civilized man. In other words, lying has been around for a long time. It appears that telling the truth is to many the function of how much information a person really needs to know. To other people, the question of morality is grounded in how much misinformation needs to be provided in order to accomplish their defensive or offensive goals for telling the lie in the first place.

In imparting a lie, many people are confronted with a set of circumstances and their own internal values that will govern how they react. The internal values are what are supposed to keep the urge to lie in check. Nevertheless, the more grave the challenge, or in other words, the perceived consequences in telling the truth, govern what some people do. Many people, before engaging in the utterance of a lie, perform an assessment of the lie that they are about to tell. Before the lie is spoken, the liar gauges the reason for the lie, how they believe it will be received, and most importantly, the risk that they will be caught in the lie. I recall one female client who was pursuing a relationship with someone else even though she was married at the time. She told me that in the pursuit of her sexual pleasures she always developed a Plan A, Plan B, and Plan C lie to tell her husband, just in case—and she never did get caught. Sometimes, the circumstances do not permit such planning (remember the investigators in the shower?) On the type of occasion when unexpected circumstances are suddenly hurled upon the guilty party, the lie is spontaneously offered as a defensive action to some perceived threat or risk. It is only after the lie is spoken that the consternation attendant to the act itself is fully realized.

If you are like me, and most other normal individuals, there are times in your life when you have made the wrong decision, or done the wrong thing, and then lied about it. First to yourself, and then to others. The feeling that is engendered by lying is painful, heavy and burdensome. But what distinguishes the truth from a lie? The truth is the sum of real things, events, and facts. A lie is not. Moreover, like it or not, and despite the fact that courts are supposed to be a bastion of truth, people lie in court all of the time. Litigants, witnesses, experts, and lawyers. It would be almost impossible for me to speculate as to all of the reasons why each of these individuals lie. For many, the lie is all about the money: earn the fee, save the property, get more property. For others, the lies are grounded in the effort to harm someone else or the need to be right. Many times, the lies are about children: the desire to validate parenting skills or to hide improper conduct with them, be it neglect, bad judgment or even child abuse.

Whether the lie is in the form of a mild distortion, omission or blatant prevarication does not really matter—it is morally and ethically wrong. And any way you cut it, if you do it under oath, it is perjury. *The Real Life Dictionary of the Law* defines the crime of perjury as "intentionally lying after being duly sworn (to tell the truth) by a notary public, court clerk or other official." This practical treatise further advises that such a "false statement may be made in testimony in court, administrative hearings, depositions, answers to interrogatories, as well as by signing or acknowledging a written legal document (such as affidavit, declaration under penalty of perjury, deed, license application, tax return) known to contain false information." I think that in my almost 20 years of practice, I saw just about all of these.

> HUMAN NATURE
> IS A SCOUNDREL'S
> FAVORITE EXPLANATION.
> —*Mason Cooley*

It is also important to note that it is not only a crime to actually be the person uttering the falsehood; it is also a crime to help someone lie. Again, *The Real Life Dictionary of the Law* defines the crime of subornation of perjury as "encouraging, inducing or assisting another in the commission of perjury, which is knowingly telling an untruth under oath." Need an example of suborning perjury? Helping a friend concoct a cover story for testimony in court about and adulterous relationship is most likely subornation of perjury. Helping a friend secret assets with the knowledge that they are doing so to conceal them during testimony is most likely subornation of perjury. Why do I say "most likely?" As is pointed out by numerous legal commentators, litigants, and even prosecutors, perjury is a crime that is extremely difficult, if not impossible, to prove. The defenses to the crime pose tremendous hurdles to a successful prosecution. It is so easy for someone to say "I made a mistake" or "I didn't understand that it said that," "I didn't understand the question" or "That's not what I meant." And as a lawyer who tried many cases, I found that extremely frustrating. So did some of my clients, who were victimized by the act of perjury. It is one challenge to attempt to articulate a logical reason why a male might be forgiven for committing adultery while a woman is not. It is an unacceptable task to attempt to justify how a spouse can be rewarded for lying. But the laws of human nature tell us that when someone is backed into a corner, lying is likely to occur.

So how bad does lying get? Just how stupid or pathological can someone be? Here is my best "worst" example. I once accompanied a friend to court. She was involved in a bitter divorce with a person to whom she had been married for 15 years. She consistently told me that her husband was a pathological liar and many of the instances of how he had allegedly lied struck me as being rather unusual under the best circumstances. I figured that she was undergoing the painful extraction from marital bliss and might not have been seeing everything very clearly. After all, nobody could have been as bad as what she described.

I was unable to represent my friend because of a conflict of interest, and I had her engage another fine lawyer to represent her. Her husband had stopped paying all of their bills in an effort to economically drain her. He did not pay the mortgages on their houses, the payments on their cars or the child support he owed. The houses were in foreclosure and the leasing companies wanted their cars back. The husband drove a BMW that he kept hidden as much as possible to avoid repossession. The creditors had already seized my friend's car, so I had offered to drive her to court.

By coincidence, as we drove to court that day, we ended up three cars behind her husband's BMW. Since traffic was creeping along, and he did not know my car, we had plenty of time to contact by cell phone the repossession agent who had contacted my friend to seek information about repossessing the car that her husband was driving. Unfortunately, because of traffic and uncooperative traffic signals, I lost him and was unable to determine where he had parked; but I knew he had to be in court. I dropped my friend off and decided to play detective. After about 30 minutes, I finally found the car. He had parked it on the rooftop garage of a hospital located adjacent to the courthouse. I called the repossession agent from my cell phone, gave him the location where he could snatch the car and quietly went inside the courthouse. I could not wait to follow this creep back to his empty parking space to watch his reaction. However, it did not happen that way.

Instead, when I entered the courtroom I found the husband on the witness stand being cross-examined about his non-payment of child support. He was crying poor, and actually doing quite a good job at it. Then, he crossed the line. When my friend's lawyer unknowingly inquired about the cars he owned, the husband testified that his BMW, the one I had just seen him driving less than one hour ago, had been repossessed *two weeks ago*. Had I not just seen this car with my very own eyes, I would have believed this jerk. He lied that convincingly, just as my friend had said. As a lawyer, I had never been the personal witness to facts that I observed being perjured—but now I was.

---

**A LIAR SHOULD HAVE A GOOD MEMORY.**

*-Quintilian*

---

I like to consider myself fairly composed under stressful circumstances, but this really offended me—I was actually astonished. I excitedly got the attention of my friend's lawyer and interrupted her cross-examination. I whispered what had happened and her eyes widened in disbelief. She played it well and did not immediately assail the husband with this new information. Instead, she asked him a few more questions about his allegedly necessitous circumstances, and then she circled back around to confirm, in passing, the information that he had given earlier regarding the repossessed BMW. He lied again. Straight-faced, convincingly, and with no apparent sense of remorse, wrongdoing or any culpability. He seemed like a sociopath. My friend's lawyer concluded her examination of the witness. Then she called me to the witness stand.

It did not take long for me to relate to the judge what I had been doing for the past hour. He was beyond irate. I had all of the details of the perjury, down to the parking space number of the spot where he had just parked. The husband, who was representing himself *pro se*, apparently had not taken quite enough punishment; he attempted to cross-examine me as to the information that I had just relayed to the court. Needless to say, his efforts were humorous (to all but him) but most ineffective; especially the part when I advised the husband that while sitting in the courtroom, I had received a call from the repossession agent confirming that he had just "secured" the vehicle.

The judge threw him in jail. His girlfriend was present in court and cried out at the injustice of the incarceration. (She later married and then divorced him.) I learned that day that some people will lie about anything without qualm. I was so incensed by the criminal actions of this imbecile that I contacted the State's Attorney to inquire about prosecution. Guess what? They declined to do so, citing the difficulty in obtaining convictions in perjury cases. It just seems it is one of those laws of human nature, people will lie and sometimes get away with it.

# A SHORT ESSAY ON MEN

During the course of this book I have postulated many different theories and notions. I sincerely believe that the thoughts expressed in this book are 100% accurate. But there is one conclusion that I can reach with 500% accuracy. No, let's make that 1000% accuracy. My conclusion is based on years of observation not only as a lawyer but also upon my own personal experience. The problem is that approximately 50% of the population will probably disagree with my supposition. What is this startling conclusion? *Men have no common sense.* Really. None. How do I know that for sure? Well, my wife told me. Tells me. And so do her sisters. And her friends. And their friends. When it comes to common sense I have learned that we (men) are cerebrally challenged.

Now I do not mean to be stereotypical, but by and large, you have to agree. Historically, men have traditionally been the leaders in our ancient and modern societies. Maybe that is why we have had wars, famine and other tragedies since the beginning of time.

Please do not misconstrue me—there are now and have previously been female leaders who have helped to shape our world: people like Golda Meir, Indira Gandhi or Margaret Thacher. But most of us never have a chance to personally interact with these great women. We just get to interact with the leaders of a different world—our wives on the ever-spinning planet called marriage.

I do not know how or why it happens, but sometime after the words "I do" leave your lips, there is a vacuum of power that apparently takes place. Suddenly, equality loses all meaning and all the rules change. Now I am sure I will be relegated (okay, returned) to the doghouse for saying this, but the entire dynamic of changing rules seems to apply marriages that ended up in my office, as well as the marriages of most people who are "happily married." It is amazing to me how men of power and fame literally cower, given a raised eyebrow from their spouse. During the day, these virile men are running billion-dollar corporations or are playing super-heroes on film and television. However, the minute they get home to their wives, it as if their spine was extracted in one fell stroke. Like pulling a cork out of a bottle. The staunch monarchs of business and entertainment become paupers in the marital court of happiness.

So why do men act this way? What is it about the dynamic of the marital relationship that frequently empowers the wife and disembowels the husband? Now I am sure that you are thinking to yourself, "Wow, this guy must really have a miserable marriage." Well, that's not true. I think that I am just being honest about most marriages. Not that I ever do it, but I love to watch the dominant male attempt to assert a view or take a position on some decision with his wife that is the subject of disagreement (I personally am smart enough not to take such a position.) I see it happen when we are out to dinner with our married friends.

Let's take Leonard and Diane. Leonard, a successful real estate entrepreneur, will say, "Mark, do you want to get a drink after work tomorrow night?" His wife looks at mine, she looks back, and the women begin some sort of an extra-terrestrial telepathic experience. It is as if the harmless question posed to me by Leonard initiates a process whereby theories, conspiracies, and hypotheses are created, then analyzed, dissected and processed at a speed that would rival the greatest super-computer on earth. Now I know what all the women are saying: "You're right—it is being processed by the female brain." But wait--all that Leonard was doing was asking was for me to go out for a drink. He just wants to spend a little guy time. Nothing more. Instead, in the time that it takes to say the words "I do," the analysis of the women has been completed and the proposal determined to be unacceptable. Diane slightly raises her left eyebrow at Leonard. Abruptly, Leonard remembers some mysterious lease that he forgot he had to complete. We are not going out for drinks anymore. And when Leonard gets in the car, he will be the subject of intense scrutiny and interrogation from Diane as to the real motives that were behind his plan for a night out on the town. Why do married men dramatically abandon their independence following the exchange of vows? Why do we consent to the extraction of the "articulated column of bones that is the central and axial feature of a vertebrate skeleton"?

Because we are scared.

Most men do not like confrontation, at least at home. For most of us, home is supposed to be a place of refuge from the madness of life in the 21st century, and that is exactly how it should be. Sure, there may be chores, screaming children, or other stressors.

But home is home; a place to sit back, watch a game, read a book or just do nothing. There are no bosses breathing down your neck or employees to keep in line. If you decide that you do not want to do anything, you won't get fired. Men are scared of confrontation with their spouses because we want peace on the home front. In almost all instances, peace is preferable to war.

Despite what many may perceive as a tone in this book that appears to be rather pessimistic about marriage, many men are happy in their marriages. They realize that the grass is not really greener on the other side. They want their lifelong commitment to be fulfilled. All of this leads us to another reason that men frequently abdicate their courageous personas when they get home. Men do not like change. We fall into certain routines and are particularly averse to surprises. If a guy has a favorite chair that he likes to plop down in, he really does not care if it looks shabby or worn out, if it is Naugahyde or leather. He only cares if it is comfortable and in the same spot where it always has been. The last thing in the world that a man wants to encounter when he comes home from a tough day at work is that his favorite vinyl leather recliner chair has been replaced with A Laura Ashley floral chaise. Fighting with a spouse might facilitate change of the most unwelcome type. Men are also scared of making a decision that may facilitate either confrontation or change. So what do people who are scared of making a decision do? They usually keep quiet, or say nothing of any real consequence. It is frequently the case that there is futility in raising certain arguments when you have done so repeatedly and failed. Sometimes the decision not to speak fails to reflect your true thoughts or views on any given point. It merely reflects a decision to disengage or not engage in the first instance.

Twice in my career, I have had people physically threaten me in such a manner that I was genuinely concerned. In the first instance, I was representing a woman who was married to a doctor, a university professor at a very prestigious university. He was simply a lunatic. We were dissolving a 40-year marriage. This academician would literally lunge at me in the courtroom. The court had to have seven bailiffs in the courtroom because I would enrage him so much that he could not hold himself back. Of course, I only wish it were my skills that caused him to go mad. I know he had a little help on his own. He called up my house once, politely asked to speak with me, and then told me, "I'm going to come over and drive my Ford Bronco right through the living room of your house and kill you." I ended up cooperating with the Commonwealth's Attorney with respect to his prosecution; it went to a jury and he was convicted.

The second incident was one that involved the husband of a woman who I had successfully represented in a divorce action. This gentleman actually threatened to kill me right in front of the judge in a crowded courtroom. He was so annoyed with me one day that he told the judge, "When I'm done here I'm going to get a rope and put it around Mr. Barondess' neck and hang him from the first tree I see." The judge said, "No, you're not. Bailiff!" They took him away. Later, he used to hand out leaflets at the entrance to the courthouse advising all who entered what a horrible person I was, and how I had destroyed his life. It was the best publicity I ever had. Other lawyers used to chide me that I had hired the guy to do it. Later he turned around and ran for Congress of the United States. I guess he believed that his lunacy would go unnoticed there. He lost.

It does not have to be as bad as murder, suicide, and false claims. There are plenty of just plain old mean, greedy people out there who do everything to make the life of their former spouse a living hell. I represented the president and chief executive officer of a large privately held corporation when he went through a horrendous divorce. His wife was just dreadful to live with, and he eventually, after sticking it out for a long time, left her for another woman. The first wife was sour and hateful, the kind of woman I would hate to set free on society. My client paid his former wife approximately $40,000 per month in alimony. He also provided for the private school tuition and college educations for both of the children, as well as $2.5 million of life insurance for each child. I told him he did not need to be so generous, but he wanted to—he had the resources to do so and he wanted to be sure that the children were financially secure—despite his ex-wife.

I received a call recently that my former client had died of a heart attack. At the time he died, he was very happily married to his second wife. I was notified about the death because his first wife filed a claim against his estate seeking that he continue to pay child support, *even though he was dead.* Apparently, the settlement agreement did not specify that child support payments ceased in the event of his *own* death. Now that is greed. The children were 16 and 17 years old, almost ready to stop receiving support. In addition, they would each collect $2,500,000 in insurance. However, the ex-wife wanted to make sure she got that support from her dead ex-husband for however many months were left. It was the ultimate bilking. He could not even escape this bitch from hell in death. But, hey, it is only human nature.

Unfortunately, I also saw some truly sad cases of physical domestic violence. Contrary to popular belief, there is no socio-economic barrier to this type of violence. The notion that a plumber from a rural area is more likely to hit his wife than the banker from Washington, DC is totally unfounded. These are people with deep-seated personality disorders, and some wear blue collars, and others white. They are people with bad problems, and their economic background makes no difference. Some women allow this type of behavior to continue because they feel they deserve it, that they have done something wrong, or believe they are in a situation they cannot escape. Some even allow it to continue because they are embarrassed to tell anyone what has happened. It is known as the "battered spouse syndrome." It is real and painful.

Verbal abuse can be just as bad. The tongue can be a mighty weapon. You can easily destroy a person, torture them, and literally make their life insufferable. Verbal abuse can make a person afraid to enter the room, keep them always walking on eggshells, and leave them worrying what they have said, done or will say and do is wrong. That, too, is very real and painful. I have seen a very dark side of the laws of human nature. Some people take joy in hurting other people. And when you get hurt, the laws of human nature usually elicit a response.

What do you do with a father, for instance, where mom has been carrying all the parenting responsibilities, dad went out and had an affair, and now they are going through a divorce? Now all of a sudden this dad, who has never shown an interest before, wants to become Mr. Mom. In addition, he is throwing it in the mother's face. You frequently see the mom try to oppose that—she is so hurt. However, I used to counsel the mom that opposing the contact was harmful. No matter what the motivating factor is that brought them to that point, if the dad was really showing an interest in the child, isn't that better to have that instead of penalizing and punishing the dad for what he has done to you?

If the attention and concern is real, and dad is showing up for the ballgames and the practices and the school plays and actively participating, that cannot be faked. Is it just a show for the court? Maybe, but if it is, soon enough the judge will see through it and the prior un-involvement will again rear its ugly head. You have to give somebody the opportunity. I used to see it all the time—people try to get more time with the children to lessen their support obligations. Of course, there will always be that type of deceptive behavior. However, other times a divorce will lead one parent to have an epiphany, and then what should the other parent do? Forever foreclose the children from a relationship with their father? Yes, there is a certain disingenuousness to this kind of behavior, but I think you have to give them a chance. The laws of human nature mandate forgiveness.

I had plenty of clients who did not tell me the whole truth or left things out. As we all know, it is human nature to hide things we do not like to confront. I could write an entire book on one gentleman. He was from a very wealthy, prominent family, but he was psychotic. He and his wife had been into a lot of very wild sex stuff—they used to go to have sex in very public places; he used to love to watch his wife become intimate with the gearshift of his Lamborghini Diablo. I could tell he was lying about many things we discussed. I remember going into court for a huge hearing, and the judge said, "Before we start, Mr. Barondess, would you like an opportunity to respond to the letter?"

I was blindsided. "What letter?"

"The 15-page letter your client faxed me last night." The judge had a bit of an evil grin on her face and I was about to find out why.

The first paragraph called her a "man-hater" and it went on from there—page after page excoriating her for the unfairness of the way she was handling his custody case. I fired the client immediately after the hearing. He threatened to sue me, even filed a frivolous bar complaint against me that was summarily dismissed…it was a big mess. He eventually got a new lawyer but wound up losing custody of his child. He was just crazy— another prime example of the kind of person I used to hate to see get divorced, because he would sucker in another innocent person and *destroy her life too.*

---

AFTER A QUARREL, A HUSBAND SAID TO HIS WIFE,
"YOU KNOW, I WAS A FOOL WHEN I MARRIED YOU."
SHE REPLIED, "YES DEAR, BUT I WAS IN LOVE
AND DIDN'T NOTICE."

---

# ADVICE TO REMEMBER

$ Lying under oath is a crime—you may get away with it for a brief window of time, but you will eventually be determined to be a liar and forever discredited by the court.

$ Do not distort the information you provide to your lawyer, opposing counsel or the court.

$ Physical abuse has no place in a marriage—do not engage in such conduct nor ever tolerate it. Be proactive and address the offending conduct immediately, including obtaining appropriate protective orders and a divorce. Physical violence committed once will usually happen again. Any person who would utilize physical violence in a relationship is suffering from a personality deficit that you will never be able to fix without intensive counseling and a sincere desire on the offending party's part to change.

$ Emotional or verbal abuse is frequently more painful and damaging to your psyche than being subjected to physical abuse. Do not engage in such conduct nor ever tolerate it—be proactive and address the offending conduct immediately, including obtaining appropriate restraining orders and a divorce. Like physical violence, verbal abuse has a tendency to exponentially increase with time and with the reinforcement that the perpetrator receives by being allowed to engage in the conduct without any perceived or actual consequences.

# MONTEL WILLIAMS
## *Scaling the Mountain of Marriage*

*It is hard for me to describe the deep feeling of love that I have for Montel. He is a Naval Academy graduate, eighteen-year Navy veteran turned motivational speaker, Emmy award winning talk show host, best-selling author, and an exercise enthusiast turned into a snowboarding fanatical lunatic. He loves his hip-hop music, wristwatches, "bling-bling," life, love and more than anything else his children. He sets no limits on what he seeks to achieve and truly believes that it is better to give than it is to receive. Montel is the founder and Chairman of The Montel Williams MS Foundation. Dedicated to finding a cure for the disease that afflicts both Montel and me, it is unique amongst charities in that 100 percent of all individual donations go directly towards research grants—Montel and corporate donors pick up the all of the expenses and overhead. I enjoy every moment I spend with Montel, be it over a glass of wine or racing with him down the slopes. He knows how to talk, and like a true friend, he knows how to listen.*

A$_s$ I wrote in my book *Mountain Get Out of my Way*, my core beliefs are simple and fairly common. I believe in hard work and dedication. I believe in restraint, responsibility and respect. In addition, I believe in setting goals and reaching them. There is nothing you cannot accomplish if you set your mind to it. I believe in love and romance. Do I believe in marriage? Absolutely—as long as you enter it with restraint and responsibility and live it with respect, love and romance.

Many people today live together, and that is fine, as long as each person is careful with their emotional and time investment in the relationship. No one likes to invest in something that pays no returns. What is it you want out of cohabitating? What return are you getting on your investment of time, affection, love, and financial support? I believe that people living together should enter that arrangement with objectives: clearly spell out where the relationship will be in six months, a year, five years, and if and when marriage is the end goal. I am a firm believer in setting goals and working towards them. If you are in a dead-end relationship, get out. If you have been in a bunch of bad relationships, take a good look at yourself and make some changes. Nothing happens by mistake. Things happen because you *make* them happen. Everything happens for a reason.

Realize that no relationship is ever 50/50. The trick is finding that special someone so you can have a relationship where you both feel fulfilled and neither feels resentful. Also, realize that everything you dislike about your potential mate is going to stay the same, if not get worse. That is, whatever they do that bugs you the first week you met them will still be bothering you ten years later. Only worse. No one changes for the better. Realize this, and only marry someone whose plusses far outweigh his or her minuses, and whose idiosyncrasies you can live with.

While many relationships begin because of some sexual attraction, a marriage can rarely survive on such a basis. You need to really like and love your spouse. You need to be able to communicate with one another about the little things in life and the major events that can be life-altering. On the door of my refrigerator in my New York City apartment, I keep a Post-it note with the quote "You must learn to speak without offending, and listen without defending." Think about it for a moment. *"You must learn to speak without offending, and listen without defending."* These are excellent words to live by in a marriage.

I said that one of my three watchwords is restraint, which I define as stopping yourself from doing or saying something that might come back to hurt you or someone else. It is exercising control or moderation. It is pulling back when your impulse is to push forward. It is keeping you from making a fool of yourself—or at the very least knowing that what you are about to do is foolish as hell.

A perfect example of a lack of restraint in marriage? *Infidelity.* It is absolutely devastating to the partner who has been cheated on. They perceive it as a personal attack—which it is—and wonder what they did wrong to cause their mate to stray. It is my belief that all cheaters eventually pay. Can a couple stay together after one has an affair or has cheated? Yes, but each person needs to determine their culpability for the affair.

Marriage is enormously difficult work. People need to stop running from the relationship and work hard together on their marriage all the time, but particularly at a juncture like this. Certainly, there is the initial consideration if this is a one-time, one-night stand or a serial problem. If someone is cheating on you all the time, there is no trust or foundation to the relationship and you should go. Find someone who will work hard with you on a mutually fulfilling relationship. Cheating is the ultimate lack of restraint. In my two marriages, I was always monogamous.

Having restraint does not mean that you cannot act with your heart, but you have to make sure your head is in the right place. Of all the things not to be entered into lightly, marriage is most certainly at the top of the list. You have to make sure you have considered all the causes and effects of what you are about to do. You have to have a relationship of 100 percent honesty with the person you are considering marrying. You must have many painstaking conversations on many, many topics: children, whether to have them, how to raise them, religion, family life, television, music, Internet, hobbies, interests, goals, wants, desires (do not omit the sexual ones), fantasies, dreams, fears, phobias, financial responsibility, and so on and so forth. Prenuptial agreements? Absolutely. It is the responsible thing to do. The reality is that marriage does not work for half of us who enter it with even the best of intentions.

I believe in responsibility and living up to one's honor and commitments, but I believe you damage yourself and your children by staying in a relationship that is dysfunctional. When it cannot be saved, you must know when it is time to go. I have learned this lesson myself, the hard way, and it is a painful thing to break up a marriage with children. The hard lesson I learned from this was that children are not anyone's possession—not the mother's, and not the father's—and that the parents must work together to ensure unimpeded, equal parenting time with the kids.

I have been married; I have been divorced; and I have four beautiful children. When my children get older and it time for them to think about marriage, I would tell them not to make the mistakes I made: the main one, which was getting married for the sake of marriage—the only way I envisioned to spend my life with the other person. There are alternatives. I would also counsel them to put more effort into what is the toughest project they will undertake, because it can lead to the biggest payoff they will ever receive in life. *I do*, I will tell them, is only the beginning. Marriage is about *"I will."* Every day, *for the rest of your life.*

# CHAPTER 10

# ALIMONY

"I don't think of it as alimony. I consider it a peace dividend."

ALIMONY, as the late great Johnny Carson used to joke, is like "feeding oats to a dead horse." Carson would always nervously titter during his opening monologues about his marital misfortunes, and somehow, he conveyed to most members of the audience a true sense of the financial and emotional frustration connected with making the payments. Of course, the fact that he was making the payments in the first place was his own fault. He made two major mistakes: first, he got married (well, at least to the wrong person); second, he got a divorce (and not just one, he magnified the glory of his financial sufferance by jumping into the marital pool several times.) Now I am only assuming that when Carson took at least a couple of his marital dives that he was not wearing a life preserver (i.e. a pre-nuptial agreement), because on some nights you could actually sense some real hostility in his ingenious wit.

Carson's monologues, like most stories that we find humorous, are funny because we can identify with them in some way. The alimony jokes were funny to the women, because Carson was rumored to be a bit of a ladies' man, so they figured, *one good screwing deserves another.* They empathized with the ex-wife and relished at the suffering she was imposing on the infidel. Men found the stories entertaining, but more along the lines of feeling sorry for the S.O.B. who got caught. They sympathized with the economic consequences. Nevertheless, both men and women understood and identified with Carson's pain of drowning in the pool of love, and nervously laughed about it in some way. In both cases, it was better that it was happening to him rather than to you.

---

**SHE CRIED—AND THE JUDGE WIPED AWAY HER TEARS WITH MY CHECKBOOK.**
—*Tommy Manville*

---

There is nothing economically that engenders more feelings of financial panic than the word "alimony." It is the bane of all men's existence. It is for many women the just and rightful compensation for perceived hardship imposed upon them during the marriage. For the reason that alimony engenders such strong emotional feelings, the word itself has worked itself in to a variety of songs performed by artists ranging from Van Halen to Weird Al Yankovic.

There are three main types of alimony or spousal support: Permanent, rehabilitative or lump-sum. Depending on your particular perspective (are you paying or receiving?), your view on the fairness of these payments will be quite different.

Permanent alimony (the type that Johnny Carson always spoke of) is the monster most men fear, and all women love. (I realize I am being stereotypical here, since alimony is gender-neutral. A court can award a husband alimony from the wife. Just ask Elizabeth Taylor or Liza Minnelli. In reality, though, these awards do not occur with the same frequency of the stereotypical version of the husband paying the wife, so for purposes of our discussion, I will stick to that example.) John Barrymore once said, "You never realize how short a month is until you pay alimony." Barrymore and Carson were referring to traditional permanent alimony, the kind of monthly financial obligation that lasts until death or remarriage. To men, paying alimony is equivalent to the feeling the contestants in *Fear Factor* endure when they are placed in tub with hundreds of the venomous arthropods of the class Arachnida (scorpions), or told that they must drink a beverage composed of blended buffalo testicles, duck feces, and sour milk. The only real difference is that the contestants on *Fear Factor* only have to suffer once; the payers of alimony get to have that feeling each and every month, until death or remarriage.

A court may grant permanent alimony in those situations where they are statutorily mandated to do so, and most frequently in the situation of a long-term marriage. It is the mentality of *I paid, now you pay*. It is an award made to allow the economically disadvantaged spouse to maintain a "standard of living." In considering an award of permanent alimony, courts typically consider a series of factors, and they usually look something like this:

- The duration of the marriage
- The health and age of the parties and their obligations to support or care (who has custody) for dependent children
- The financial obligations of the spouses, including their earning capacity
- The liquidity of the parties' assets
- The income, means and assets of the spouses
- The earning capacity of the spouse who seeks alimony in consideration of all the other circumstances and the time necessary for the recipient to acquire appropriate

education, training or employment
- Any other circumstances that the court deems relevant

Did you catch that last factor? It is the embodiment of what is known as the "sound discretion of the court." It gives the court the opportunity and latitude to afford a party consideration of points that may not be encompassed by the other factors. Things like, *"I really like you"* or *"I think you are the scum of the earth."* It is sometimes difficult to examine a party's financial statement and determine whether something is a legitimate need or not a legitimate need. It is up to the court's discretion. I have worked on divorces where people legitimately spent $80,000 a *season* on clothes. That is what the level of their lifestyle was; the standard to which they had become accustomed.

> ALIMONY:
> A LATIN TERM FOR REMOVING
> A MAN'S WALLET
> THROUGH HIS GENITALS.
> —*Robin Williams*

In any event, it is the totality of these typical factors that will delineate the pain or joy of the alimony determination. Keep in mind, these payments are for life, until your spouse dies or remarries. Yes, the payments are tax deductible (oh boy!) and subject to future modification by the court because of changed circumstances, but all in all, most of my clients took no solace in those points.

The next type of marital severance payment is known as rehabilitative alimony. I personally feel that this type of alimony is the most fair and reasonable. It is not punitive to either spouse and revolves around the realistic needs of a spouse following the unexpected circumstances of divorce. With rehabilitative alimony, you do not receive a life sentence. Instead, you are sentenced to a few years, but sorry, no time off for good behavior. There has definitely been a move toward rehabilitative alimony in recent years; the idea that each spouse will contribute to their own support after divorce. I think that is more of a societal trend. Our country is not full of Ozzie and

Harriet-type families anymore. There are more and more professional women out there working. Most people, in fact, are out there working, and those who are not are usually at the high end of the income scale and at that point, their working does not make any difference.

The heydays of the alimony lottery are long gone. As the economic gap between the genders decrease, and the ability of most women to procure *bona fide* employment opportunities increase, the justification or necessity for courts to do anything other than to help get the economically dependent spouse back on their feet has ended—unless of course, the Judge does not like you. In that case, expect something towards the upper end of the sentencing guidelines.

Finally, there is lump-sum alimony, which to put it in crude terms means handing over one payment to make someone go away. "Here's $100,000, now *get out of my life*." Sometimes courts will set a lump sum and then allow it to be paid in installments. Some jurisdictions make the lump-sum alimony payable even if your spouse remarries. Frankly, there cannot be much worse in the divorce game than having to pay your ex-wife alimony after she happily remarries—it just strikes me as wrong.

Keep in mind that alimony is not a property division. It is above and beyond the distribution of the marital assets. That being said, the divorce attorney's first job is to divide up the property to see what each side has, figure out what their income-producing assets are going to be, and what their living expenses will be as a single person. All that must be established before determining what the needs of one party are versus the means of the other party to provide support. In a nutshell, you whack up the property then divide the marital property pie, so to speak. After you divide the pie, alimony is basically the whipped cream you put on top. Moreover, as we all know, it is the carbs and the calories that will kill you.

So now that we have the general legal framework in mind, let's see how alimony can be deemed unfair to both sides. It really shows you how marriage and divorce can both be considered losing propositions: The following scenario is quite common, especially in areas like Washington, DC. Let's say you have an Admiral. He is 55 years old and has been in the Navy for 35 years. He got married as an Ensign, has worked extremely hard, valiantly served his country, and with a service record that long, most likely has served in actual wartime. During that same time, he has been subsumed by his career and grown more distant to his family, and most importantly his wife. When he returns from his distinguished service, the land that he has worked so hard to defend seems to be overtaken by enemy troops. The homeland is far from secure, and the couple married for 36 years is now sadly about to become yet another statistic.

By federal law, the Admiral's wife will get half of his pension upon the entry of the divorce, whether she was a great wife or just a miserable witch. So now, the Admiral gets divorced and is only going to receive $40,000 a year instead of the $80,000 he had counted on and worked for his whole life. He may be able to go out and get a consulting job with Lockheed Martin, Northrop or some other "Beltway Bandit" after he retires, so he can earn some additional income (which the wife will also benefit from, because she will be able to seek support for whatever that increase is.) However, let us assume the Admiral is tired—he has done enough work. He just wants to take up golf, relax and read some old war stories. Maybe do a little charity work. However, since the Admiral has the ability to obtain employment, a court may constructively charge him with that income, even though he is not actually earning it. He will need to pay his wife alimony because neither one of them can survive on $40,000 per year pretax income. Therefore, the retirement of the Admiral will be short-lived. It seems that all of the negative economic and societal pressures have converged to create *"The Perfect Storm."*

Frankly, I always found these circumstances inherently unfair from the perspective of the Admiral. Now let us look at the same circumstances, except from the wife's perspective. Most likely, she has worked in the sense that she supported the Admiral's career for 35 years; but at the end of their marriage, she has no job experience or quantifiable skills (wives of military officers do work, even though their time is uncompensated. The social duties and moral support of the spouses of officers and enlisted personnel is truly trying, especially during deployment in wartime. The higher the rank of your spouse, the more duties you concurrently and involuntarily acquire). In most cases, while the husband has been out protecting our shores, the wife has been dispatched with the responsibility of raising the parties' children. In other cases, the wife may have no children, and instead occupied her time with the duties I previously described. Now, the Admiral is finally home, and the marriage has collapsed. What will she do at that point in time? She is kind of out of luck. She has relocated all over the world. She has no roots. She is in a simply terrible position; a very bad place to be. If she had children, they could now be a source of comfort and support to her—but they have their own lives. If she has none, she probably has no support system around her. Imagine that, an example where a divorce with kids might actually be easier on someone than a divorce without kids. One could not reasonably expect a woman who is probably 55 years of age or older and who has been "unemployed" for 35 years with no marketable skills to become self-supporting. It is just not a likely occurrence. Moreover, the fate of the Admiral's wife is even more untenable than that of the Admiral. At least he has the option to generate substantial outside income. The Admiral's wife needs alimony—but there is not enough income available for a reasonable award. As you probably realize now, conceptually and practically, alimony seems unfair in both circumstances.

A well-versed divorce attorney is capable of doing a good job for either the Admiral or his wife. To make it a little bit more interesting, let us just interject two more facts: The Admiral has a girlfriend, and she is pregnant. Notwithstanding these facts, a skilled divorce litigator can construct the Admiral as a distinguished military veteran who had devoted his life to serving his country. After a lifetime of traveling around the world in service to our country, he found himself involved in a very unexpected love situation. It was nothing he could have expected or imagined. He appreciates everything his wife has done for him, and wants to provide for her within his economic means. Nevertheless, at this stage in his life he believes that he is entitled to enjoy the remaining days on the earth. He should not be kept hostage in a relationship that he is no longer committed to or that fulfills either party. It is untenable that his wife be permitted to hold a financial gun to his head to keep him in an unhappy marriage.

Counsel for the Admiral's wife will paint her as a victim. They will point out to the Judge that this woman had devoted her entire life to advancing her husband's career, sublimating any career ambitions of her own and any desire for children in the service of her husband. They will no doubt stress the wife's reasonable position: "If he wants to go, fine, I can respect that, but I have already been emotionally traumatized. Do not financially traumatize me as well." See how important it is to have a *skilled* attorney?

As troubling as these issues may be in the context of an "ordinary" divorce, I cannot even imagine the frustration that must have been felt by the husband in the following case that was decided by the Ohio Court of Appeals in 2004. In the case of *Moore v. Moore,* the parties' marriage ended after a quarter of a century. Following the dissolution of the marriage, the trial court entered an order providing to her spousal support or alimony. The court also reserved jurisdiction to modify the award of alimony in the event that Mrs. Moore started cohabiting with an unrelated male. Nothing unusual, right? Well, not yet. It appears that following the award of alimony Mrs. Moore decided she was not happy being Mrs. Moore. Instead, she wanted to become,—and actually did become, Mr. Moore. That's right, she had a sex change operation and was now a male. And not only did Mrs. Moore become Mr. Moore, the new Mr. Moore even had a girlfriend. Accordingly, the old Mr. Moore wanted to terminate the alimony obligation that he had to pay to what was now the new Mr. Moore.

Unfortunately for the old Mr. Moore, the Court of Appeals ruled that the new Mr. Moore was entitled to continue receiving alimony from the old Mr. Moore. The court held that the new Mr. Moore's "sex-change, without more, provides no basis for the court to revisit the spousal support provisions of the parties' decree." So, even though the old Mrs. Moore was now the new Mr. Moore with a new girlfriend, that was not enough to relieve the old Mr. Moore of the obligation to pay support. I am not sure what the moral of this anecdote should be. Since two persons of the same sex living together could not legally marry in most jurisdictions (including Ohio), it seems somewhat odd that you can skirt around such a problem by a few surgical procedures. Anyway, if anything it would appear that the ties that bind you forever do so even though the woman you married may now be a man. Go figure.

Before closing our discussion on alimony, I must make mention of another creative attempt made by those to create a right to alimony, even though they have never married. That was the challenge that faced actor Lee Marvin in 1976. In a California courtroom, Michelle Marvin sued Lee Marvin (same last names, but they were never married) claiming that they had a marriage-like relationship and that she was entitled to support as if they were married. The court denied Michelle's request, but in doing so did find that she had a right to sue based on her claims of a significant relationship arising out of cohabitation and that others could do the same. This action gave rise to what is now affectionately referred to as "Palimony." It also means that if you are considering living with someone, you may need a cohabitation agreement, which is essentially a prenuptial for the unmarried. It seems that everyone wants to get in on the gift that keeps on giving.

Speaking of gifts, one of the best (or worst) gifts I ever heard of was from a friend who had an award of permanent alimony entered against him. On the first Hanukkah following their divorce, his ex-wife sent him a nicely wrapped gift box. Now I personally would not have opened such a box without screening it with a metal detector or until it was inspected by my friendly explosive ordinance disposal team—and I would have been right. Because inside the gift box of my friend was a bomb of a different sort: the wife had placed twelve self-addressed stamped envelopes. One for each month the husband was to make an alimony payment during the next year. *Happy Hanukkah! Kaboom! Happy New Year!*

Now there could be several messages here: First, if you want to avoid any chance of alimony, do not get married or divorced. Two, if you must marry, execute a pre-nuptial agreement that limits your liability. Three, *always be leery of gifts from former spouses.*

---

**I RESOLVE THAT IF I EVER GET HIT IN THE FACE WITH RICE, IT WILL BE BECAUSE I INSULTED A CHINESE PERSON.**

*—Johnny Carson*

---

# ADVICE TO REMEMBER

$ There are only three true means to absolutely avoid the payment of alimony: never marry; never divorce; or, execute a valid prenuptial.

$ Each passing year of your marriage increases the statistical likelihood that you will pay alimony at the time of your divorce.

$ If you encourage your spouse to stay home and forego a career, you are increasing the likelihood that you will pay alimony at the time of your divorce.

$ Be cognizant of the standard of living that you are creating during the marriage—you will be reminded about it at the time of your divorce.

$ Once you begin making support payments in a certain amount, you create an expectation of the continued receipt of those monies.

$ Never try to economically starve a dependent spouse—the court loathes parties who attempt to economically punish the other spouse by withholding reasonable support.

$ Remember the tax consequences associated with the payment and receipt of alimony—failure to afford these issues correct consideration can be economically devastating.

$ The court is most likely to make the best judgment considering alimony if you avoid the extremes. Do not request that the court order an unreasonable payment—alimony is not designed to punish the payer spouse.

# LARRY KING
## *Live on Love, Marriage & Divorce*

*Larry King remains the master of the airwaves, with over 40,000 documented interviews to date. Millions of viewers around the world welcome Larry into their homes five nights a week. Like many of us, Larry has also had his share of ups and downs in the worlds of love, marriage and divorce. Since I offer my personal comments and deep affection and love for Larry and his wife Shawn elsewhere in the book, I will not repeat them here. I will take a moment to tell you that Larry is married to the most unbelievable lady, the vivacious and stunning Shawn Southwick King. I will be honest and state that I was skeptical about the marriage and was sitting at the foot of Larry's hospital bed as the vows were exchanged. A more formal wedding followed, where Jane Fonda was maid of honor and Ted Turner was the best man. After a reading by Al Pacino, the King marriage was re-affirmed. Larry and Shawn love each other dearly, but still leave enough room in the relationship so that they each can pursue their own interests, including Shawn's recording career. Here are some of Larry's thought-provoking comments and advice that you will never ever hear on CNN, spoken in his own words.*

A 98-year-old man and a 97-year-old woman are getting a divorce after 75 years of marriage. The judge leans over as they're standing in front of him and asks, "What are the grounds?" The man looks up and says, "*Enough is enough.*" That's pretty much what this whole book is about, isn't it? When is enough, *enough?*

Divorce is a very popular legal concept in America. We as citizens would never abandon our right to it. If someone proposed a bill to wipe out divorce it wouldn't make it out of committee. The Catholic Church, as much influence as it has in America, couldn't get one vote for that bill. *Ban divorce…divorce is illegal…*that would never play. Yet in a marriage ceremony we still say it's for life.

Now I've been married six times, but I've only been in love three times. The other three times I still don't know why I got married, because I have loved only three women in my life. You know you're in love when the slightest little "I can't make it today" is a major calamity. If you're not in love, it doesn't mean a thing. That's one sure-fire way you can tell whether or not it's love…when you get upset because you can't reach the object of your affection on the phone. When someone can make your day or ruin it by the most innocuous act. If she casually says, "Call me at ten," and then she's not there at ten, or eleven, or twelve, or one…your day is just ruined. That is love.

I remember when I was dating my wife Shawn, she was in Nashville recording, and I was in Philadelphia interviewing Colin Powell live. I phoned her all day long but never got a call back. I was never able to reach her, because she was locked in a recording studio. I was so upset…I went on the air with Colin Powell, and during the breaks I kept telling him, "She hasn't called back…she hasn't called back." When the show was over Colin called her himself and said, "Listen, either go with this guy or break it off, because this is going to kill him." It's funny now, but it wasn't then.

What I would tell a man planning to propose? If you are considering asking someone to marry you, make sure the answer is going to be yes. Really, never propose if you're not sure of the answer. That is the number one mistake men make. No one needs that kind of rejection.

But look, more importantly you've got to really think about it. Put your head into this decision along with your heart. It's the hardest thing in the world to do, because the heart certainly wins most of the time. A big mistake people make when contemplating marriage is going only by their hearts. The heart is all, and the intellect has no bearing on their decision.

I have never met a guy yet who wanted to get married who said, "Let me see now…let me weigh the options…" as he would a business deal, or a job offer, or a contract negotiation. Make a list, here are the plusses, these are the minuses…. When you're in love, you don't think that way. If you are in love, she'll be a good mother. If you are in love she's the best, she's absolutely perfect!

So if I was going to give myself or anyone else some good advice, it would be think and think and think again. Picture everything. Someone once told me, Picture your mate in the bathroom going on the toilet. Does even that vision still pep you up? There was a great scene in a Charles Grodin movie where he falls in love with a gorgeous girl and marries. He and his wife are on the first night of their honeymoon in a motel room in Florida, he's lying in bed, newly married, and she goes into the bathroom, which is right next to the bed, of course, because it's just a single motel room. He hears the flush…and the camera zooms in on his face, and you can just see it…that look…"Oh shit." Just the flush. The end of romance.

I would tell my sons Chance and Canon, if one of them came to me and said, "Dad, I really love this girl and I'm thinking about asking her to marry me,"—I'd tell them to be very careful if they were under the age of 25. Under the age of 25 is just too young, and I would encourage them not to marry. I think the national average for the age of males upon their first marriage is now 27—females, I believe, is 24. It used to be, only twenty years ago, 21 and 20. Males in Utah still marry at age 21, because of the prohibition on sex before marriage.

What I would tell my sons or anyone else is to really know the person you are considering marrying. It is very hard when you are falling in love…that glow period…rational thought flies out the window. For example, Shawn is a firm believer in her faith, Mormonism. When we were going together she said, "We are going to raise our children Mormon?" and I said "Absolutely!" I did not even hesitate, because I am not very religious. Now, years later, I want our kids to learn about other religions.

Now I know they are going to be raised Mormon, but now I really want them to study other faiths and make their own decisions. I most certainly would not have made such a big decision and answered so quickly if I had not been in that altered state.

What will cause a marriage to fail? Financial pressure, dishonesty, loss of a child…I think the statistics for couples who split up after losing a child are as high as 80 percent. When a child dies, so often the marriage ends. The guilt, the anger…it's a terrible thing on top of a tragedy.

A marriage can technically survive adultery, but it's never the same afterward. I could go home right now and tell one of two things to Shawn. One: "I've lost my job and all our money in a failed investment. We're wiped out. We have to live an apartment because of this investment I never told you about." Or, "I'm sleeping with your friend Donna." Believe me, I would pay a much higher price for the second admission. The marriage might survive, but it would never be the same.

One of the best qualities in a woman? Genuineness. As George Burns said, "If you can fake that, you got it made." A sense of humor. That's a big one. The ability to keep balanced, not too moody. Even-tempered, yet mysterious. We all want a little mystery.

I don't have the answer to longevity of a marriage…that one I don't know. You know, sometimes I think I've learned a lot about women in my life, and sometimes I don't think I learned much at all. My favorite quote on the subject is from Stephen Hawking. The man writes through his teeth, he's in a wheelchair, can't talk or move, yet is one of the most brilliant men the world has ever known. I had him on my show interviewing him. He was answering all my questions on his machine. As I said, this is one of the smartest men in the entire world: astrophysics, the history of the universe, Big Bang theory, you name it. I asked him, "What puzzles you the most?" His answer? "*Women.*" We'll never know. *Men will never know.*

# CHAPTER 11

# CUSTODY

*"I put them up after the divorce so he knows his father is still a part of his life."*

There is no aspect of marriage, and for that matter divorce, that engenders more potential emotional or financial mayhem than children. I certainly appreciate that any normal parent loves their children, wholly and unconditionally, and typically wants to spend as much time as possible with them (until they become teenagers). Unfortunately, parenthood is not limited to those who are "normal" and hence, a wide variety of aberrant circumstances ensue as a result. For many, the transition to parenthood marks the real coming of age to signify adulthood. The responsibilities attendant to being a "good" parent can be daunting to most couples. The prospect of facing those responsibilities alone are even more terrifying.

Creating a child is by far the easiest part of being a parent. It is almost akin to marriage. In a matter of a few seconds, the damage is done. For many, planning the marriage ceremony is stressful but still fun. You have wedding showers, pick out a dress, plan the wedding and reception, find romantic places for a honeymoon and fun things like that. Same with having a child: you get to have baby showers, pick out baby clothes, decorate the baby's room and select names. But after all is said and done, the honeymoon is over and the baby is born. Sure, there is joy following both events. But how long will it last? Soon there are bills to pay, problems to solve and diapers to change. The romantic blur of young lovers and parents begins to fade. The bride you swore to love forever now gets on your nerves like a pimple you just cannot pop. Your beautiful little girl is now fifteen years old, and if your perception is even remotely accurate, a good candidate for exorcism. The bottom line is that after the marriage vows are made and the baby is born is when the difficult challenges of these relationships begin. Getting there is easy, maintaining your sanity after doing so is a whole different subject. And as you already know, since half of the people that are reading this book have already been divorced, or will be divorced, it is readily apparent that this success is fraught with challenges.

It always amazed me to see how two people who created a child out of publicly-pronounced love, could become so embittered and hateful to each other—to the point that the welfare of their own children would become secondary to their own agenda, usually out of retribution to their former spouse. Custody litigation is the pinnacle of the battle in divorce war, and more frequently than not it leaves the children permanently injured with the shrapnel of the battle.

There are innumerable books and studies available that examine the effect of marriage and divorce on children. I do not intend to recapitulate them in this book, but rather, to offer you a few examples of how bad it can get if you do not handle a custody situation correctly. But before doing so, we must first reflect upon the age-old question, is it better to endure an unhappy marriage for the sake of the children? I am a firm believer that it is not.

If you are miserable and unhappy, your children will be too. Children, even the very young ones, are incredibly perceptive. They can readily sense an atmosphere of trust and love, and have the equivalent of emotional radar when it comes to unhappiness and hostility. You may think you are fooling your kids, but they know when Mom and Dad are really happy, and when they are really not.

Most of us are taught that we are to set an example for our children. Most good parents try to do exactly that. Do we mess up? Well, I know that I do—all of the time. But if your intentions are positive and your desire sincere, you will maintain a proper course that should enable your children to be the best they can be. So, that being the case, what is the point of the example being made when you are far from satisfied but remain with someone who destroys the very joy of life? Some argue that doing so evidences maintaining commitment. You made a deal, and it is important to keep it. Well, while that is certainly admirable, it is also plain stupid. If I promised my wife and kids that we would paddle down a particular river in a canoe, I would certainly take the trip. I will navigate the waters to the best of my ability, even through the turbulent sections. But when I see the 200-foot waterfall ahead, I am going to get to shore immediately. I am not going to waste time trying to paddle upstream—I will eventually fail. Now at that juncture my spouse has a choice: to safely help me to get the canoe to the shore with the kids, or not to help, causing us all to plummet down the falls. As it turns out, sometimes you end up doing all of the paddling by yourself. Some people reach the shore, others become casualties.

The decision to divorce is much the same. Sure, it may be a frightening experience that children remember, but that experience is preferable to plunging down an abyss and drowning. I heard two children speaking the other day when one child expressed in bewilderment to the other, "Your parents weren't married before?" While this may be a sad statement about the status of our marital society, it was also a stark commentary

231

about the reality of life in America today. People get married, have kids, and get divorced. It is all part of the American Dream—I mean the American reality. There is no longer a stigma, "Don't play with Anne's kids, she is going through a divorce." Instead, it is just another step in the modern maze of our lives.

Now that we have discussed the reality that people with children might be making a good decision by divorcing their spouse, what really happens when they do? I am sure that everyone reading this book knows of some horror story involving a bitter custody dispute. It happens every day, and wreaks undue emotional and financial havoc on both parties and their children at a time when those resources are usually most depleted.

Let's review some of the basic options you may have should your family become divided. First and by far the best way to handle this incredibly difficult situation is to reach an agreement with your spouse as to the parenting plan you will have for the children. Depending on your circumstances, this plan can be regimented and detailed or open and ambiguous. The key is to simply reach a mutually acceptable plan as fast as humanly possible. In order to reach agreement both parties need to first understand that the children are not chattels. Children should not be treated in the same manner that is utilized in dividing bank accounts, furniture or the family pets. It requires a willingness to be completely selfless. It requires an understanding that the children are more likely than not innocent bystanders, and they have no interest or desire in facilitating acrimony between their parents.

Second, you can decide to file a custody action as part of your divorce and ask the court to decide all of the details concerning the arrangements pertaining to your children. Now if you elect this alternative, you will be relegating yourself to a process that was not in any respect designed to protect you or your children from harm. Because while the court is always supposed to act in the "best interests of the child," the other litigant (your soon to be ex-spouse) and his or her lawyer are not so obligated. Neither are the therapists that you and your spouse may retain, the expert witnesses, the in-laws, pastor, co-workers, lovers, ex-spouses, neighbors, friends and former friends. And trust me, everyone will have something to say. I remember one case where a sister was mad at my client who was going through a difficult divorce where the custody of the children was at issue. This person, part of the flesh and blood of my client, actually wrote a letter to her spouse's attorney extolling fraudulent reasons why her own sister should not win custody out of her own hatred for her sister. It was such a despicable act. It came full circle on the sister when she ended up going through her own divorce. My client won, and I understand the sister ended up almost losing custody of her own child (without any input from my client). The point is that when you enter the arena of custody litigation, anyone and everyone seems to want to get involved. And like marriage, it is often for better and for worse.

Third, you might engage in what is known as an alternative dispute resolution process, or mediation. In many instances, your participation in this process may actually be judicially mandated. After all, courts have come to the conclusion that if people actually sit down to discuss problems and potential resolutions, they can frequently resolve the underlying dispute. Nonetheless, as we have discussed, mediation is a viable option only if the parties and their counsel believe that it is. If they do, the mediation process can help to give the parties a "nudge" in the right direction. Mediation is frequently confused with arbitration. Arbitration is a process whereby a third party (a lawyer or perhaps a retired judge) employs their skills to independently decide a case according to rules agreed upon by the parties or the organization administering the arbitration. Arbitration is still an adversarial process, but it allows the parties to choose who decides their case, the rules for doing so, and it avoids the backlog normally attendant to our congested judicial system. The rights of appeal from an arbitration are extremely limited, so you need to be fully versed in the options you will actually have in the event that things do not go as well as you and your lawyer planned. Arbitration also provides an ideal venue for keeping highly personal custody issues confidential. Arbitration proceedings are closed to the public (unless otherwise agreed) so you can keep more of the dirty laundry pertaining to these sensitive subjects off the public clothesline. Typically, this is better for both you and your children.

Mediation remains a process of conciliation. It is designed to reach an agreement as opposed to just a decision. A good arbitrator is not necessarily a good mediator, and that distinction is critical to the success of the process. Just as you are charged with undertaking a degree of due diligence with respect to the selection of your lawyer, the same responsibility is incumbent upon both you and your lawyer when deciding to involve an independent party to help you resolve or decide the welfare of your children.

Once the determination has been made as to the type of process that will be utilized in deciding how custody will be decided, you will then be faced with a plethora of choices concerning how the children will be handled. The traditional choices are sole custody, joint custody, shared custody and split custody. Keep in mind that there are variations on all of these themes, depending on the facts of the case and the law of each jurisdiction. Sole custody is the one with which most folks are familiar. One parent is charged with the responsibility for caring for the children and making all of the important decisions pertaining to the children, with the non-custodial parent usually having a fixed visitation schedule. Joint custody, a trend started in the late eighties, is better explained by stating what it is supposed to be, rather than what it has become. Joint custody is supposed to be an arrangement by which the parents share in the responsibility for making important decisions for the children. It does not imply or reflect any equal or joint time sharing with the children, rather simply how the decisions, schools, residence, doctors are determined. Unfortunately, joint custody has become a label of validation, for most. More often than not, dads want to be able to stand by the water cooler at work and advise their co-worker, "Yes. We have joint custody." It is more about their own best interests as opposed to the best interests of the children. Joint custody has also become a tool of control and manipulation.

People use the rights grounded in joint custody to obtain results in other areas of the parties' relationship. In other words, if you give me that, I will not ask for the court to do this with respect to the children. It is a disgusting but routine occurrence.

In my experience the label of joint custody usually belied the fact that one party, usually the one with whom the children maintained their primary residence, did most of the day-to-day chores associated with parenting. That includes the doctor's appointments, homework nagging, chauffeuring, etc. More importantly, the party who is engaging in those activities is the parent who is actually exercising the most influence and control over the development of the children. I do not mean to imply that the other parent cannot still play an important role is the upbringing of the children. As is the case with most everything in life, you get out of it whatever you put into it.

Frequently, I would encounter parents who did not actually want joint custody and the real responsibilities attendant to it—they just wanted the label. And even more frequently, I would encounter a parent who was opposed to joint custody, since up until the date of the divorce they had actually been discharged with the responsibility of raising the children. Joint custody is a legal fiction, and the essence of what it means is defined by the rules you and your lawyer craft. I would often convince clients to accept an award of joint custody because the definition of it in their own case had been so eviscerated by the terms of the agreement we had negotiated. In essence, sure, you have joint custody, but I decide where the kids live, the schools they attend and the doctors they see. Impotent joint custody, if you will.

Shared custody is the actual sharing of physical and legal custody of the children. This means both time and decisions and is rarely awarded except in the most unusual situations. Split custody is dividing siblings between parents. Frankly, absent the most unusual situations, this is a dreadful way for children to be raised. Children who are at each others' throats to the point they are at emotional or physical risk of harm is usually the only justification for making such an award.

Courts are permitted in most jurisdictions to admit into evidence the preferences of the children regarding their custody. However, depending on the age and circumstances of the children, the court may totally or partially accept those preferences or reject them in full. I recall one case where two children, ages 12 and 15, both wanted to live with their father, and they were very vocal about their desire to do so. The problem was that they had been brainwashed by him into believing that their mother was the most evil creation since Hitler. The court, however, and the expert witnesses involved saw through the madness of the father and knew he was a strong candidate for diagnosis of multiple psychiatric disorders and awarded the mother custody, over the opposition of the children.

Now that we have a basic understanding of the methodologies used to resolve custody disputes, and the types of custody awards that are made, what type of people end up in these horrific battles pitting parent against parent, and frequently parents against the wishes or their own children? I believe that the participants can usually be lumped in to on of three categories. Let's deal with the easiest one first:

Individuals transgressing through the battlefield of divorce inherently rely upon the direction of their commanders, i.e. lawyers. Not to beat a dead horse, but sometimes lawyers do not take the time to explore the best interests of the children or their clients when deciding to launch the first strike in a custody dispute. In the opening days of a divorce, while the wounds are so fresh and tender, it is easy to place damning allegations in a sterile pleading against your spouse. It may be something that is true but really does not need to be said, or perhaps said in the way your lawyer has pled it. The result of such an action is that it is extremely difficult to take back those words that felt so good to hurl back then, when you were really angry or hurt. Since you cannot take back the words, your spouse may respond with words of a similar level of vindictiveness, and the snowball

ball begins to grow. It usually ends up with an avalanche of emotion months later, frequently without survivors. The point to be taken is that your lawyer can be responsible for leading you headlong down a path of destruction that you never really intended. Assess your emotions and read and then re-read a pleading before you let your lawyer file it. Think about whether or not the pleading is really something that your children should read about their mother or father in the years ahead. Do the means actually justify the end?

The second group of custody cases falls into the category of people who hate each other so much or are so

> **WHENEVER I DATE A GUY I THINK, "IS THIS THE MAN I WANT MY CHILDREN TO SPEND THEIR WEEKENDS WITH?"**
> —*Rita Rudner*

mentally imbalanced that they throw out every nuance of parenting undertaken by each for analysis by the court, so much so that the head of the Judge actually begins to cave in. They bring up the time little Alec drank out of a mud puddle at the amusement park while Dad had his back turned. They bring up the fact that they accompanied Russ to the Boy Scout meeting. But they also usually bring up the hateful rhetoric accusing the other of being a terrible parent, of being uninvolved, of always making poor decisions. You could literally take transcripts from thousands of custody cases and hear the same things over and over again. All economic classes, all races, in every single state. Pure vengeful unmitigated hate.

These same individuals are also the ones who use the children as economic leverage. It is in essence the ultimate blackmail—give me this or I try to take the kids. It is for them all about the money, and the children are only a convenient means to accomplish an economic objective. As contestants in the battle of the children (not really for the children, because their interests are secondary), the party only cares about inflicting pain and suffering on the other spouse, or vindicating their own name or reputation. While these cretins are quite a boon for the divorce industry (and loved by the sleaziest of lawyers) they are devastatingly harmful to themselves and especially the children.

The people in this last group are the origin of the horror stories about the children of divorce. I remember one hard-fought case where the parties really despised each other. The kids, a young boy and girl, were obviously being used in the process in a harmful way by the parents. I tried to keep control of the situation as much as I could (as did the other lawyer), but the bitterness between them was overwhelming. About ten years later I ran into my client at the local mall. When I inquired about the children, I was told that the cute little girl I remembered was now working at an escort service. My guess is that the bitterness of the divorce played a role in her decision to denigrate herself as a woman later in life. Another example? I just received in the mail a scholarly book from a proud client. It was written by his son, who had survived a very bitter and contested custody dispute. What I found particularly fascinating about the book was that it was dedicated just to my client, his father, with no mention of his mother. *Children remember.*

People frequently ask me what was the strangest custody case I was ever involved in, and I always think of the same one. Let me set the stage. Washington, DC is a huge community with pockets of poverty, a large affluent middle class, and many areas where a 7,500-square-foot home is, well, ordinary. My client lived in one of those areas—Potomac, Maryland—in a more livable home of some 16,500 square feet. My client was the Mom, a practicing emergency room physician. She was very quick on her feet, brash and a loving parent of two pre-adolescent children. Her husband was a successful lawyer representing trade associations, which are all the rage in Washington. They were an extremely well-to-do professional couple and seemed to have an ideal situation. The only problem was that the husband was a homosexual, a fact that he only acknowledged just as the children were set to begin their teenage years. (You are probably thinking, not another gay story about sex in the church, right? No, don't worry—this is much better than that.) As it turned out, the wife took a very mature approach to this announcement and did everything she could to make this development tolerable for the children, and the pending divorce as painless as possible. The parties separated, but both continued to live in their huge mansion; it was big enough that they could both live comfortably there, albeit separately. My client lived in the main bedroom suite, while the husband set up his living arrangements in the unoccupied housekeeper apartment on a lower level of the home.

Things were going along as well as could be expected under the circumstances until the husband decided he was going to be even more open about his sexuality. He decided to move his lover in to the house. Unannounced. The lover moved in downstairs into the servant's apartment and things went on that way for some time. Then, in another step towards his own self-fulfillment, the husband decided that he was not a servant in the home; it was just as much his house as his wife's, so why should he and his lover be relegated to the servants apartment downstairs? The husband decided that he should be back upstairs in the master bedroom. Exercising more judgment than the husband, his lover felt "out of place" in the bedroom and declined to move upstairs. My client refused to let him occupy the marital bed, but the husband was not to be frustrated in his desire to reclaim his territory. The husband, demonstrating the creativity found only in Washington lobbyists, decided to place a mattress inside the walk-in closet inside the master bedroom and started sleeping there. He came up there every night and slept alone. Now, keep in mind that the closet was not the typical closet like most of us have. Their closet was the size of a comfortable efficiency in New York City. Nonetheless, it was a closet. Think about this for a second…this was the case of the lawyer who came *out* of the closet, only to go *back* into the closet.

Despite these extremely odd arrangements, everyone was living together more or less happily. Over time the wife got to know the husband's lover. You guessed it, the lawyer's lover started to take an interest in the wife—he was apparently beginning to question his own homosexuality. Given the lover's feelings towards the wife, he believed that he might in fact be a bisexual. So why is this the strangest custody case? My client and the husband's lover became lovers, and my task was to remove the husband from the house so the wife could pursue her relationship with the husband's lover. Eventually, the husband learned of the relationship, broke up with the lover and moved out of the house. He made my job much easier. Guess who ended up with custody?

I have deliberately omitted countless stories of pain and heartache that typically accompany a custody battle. The story about the father who sexually abused his daughter with the stem of a baseball pennant from a team he did not like. The mother who was a nurse and inexplicably stole surgical tools, like scalpels and cauterizing equipment, and kept them in a drawer for her kids to find. They found them. Imagine the results of two young children playing with sharp surgical instruments. The mother who objected to a child going on visitation with the father and carried a protest sign to the airport and stood at the gate as they departed. The mother who watched and laughed as her toddler child who could not swim fell into the pool and tried to stay above water. The mother who told her husband in response to his call to her to speak with their three-year-old child, that their son was not actually there, that "He was with God." The wife did not know that the phone call was being recorded (which was legal in this particular jurisdiction, if one party consented). The tape of that conversation and the ensuing panic on the part of the husband was probably one of the worst and most chilling phone calls I ever heard, and one of the worst episodes I had ever encountered in court. The judge turned pale as she listened in horror, and I was left to explain the inexplicable. These tales are true, tragic and just not humorous.

Despite all the laws that are supposed to guarantee equal protection under the law, discrimination is still alive and well in the area of child custody. For decades, the presumption of "tender years" governed, that being that children of tender years were presumed to be better cared for by their mother. This presumption has been abolished by all states, yet I still found that no matter how great the father was, he seemed to always have an extra burden placed on him. The maternal influence on the judiciary seemed to always play a substantial role, causing decisions to be rendered against wonderful fathers who were able to provide for the care of the children just as well (and sometimes better) than the mother. The laws are gender-neutral, but just as it is generally more acceptable for a man to go out and commit adultery, it is also more acceptable for a woman, no matter what kind of mother she is, to retain custody. This is not fair, and it should not be that way, but it is another one of those things that just is.

An entirely different subsection of child custody cases are the issues surrounding child support. Child support is different than spousal support, the latter funds allegedly to be used for the support of the children and not the spouse. Of course, in reality, it is difficult to bifurcate the actual dollars and cents since the housing, utility and food costs are difficult if not impossible to segregate.

The amount of child support to be paid used to be subject to wide discretions of judicial latitude and discretion—or indiscretion depending on your perspective. Over 10 years ago, all states were mandated by the federal government to adopt "child support guidelines" to develop more uniformity in the award of child support. Keep in mind, they are only guidelines, and the courts are still permitted deviate from those guidelines provided that some reason for the deviation is articulated, usually in a written order. In the upper income cases, the discretion of the court is greatly expanded and its latitude substantially increased. Typical factors relied upon by the court in awarding child support are as follows, but as I have noted, each state has their own unique set of factors and mathematical computations as to how the support amount is determined. The following is an actual statutory excerpt from the Commonwealth of Virginia, and it provides a typical example of the scope and factors to be considered in awarding child support. It may be a bit on the complex side for this text, but I thought it was important to give you just a little flavor of the intricacies of a typical child support law. Keep in mind, I have omitted the pages involved in actually doing the mathematical calculations, which would give most readers (and lawyers) a nice migraine headache:

B. In any proceeding on the issue of determining child support under this title or Title 16.1 or Title 63.2, the court shall consider all evidence presented relevant to any issues joined in that proceeding. The court's decision in any such proceeding shall be rendered upon the evidence relevant to each individual case. However, there shall be a rebuttable presumption in any judicial or administrative proceeding for child support, including cases involving split custody or shared custody, that the amount of the award which would result from the application of the guidelines set out in § 20-108.2 is the correct amount of child support to be awarded. Liability for support shall be determined retroactively for the period measured from the date that the proceeding was commenced by the filing of an action with any court provided the complainant exercised due diligence in the service of the respondent or, if earlier, the date an order of the Department of Social Services entered pursuant to Title 63.2 and directing payment of support was delivered to the sheriff or process server for service on the obligor.

In order to rebut the presumption, the court shall make written findings in the order, which findings may be incorporated by reference, that the application of such guidelines would be unjust or inappropriate in a particular case. The finding that rebuts the guidelines shall state the amount of support that would have been required under the guidelines, shall give a justification of why the order varies from the guidelines, and shall be determined by relevant evidence pertaining to the following factors affecting the obligation, the ability of each party to provide child support, and the best interests of the child:

1. Actual monetary support for other family members or former family members;

2. Arrangements regarding custody of the children;

3. Imputed income to a party who is voluntarily unemployed or voluntarily under-employed; provided that income may not be imputed to the custodial parent when a child is not in school, child care services are not available and the cost of

such child care services are not included in the computation;

4. Debts of either party arising during the marriage for the benefit of the child;

5. Debts incurred for production of income;

6. Direct payments ordered by the court for health care coverage, maintaining life insurance coverage pursuant to subsection D, education expenses, or other court-ordered direct payments for the benefit of the child and costs related to the provision of health care coverage pursuant to subdivision 7 of § 20-60.3;

7. Extraordinary capital gains such as capital gains resulting from the sale of the marital abode;

8. Age, physical and mental condition of the child or children, including unreimbursed medical or dental expenses, and child-care expenses;

9. Independent financial resources, if any, of the child or children;

10. Standard of living for the family established during the marriage;

11. Earning capacity, obligations and needs, and financial resources of each parent;

12. Education and training of the parties and the ability and opportunity of the parties to secure such education and training;

13. Contributions, monetary and nonmonetary, of each party to the well-being of the family;

14. Provisions made with regard to the marital property under § 20-107.3;

15. Tax consequences to the parties regarding claims for dependent children and child care expenses;

16. A written agreement between the parties which includes the amount of child support;

17. A pendente lite decree, which includes the amount of child support, agreed to by both parties or by counsel for the parties; and

18. Such other factors, including tax consequences to each party, as are necessary to consider the equities for the

parents and children.

C. In any proceeding under this title or Title 16.1 or Title 63.2 on the issue of determining child support, the court shall have the authority to order a party to provide health care coverage, as defined in § 63.2-1900, for dependent children if reasonable under all the circumstances and health care coverage for a spouse or former spouse.

D. In any proceeding under this title, Title 16.1 or Title 63.2 on the issue of determining child support, the court shall have the authority to order a party to (i) maintain any existing life insurance policy on the life of either party provided the party so ordered has the right to designate a beneficiary and (ii) designate a child or children of the parties as the beneficiary of all or a portion of such life insurance for so long as the party so ordered has a statutory obligation to pay child support for the child or children.

E. Except when the parties have otherwise agreed, in any proceeding under this title, Title 16.1 or Title 63.2 on the issue of determining child support, the court shall have the authority to and may, in its discretion, order one party to execute all appropriate tax forms or waivers to grant to the other party the right to take the income tax dependency exemption for any tax year or future years, for any child or children of the parties for federal and state income tax purposes.

Not much fun, huh? Do your children a favor—before you decide to have children, make sure that you really want to spend the rest of your natural life with the other parent. Sure, there is a 50 percent likelihood that your decision will be wrong, and that you will have children and then divorce. You must always be cognizant of the shock and pain a divorce causes a child, and you must place their interest in the forefront. When I went through my own divorce, the worst part of the entire experience was telling my then-four-year-old son that his mother and I were getting a divorce. He clapped his hands over his ears and ran out of the room crying. It was the most agonizing moment of my life, one I would never want to relive. The pain and agony of divorce is often seen most vividly in the hearts and eyes of your own children.

A MAN AND HIS YOUNG WIFE WERE IN COURT BATTLING FOR THE CUSTODY OF THEIR CHILDREN. THE MOTHER ARGUED TO THE JUDGE THAT SINCE SHE BROUGHT THE CHILDREN INTO THIS WORLD, SHE SHOULD RETAIN CUSTODY OF THEM. THE MAN ALSO WANTED CUSTODY OF HIS CHILDREN, AND THE JUDGE ASKED FOR HIS RESPONSE. AFTER A LONG SILENCE, THE MAN SLOWLY ROSE FROM HIS CHAIR. "YOUR HONOR, WHEN I PUT A DOLLAR IN A VENDING MACHINE AND A PEPSI COMES OUT, DOES THE PEPSI BELONG TO ME OR THE MACHINE?"

# ADVICE TO REMEMBER

$ The decision to procreate will last a lifetime—do yourself a favor and spend a few years with the person you are considering parenting with before you embark upon this lifelong experience.

$ Children remember forever how each parent treats each other and them during the period surrounding a divorce—treat your children and spouse with respect on custody and visitation issues.

$ Do not attempt to use the children as a tool for retribution against a spouse or to gain leverage in other aspects of your divorce.

$ Court systems were not designed to determine the custody of children, and your resolution of those issues will almost always be better tailored to your children's interests than what a court will do.

$ Your children have a different experience and relationship with your spouse than you do—do not try and change the relationship to fit your own desires, needs, or wants.

$ Children have no desire to be included in the potential war against your spouse—do everything possible to keep that out of the war zone and handle all communications regarding their interests directly with the other parent or through counsel. Never communicate through the children to the other parent.

$ Forget about the labels and day counting frequently advocated by lawyers in association with child custody and support matters. The court (and your children) will forever appreciate a parent who is concerned only about the child's best interest as opposed to a parent's ego validation or economic concerns.

$ Make sure that you only enter in to an agreement that you know you can comply with. Do not settle a case on terms that you find offensive or that you have been pressured to accept. In reaching an agreement regarding children, you must take a step back and think about what is really best for them, not you, in the long run.

💲 Judges are faced with terrible cases of abuse and neglect on an almost daily basis. Keep that in mind when you are considering raising concerns about the "parenting" of your soon-to-be former spouse. To an independent party, how will the alleged conduct actually be perceived by them? Is the conduct really harmful?

# DR. STANTON SAMENOW
## *Parentectomy and other mistakes*

*Licensed in Virginia since 1972, and in full-time practice since 1978, Dr. Stanton Samenow is an internationally acclaimed forensic clinical psychologist. His book, **Inside the Criminal Mind** is the preeminent work on why criminals behave as they do. He has written other books as well on parenting and other subjects, and most recently published a book on the rigors of child custody entitled "In the Best Interests of the Child." The opinions of Dr. Samenow are frequently sought in custody and visitation matters throughout the country, and he is often appointed by the court or appointed through a consent order of the attorneys. In 90% of the hundreds of cases in which he has been involved, he was named the independent evaluator to assist the court in making the ultimate decision regarding the children. Stanton Samenow is a man whose opinions I respect, even when he was retained as an expert in litigation against my own clients. I knew that if Dr. Samenow was involved, I would be faced with a no-nonsense, honest opinion regarding the facts of the case. I hope that you will find informative his unique perspective on marriage, divorce, lawyers, marriage counseling, custody and the mistakes we all can make.*

The number one mistake divorcing parents make is to lose sight of the big picture. The big picture is that their child has already suffered a tremendous loss—that of the family in which he or she grew up and lived in. He no longer has that life and that family. Even if that family was in turmoil, even if the family was marred by financial trouble or instability or even abuse, it was that family that the child woke up to every single day. The second biggest mistake parents can make is to put their child under pressure, either directly or indirectly, so that he feels he has to make a choice, and feels there is the threat of the loss of another parent. The attempt to diminish or eliminate from a child's life somebody whom he loves and is attached to is a terrible mistake during divorce. I would strongly counsel against what I term a *"parentectomy."*

I actually have a great deal of respect for domestic relations attorneys, and most I have dealt with have been very fine professionals. However, if there is one mistake they tend to make, it would be the lawyer gets so close to his case that he focuses on litigating and battling and winning the advantage. If there is some reasonable possibility of taking the more amicable course, they sometimes do not, because they are so close to their client that they throw fuel on an already burning fire rather than trying to quell it and see what kind of amicable settlement can be reached.

I would tell divorcing parents several things, after reminding them to bear in mind that you and your spouse or soon-to-be-ex-spouse are always and forever going to be the parents of this child. You will always be bound together in that way. You certainly don't have to love your ex-spouse or even like them, but bear in mind that your child is attached and does love his other parent, so do everything you can to foster and encourage that child to have a relationship with your ex-spouse. Obviously, the exception would be those relatively few cases where the other parent represents some kind of real danger to the child.

Do not force your child to compartmentalize his existence with each parent. In other words, let him feel free to express positive thoughts and emotions about the other parent. Encourage him to talk about his life with the other parent—and when I say encourage, I do not mean grill. Your child should feel that he can talk about either having a good time or any problems he might be having at the other parent's. He should not feel like he has to live two separate lives.

Do not get sucked into or engender any competition with the other parent for the affection of your child. That means emotionally, financially, or in any other way.

Communicate in a businesslike fashion with the other parent the necessary information about your child's health, education, activities and general welfare so he can have as seamless an existence as possible. Your child's welfare should not fall through the cracks because the two of you cannot communicate properly. That communication should be handled in a courteous and businesslike way — even if it has to be handled through e-mail.

Each and every situation is different, and every case has to be looked at in terms of the personalities involved and their dynamics. I am *not* a person who presumes that joint custody is automatically the best way to go. I make no assumptions going in. Clearly, it is in the best interests of the child to have a relationship with both parents, assuming both are fit. But that in and of itself does not necessarily assume joint custody from the beginning. I think you have to enter every case with a clean slate as far as your own mindset, and really recommend what you think is going to serve that child best.

In my experience, marriages fall apart for one of several reasons. One is that the parties thought they knew each other, but really did not take the time and make the effort to know each other well enough prior to getting married. I understand that people never truly know each other until they have had many, many, years together; and even then, they may feel they do not fully know the person they married, but marrying too soon certainly exacerbates this problem. Another problem is couples who are more in love with the idea of being married than knowledgeable about their partner and what marriage actually entails. They have unrealistic expectations, both of their partner and about what marriage means. They think that being married, in and of itself, is going to be such a great thing and transform their lives, and that may or may not be the case. When I got married 34 years ago, I was given a banner that said, *"Love is a lot of hard work."* That is absolutely true, and I think one powerful reason that marriages don't make it is that either one or both parties are not willing to put in the requisite effort to make it work and seek responsible help if is needed.

Of course, marriages can run into other problems, such as affairs, alcohol abuse, an absent parent who leaves the child-rearing entirely to his or her spouse…but these are all contributing factors. They are basically personality deficits on the part of one of the parents which certainly contributes to the breakdown of marriage. Now some will disagree with me, but I think that having an affair certainly demonstrates a personality deficit on the part of the person who has the affair in the marriage.

Can a marriage survive an affair? Well, sure. Can a house be built on a cracked foundation? Of course. Nevertheless, once the distrust and sense of betrayal is there, the marriage will never be as strong and solid again. Certainly, some marriages do survive an affair, but something has changed forever.

If a client of mine were considering having an affair, I would ask them to tell me what he thought the ramifications of such an affair might be: A, if it were found out; and B, if it were never found out. I would want to engage in a very thorough discussion. I would want to know what this person's thinking was; see if he's really even thinking rationally or correctly estimated the likely consequences. If I were asked for my opinion—and I might give it anyway, asked or not—I would say "Don't do it. If you were to have sex with somebody outside your marriage, then you better look at your marriage and decide whether or not you want to stay in it."

I think that marriage counseling does *not* work for countless individuals, for two reasons. One is that there are many people out there who call themselves marriage counselors who are ineffective, to say the least. Number two, unfortunately I think that marriage counseling is often thought of too late. Even if you have a very competent counselor, once a certain point has passed, so much has happened that it is unlikely that any counselor can help repair it. For the people I typically see, it is usually far too late for marriage counseling. It can be quite effective; unfortunately, it often comes too late to make any difference.

Now even in the most solid of marriages there are certain recurrent themes of disagreement that come up. Whether it's sex, or in-laws, or differences in child-raising, or money, everybody has certain areas where they disagree. Nonetheless, I think if you can pinpoint an area where you and your spouse consistently cannot come to a meeting of the minds, and resentment is building, it's time to say, "Maybe we should talk to somebody about this."

I would say that I am probably considered quite conservative on this matter, but it is my belief that parents should stay together for the sake of the children, except in cases where there is a danger to the child—either actual physical danger, or where one parent is so impaired that the child is not safe with him or her. In that case, a break-up is probably the best idea. If there is so much conflict and so much anger that the child is constantly being caught up in it, tossed back and forth like a badminton shuttlecock, and things just seem to be getting worse and worse, and counseling has failed and everything else…. If the couple has made reasonable efforts to resolve their problems and there is nothing but continued turmoil, I certainly would not say that the best prescription is to stay together for the next ten years for the sake of the child.

The pain of breaking up the family and the loss of the family unit must be counter-balanced by the child being relieved of being in the crossfire of the parents. I think that people must work and should be encouraged to work on their marriage—and it is immoral not to work hard on their relationship. No one should simply give up until every option is exhausted. You have a moral obligation to your child, and that obligation must be fulfilled. If in good faith you and your spouse have tried everything possible, and there is no amelioration of the situation, then I guess you call it quits. *But, only then.*

I would have to know a fair amount about someone personally before I could judge if he or she was ready to marry. I would want to know how well he believes he knows his intended, what is the history of the relationship so far, what does he think are the differences they have now, what differences does he see arising in the future, how has he handled any differences so far? Then there is a whole host of other questions to consider, such as, Does she want to have children? What faith will they be brought up in? Will she work after she has a child? What about childcare? I believe that people need to think about these things and talk about them so they do not just fall in love with the idea of being married and think that marriage is going to be this great easy ride and they are going to have kids and be a big happy family. You need to have realistic expectations of marriage and of your partner.

Everybody has his or her own definition of love, but to me, first there has to be a very strong friendship. I think that marriages in which each partner is the best friend of the other have an excellent foundation. There should also be physical attraction, chemistry. Respect is also very important. You can respect the person you are in love with or married to even when your opinions differ from theirs; that is, you respect who that person is and where they are coming from. It does not mean you love everything about them, but it means that whatever minuses there are, the plusses far outweigh them. Common values and interests shared in common are also important. I know this sounds very cerebral and intellectual, but love and marriage is not just romance. As I said, it requires a lot of hard work.

Marriage does work, but it takes a lot of effort, thought, compromise, perspective, devotion, dedication and hard work. When people go into it properly prepared, it can be a great thing and wonderfully enrich your life. Marriage is great—*I highly recommend it!*

# CHAPTER 12

# DIVIDING UP THE PIE

"Some people say you can't put a price on a wife's twenty-seven years of loyalty and devotion. They're wrong."

Through the last eleven chapters, we have traversed the painful journey through perceived love, the decision to marry, and some of the reasons why marriages dissolve. We have also discussed a number of the processes and persons who you will encounter on your gleeful path to freedom (no doubt only to repeat the process, as set forth in the next chapter). We have noted on multiple occasions the agony and misery attendant to the process of the extraction of love, and the heavy financial cost of doing so. However, at the end of the day, where does the process leave you financially? What is fair? How is it determined? What should you realistically expect to pay or what will you have left when you start to calculate the cost of living the American Dream?

Dividing up the marital pie is a process that triggers a variety of responses, ranging from anger and frustration to fear and desperation. Depending upon your perspective, you might be faced with anger and hostility about not getting a large enough slice of the pie. On the other hand, you could be confronted with similar anxiety, fear and desperation over how much that slice of pie might cost you.

In order to comprehend what steps you may take before you get married in order to maximize your potential recovery of marital property, or to ultimately minimize the economic harm of your trip down the aisle, it is first incumbent to fully understand the general definitions of the terms we will be using. Keep in mind, this is not a legal treatise, and as we have discussed in prior chapters, there are always deviations to every rule depending upon where you live, or more appropriately, where the court is located that will ultimately be deciding the issues related to the disappearance of your property.

The first category of property is marital property or community property. Marital or community property is typically that property which has been acquired by you or your spouse during the course of the marital relationship. Depending upon where you live, the property continues to accrue for the benefit of the marital estate until either the date of your separation, or in some states, until the date that you actually are divorced. It is safe to assume that if the property or income was created, generated, or earned during the time from when the pronouncement was made that you were married, through the time of the announcement that you and your spouse have separated, that the property is most likely going to be thrown in the marital or community pot.

The second category of property is separate property or conversely, non-marital or non-community property. Separate property is that property that was acquired by either you or your spouse before the utterance of your sacred marital vows, was inherited by you, or was gifted to you by a third party. In some states, separate property includes that property that is directly traceable to these same three sources. Separate property may also include, depending upon where you happen to live, that property acquired by you subsequent to the date of your separation. Separate property may be defined to include the appreciation on the value of separate property. I mentioned to you that gifts from third parties are exempted from inclusion in the marital estate or community. Notice that I did not mention gifts from your spouse, which are generally subject to be freely tossed in the marital pot.

Most clients found the fact that a Christmas, birthday or even anniversary gift given to them by their spouse could at the time of the break-up of the marriage be in essence counted as just another bank account or couch. Especially infuriating were the gifts given to a client by their spouse as a peace offering for some act of marital misconduct. You remember Kobe Bryant giving his wife the $5 million ring after his "consensual sex" in the lodge in Eagle County, Colorado. Well, when they eventually get around to divorcing, it will probably end up getting whacked up too. The gift issue would also rear its ugly head frequently when it came to real property. Why? Invariably, some spouses' parents would have given one party some sum of money utilized to acquire their first property, let's say for purpose of our discussion, $10,000. Suddenly, fifteen years later when the marriage has broken down, the spouse whose parents made the gift suddenly claims that the gift was made just to her, not to the two of them. By doing so, the spouse will suddenly turn marital property into separate property, and then claim as separate property any appreciation on the property attributable to the "gift," and the amount can be significant.

Therefore, for purposes of simplicity, you need to look at what you had before the marriage, assume that that property is your own, and consider everything that you earn or acquire after the date of marriage to be something to be shared with your beloved. But be forewarned—you can turn separate property into marital property by mixing up your separate property with property that you acquired during the marriage. There are other classifications of marital property, such as part separate, part marital, commingled, transmuted and hybrid property. Any discussion of these variations exceeds the scope of this book and is excruciatingly boring as well.

> I AM A GREAT HOUSEKEEPER.
> I GET DIVORCED.
> I KEEP THE HOUSE.
> —*Zsa Zsa Gabor*

Now that you have a basic understanding as to how property is classified, you must next appreciate how the property will be valued. Personal property, things like bank accounts, stock accounts, cars, furniture, jewelry, and so on are valued according to their actual fair market value. That does not mean what you paid for it, what you wish it was worth or what it may be emotionally worth to you (pets are personal property). It is the value or price that a willing seller would sell to a willing buyer, neither of them being under any compulsion to sell or buy. Real property (real estate including your house or condo) is valued at fair market value as well. Businesses and professional practices (law firms, accounting firms, medical practices) are where the real variations in value are found. It is in valuing these entities or interests where tremendous value can be created at the hands of a skilled lawyer and forensic accountant or effectively made *de minimis* at the crafty hands of another. The valuation of pensions is an art in and of itself, and typically requires the utilization of an actuary, if the pension is not to be divided on an "if as and when" basis, meaning that when your spouse starts receiving it, you get a percentage share of it as determined by the court, as opposed to the calculation of its total value as just another piece of the marital pie. Frequently, the value of a pension or profit sharing plan can easily eclipse the value of all other assets. In addition, I am sure that most of you may have heard the stories of the secretaries that became millionaires overnight when the small start up company they worked for (like Google or Amazon) had given them stock options in lieu of ordinary compensation. Stock options and other employee perquisites (country club use, private planes, expenses accounts) all need to be assessed in creating the right recipe.

You either reside in a state that is an equitable distribution state or a community property state. Community property is easier, so let's get that out of the way first. You are in a community property state if you live in California, Nevada, Arizona, California, Idaho, Louisiana, New Mexico, Texas, Washington and Wisconsin. If property is determined to be part of the marital community, you get half upon divorce. It is just that simple. Forget about who did what to who during the marriage, as long as you were not stealing from the community property. As you can imagine, most of the fighting is about what is going to be defined as part of the community and what its value actually is.

All other states are equitable distribution states. In those states, the rule of 50/50 does not apply. Instead the courts, following a series of factors enacted by their respective legislatures, analyze a series of factors and arrive at a fair and equitable distribution of the parties' property. Keep in mind that fair and equitable absolutely does not mean equal. I have seen scenarios where one spouse receives *all* of the parties' marital property—and it was fair and equitable. The type of factors that courts typically consider varies by each jurisdiction, but some common factors are as follows:

• duration of the marriage
• economic and non-economic contributions that each party has made to the acquisition or preservation of the marital estate
• age and health of the parties
• liquidity of assets
• tax effects
• the earning capacity of the parties
• the reasons for the breakdown of the marriage
• any other circumstances that the court deems relevant

Once again, it is this final ubiquitous factor (remember it from the Alimony Chapter?) that affords the court the unparalleled discretion to either reward or crucify you. Constructing an equitable distribution award is almost completely dependent upon you and your lawyer providing the court with the requisite evidence to yield a result that you will feel best represents your contribution to the recipe that has composed the marital pie. The simpler the ingredients, the better the pie usually tastes. Nevertheless, remember, use only the finest ingredients, and leave the extraneous junk out—once you put this pie in the oven to bake, you can't change the essence of its taste, nor how palatable it will be to others.

If an affluent couple is the subject of a distribution of property, there is more flexibility on the part of the court and parties in terms of how much money someone receives or pays. The husband may have to pay his wife $10 million, $20 million or even $30 million. Now, does the difference between a $20 million-dollar settlement and a $30 million-dollar settlement change either the husband or the wife's life substantially, or for that matter in any meaningful way? No, of course not. However, to a couple like you or me, the difference between who has to pay off the MasterCard bill before the divorce is settled may make a huge difference in the quality of their lives. Keep in mind that when it comes to divorce, the rich and poor have the same basic laws. The same rules, just bigger stakes and skilled advocates to facilitate their best application. Donald Trump gets a divorce in the exact same way that a maintenance worker in Trump Tower does. The same essential paperwork is filed in the same court; it is only the quality and volume that differs. The process is exactly the same for everyone; it is just that Donald Trump has more assets. He may have to divide a penthouse here, a private plane there, and a business with branches all over the world; whereas the maintenance worker has to divide up his Swatch watch collection and two dogs and a MasterCard bill. The underlying legal process, however, is exactly the same.

When I look through my old files and see all the motions for return of personal property, it reminds me of just how petty things could and often did get. I did so much work for couples worth literally millions and millions of dollars, and they would have me filing motions for the return of a piece of china or crystal. Maybe some scuba gear or assorted tools. It was ludicrous. Talk about a wife cleaning house…I will never forget the woman who literally took the *carpet runner on the stairs* that had been nailed down. She was just that mad.

> ## A DIVORCE IS LIKE AN AMPUTATION: YOU SURVIVE IT, BUT THERE'S LESS OF YOU.
> —*Margaret Atwood*

I also chuckle when I think about a motion that I had to defend regarding the valuation of personal property. I was representing a woman who was the manager of a Victoria's Secret store. Her husband was extremely discontent at the breakup of their marriage and wanted to inflict as much pain and suffering upon her as possible. The husband and his intellectually challenged counsel decided that my client had spent a small fortune on lingerie and other intimate apparel during her years at Victoria's Secret, and accordingly, there was significant marital property in her dresser drawers that should be subject to valuation. I am guessing that you might be rolling your eyes at this point saying, "No, this cannot be true; he is obviously making this up." My only saving grace here is that by coincidence, my parents were visiting me and I had invited them to come to court with me that week so that they could see the benefit of all of the hard-earned dollars spent by them on my higher education. My parents witnessed the whole argument. The lawyer for the husband actually sought the appraisal of the used underwear, bras and sleepwear so that its value would be included in the marital estate. Now I admit, my client had essentially enough lingerie to stock one—okay, maybe two—small stores. Nevertheless, valuing used underwear? What kind of an expert does this take anyway? Wouldn't you love to hear their statement of qualifications on the witness stand? I made all of those arguments but especially enjoyed asserting that the husband simply wanted to engage in this fiasco for his own prurient interests, just to get one last glimpse of his wife's bras and lace panties. The judge was holding back his own laughter and disgust and ended up allowing the husband to value the lingerie if he could find an expert to do so. However, the appraisal of the underwear was to take place out of the viewing of the husband. When we left court after the motion was finished, my parents asked me to repay them all of the money spent by them for my law school education.

Marital fault can still play a role in certain states when it comes to dividing up the property, but most courts look for some nexus between the marital misconduct and economic harm to the parties. I remember one case in North Carolina where a woman sued her husband's girlfriend for tortuous interference in her marriage and intentional infliction of emotional distress, and she won a $400,000 verdict. I was on a television program commenting about it, and I said, "This case proves why North Carolina is known for its barbeque and not its jurisprudence." Geraldo Rivera said words to the effect, "Well, Mark, I guess you won't be getting any cases in North Carolina in the future." But that is just ridiculous. Alienation of affection statutes were abolished everywhere except, obviously, in North Carolina and I believe one other state. With good reason, because what, we don't have enough divorce litigation alone without going around suing everybody else over breaking up a marriage?

Is a bigger piece of the pie going to make you feel better? Some people would say yes, but I would say that people who want to feel better *will* feel better, whether or not they get a large slice. Certainly money makes everything easier. Life is easier when you don't have the stress of economic woes to deal with on top of a divorce, but other than that, the rich folks will tell you that the process is just as painful.

You now have completed a basic primer on the laws regarding the division of property coincident with a divorce. Not exactly exciting reading, but nonetheless important information in assessing a decision to marry and to divorce. In the advice to remember section that follows, I have set forth a few general rules and observations that I have made over the years to make the whole process easier. I am not going to repeat the issues that we have discussed in prior chapters, such as prenuptial agreements, retaining the right lawyer and expert witnesses. If you have not figured out the importance of those points, you might as well just title everything in the name of your spouse and walk out the door (leave them your checkbook too).

I BELIEVE IN MARRIAGE...BUT THERE AIN'T GOING
TO BE NO EQUALITY. IF YOU WANT TO BE EQUAL WITH ME,
YOU CAN GET YOUR OWN ROLLS-ROYCE, YOUR OWN
HOUSE AND YOUR OWN MILLION DOLLARS.

—*Muhammad Ali*

# ADVICE TO REMEMBER

$ Any gifts given to your beloved before marriage are gone forever —save the good stuff for after the marriage.

$ Keep all of your assets separate to the largest extent possible, both before and after marriage—checkbooks, stock accounts, real estate, everything.

$ If you elect not to execute a prenuptial agreement, consult a tax and estate lawyer who can secure and title your existing assets in a manner to shield them from attack before the date of your marriage.

$ If you are to receive a gift from your parents or a third party, make sure that they document that the gift is just for you, not for the both of you (that includes family heirlooms you do not want to lose).

$ Do not attempt to hide assets. If you are caught, you will forever regret the consequences judges despise people who do this.

$ Substantial gifts between spouses (expensive jewelry, art, cars.) should be presented as good investments for the family, while bringing joy at the same time.

$ Keep track of documents that establish the source of the acquisition and value of property, and keep a copy of them in a location outside the home.

$ Have your spouse explain the tax return before you sign it and make sure you get a copy so you can review it at your leisure.

$ Be realistic in assessing your ability to successfully value or devalue assets.

$ Pick your battles—a couch is just a couch—let it go and buy another.

$ Do not be greedy-judges have a disdain for overreaching.

$ Do not be cheap-judges will not like you either.

# DONALD TRUMP
## *The Art of the Marriage*

*I first met Donald Trump in 1998 at a dinner with Larry King at the 21 Club in New York City. I was there with my soon-to-be wife, and little did I know, Donald was there with his future wife as well, Melania Knauss. When I first met Donald, I was instantly struck by his candid, down-to-earth manner. He was intelligent, kind, and not at all the abrasive controversial billionaire we now watch fire people week-*  *ly on* **The Apprentice**. *He was just a great guy to talk with and listen to: a wonderful raconteur. Over the years, we would get to spend more time together —I was even fortunate enough to present Donald with the prestigious Larry King Heart Award.*

*When you enter the offices of "The Donald" you must first pass through a security guard to enter the express elevator to his offices on the 26th Floor of the world famous sanctuary of luxury and power on New York's Fifth Avenue, Trump Tower. Next, you enter through one set of secured glass double doors to his opulent suite. To reach Donald's office you need to pass through yet another set of secured glass doors and then the wooden ones that allow access to his hallowed chamber. The view from his office is incredible, from Central Park straight down to the Statute of Liberty. Moreover, for Donald, it is an easy commute—he just lives forty floors above.*

*Donald, while lucky in the world of business, has faced challenges in the game of love. He was married to Ivana for many years, then Marla for a brief stint. We had dinner once when he was going through his divorce with Marla and she was challenging their prenuptial agreement. Donald told me then that he could settle the case by just paying another million dollars to Marla, but "A deal is a deal." As noted previously, Donald is now married for the third time and he wants this to be the last. I respect the candor, courage and accomplishments of America's favorite tycoon, Donald Trump. Here are some of his thoughts and advice on rolling the dice of marital happiness.*

These days, the odds for the survival of a marriage are not very good. Marriage is not a contract written in stone. I am not saying it is not a big deal—I think it is a very important part of life and I take it very seriously. However, one has to be practical and objective. There is a lot of reality in marriage—just like in business.

Just about every rule that applies to business also applies to marriage. Whom you marry is one of the biggest business deals you will ever make. Be aware, focus, and know that relationships evolve, just as businesses do. Compatibility is hard to guess at, and since marriage should not really be left up to chance, I think it is better to live with someone first.

Pre-nups are the responsible, sensible thing to do. Always get a prenuptial agreement, whether you are a man or woman. Realize that marriage is a serious endeavor, and treat it that way. It should never be approached or handled in a haphazard manner.

You have to marry someone with whom you are completely at ease. Any time I hear people talking about 'working' at their relationship, I know something is off. If you have to work at it, it is not right to begin with.

Marriage should enhance your life, and very positively, just as your job or work should. That is the main question to ask before marrying someone, and also about your work. The same question applies when considering divorce. Negative relationships are not good for anyone, at work or at home. The main lesson to learn from a divorce? How to recognize and avoid the same mistakes, next time.

Everyone has his or her own definition of a workaholic. People who run their own businesses will not be working a straight nine-to-five schedule. We all know the boundaries of what is too much. When one aspect of life starts to eclipse the others, something is out of line and needs to be brought to attention.

Money problems are money problems, whether the sums are large or small. That being said, having money is better than not having money. Having money can make life a lot easier…

# CHAPTER 13

# THE SECOND TIME AROUND

*"She married and then divorced, and then she married and divorced, and then she married and lived happily ever after."*

Perhaps it is a mere coincidence, but I just noticed that this chapter on remarriage is Chapter 13. The all-time lucky number. The floor number they omit from most buildings and the one date of the month you hope does not fall on the Friday of your big interview.

You might be asking yourself why in the world would you want to get married again after enduring the potential for pain and agony described in the previous twelve chapters? There could be several reasons. First, you may not have read this book before your beginner marriage. See, all first marriages really are just trainer marriages. Unfortunately, we do not get training wheels, so when we take a wrong turn, most people fall down and get hurt. Sometimes the injuries can be minor, and for others, like Laci Peterson, the injuries can be fatal.

Most of us who have been married previously share a variety of common factors. We were probably too young; listening (or for that matter, not listening) to the advice and counsel of our parents; we were idealistic in our perception of love and were unrealistic about the realities of the obligations of marriage; we thought that "I do" meant forever and we believed that we could change the "bad habits" of our spouse; we may have believed that we made a commitment and that commitment should be kept, sometimes for the sake of the kids, other times out of guilt; we may have felt that we only cheated once (or were cheated upon once) and that it would never happen again; we all probably felt the disquieting silence of awakening in the night, as our spouses slept, completely unaware of the questions pounding our conscience as to whether to take the plunge, separate and forever change our life as we then knew it.

---

MARRIAGE IS THE TRIUMPH OF
IMAGINATION OVER INTELLIGENCE.
SECOND MARRIAGE IS THE TRIUMPH
OF HOPE OVER EXPERIENCE.

---

Second, despite having fallen down and gotten hurt, most people get back on the bike and try to ride again. Why? Because there is a pleasurable aspect to marriage. There is no other institution that provides the rewards of a marriage, despite its high risk of failure. Just ask any spouse who really loves, cares for and appreciates their "other half." To them, their life is not whole without the other person. Since the passing of my father, I have become even more attuned to the ramifications of the loss of a spouse. I have observed the pain and suffering, the lack of "oneness" that seems to torment my mother each day. After being with someone for fifty years, they become a part of you, for better and for worse. Notwithstanding all of the ranting contained in this book, I do feel that the institution of marriage is sacred, important and very well-suited to many people—just not for everyone. For those of us who have tried to ride again, we do so with the knowledge that guiding the relationship safely requires a steady balance, hard pedaling up the hills, avoiding the numerous potholes in the road, and hopefully long stretches when we can just coast along and enjoy the scenery and comfort of our riding companion.

The third reason you may remarry is that there is a vacuum of common sense in your brain when it comes to relationships. Included in this category are hopeless romantics, and those who are simply so insecure that they cannot be alone for any protracted period. These are the folks who jump from one relationship to another, changing significant others at will.

If there was ever an area where people tend to repeat the same mistakes, it is in the arena of personal relationships and marriage. There usually is a period after a separation or divorce when the words "I will never get married again" are spoken. These are what I typically refer to as "famous last words," as most people will get married again. I found that much of the success of a second marriage depended upon how quickly the remarriage occurred. I hate to be so simplistic, but please, do not immediately jump from one marriage to the other. Sometimes people are so disenchanted with their first or existing marriage that they fail to fully appreciate the dynamics behind the new relationship or marriage under contemplation. All they can think is, "I know I can't live with someone who does *that*," (whether that is drinking, or cheating, or being a workaholic, whatever it is that they believe caused their divorce). They run to another person, remarry and realize, "Oh my God, there's a whole new set of problems with this other person!"

*The grass is almost never greener on the other side.* Sometimes it is, but the odds of you finding it are extremely remote. Everyone has to understand and appreciate that, and then act or not act accordingly. There are married people out there, having affairs, and then cheating on their lover too. Some people are not happy with their wife but feel they cannot terminate that relationship, so they start up an affair with someone else. Then they become bored by their lover, and seek another. They always think the grass is greener, that something better is out there.

To many, remarriage is simply the exchange of one set of problems for another. The advantage of staying married is that you know the problems that you are dealing with. You know what to expect and not to expect. When you get remarried, you may think you know what you are dealing with, but are rarely correct in that assumption. You will find that the passion, excitement and allure of the new relationship will fade at some point. Moreover, when the sun sets on all of the fun and games, you will see your mate in a completely different light. You will have discovered that your expectations for the relationship have not been realized. The question is, will the picture be more pleasing than what you previously had, or will you wish you had the old picture back?

When people remarry, they seem to marry the exact same type of person they divorced in the first place or they marry someone who is the complete opposite. The wife married to the heavy drinker finds someone who completely abstains from alcohol. The husband who was married to the prudish wife marries a nymphomaniac. The wife who had a frugal husband finds one who will spend lavishly. The husband who is the victim of a cheating wife marries a homely bride, reducing his risk of an adulterous recurrence. The wife previously married to the workaholic finds a 9 to 5 man.

---

**THE HAPPIEST TIME IN A PERSON'S LIFE IS THAT
PERIOD OF TIME BETWEEN THE FIRST AND SECOND MARRIAGE.
THE PROBLEM IS, WE DO NOT REALIZE THIS UNTIL
THE SECOND MARRIAGE.**

---

I do not wish to appear any more skeptical about remarriage than I am about marriage itself. The problem is that although you may not have gotten it right the first time, statistics tell us that you will not get it right the second time either. In fact, it is statistically more likely that your second marriage will fail than your first marriage. That's right, there is a higher percentage of second marriages failing than first marriages. In fact, some statistics demonstrate that the divorce rate for second marriage can approach 70%. Promising, huh?

Now many people feel that following a divorce that they may not be as desirable as "new goods." Let me assure you that anyone who ascribes to that view is not someone you would want to be with in any event. Remember the saying of my father-in-law, "There's an ass for every seat." There are numerous advantages to marrying a person who was previously married. First, they hopefully have a much better understanding of the obligations, benefits, and yes, duties attendant to the role of spouse. Second, they are probably more mature for the experience of having been married and are typically are more cautious about wanting to dive into the marital pool again. However, keep in mind, this only applies to the good ones. There are a multitude of real rejects and losers out there, people who were married before and were discarded for very good reason. Unfortunately, you may not find out the reason they were discarded until it is too late. Because of that lack of knowledge, you may get to go through the whole divorce process again.

People understandably feel horrible when they are the one being left, or being asked for a divorce, but I always asked and encouraged my clients to look at it this way: If you are being left, you are being given another chance to find someone who will really be good for you, to you, and with you, as opposed to being stuck with someone who is none of these things. If you can rise to the occasion, undesired events can certainly be a blessing in disguise. If you can accept the fact that yes, this man (or woman) is leaving me, but realize that you are not being appreciated and have so much to give to someone else, it is a tremendous opportunity. It is a whole new second chance for a new life. After the shock, mourning, grief, anger and bitterness, you have been granted another prospect, a brand new beginning.

Today we are inundated with ads—televised, published and e-mailed to us daily—revealing opportunities to find the perfect Miss or Mister Right. Given modern technology, we can now pick a potential spouse by age, color, religion, height, weight, sexual preference, hobby, never married, widower, hair color, you name it—you don't even have to leave the house to do it. Some people utilize the traditional classified ads, and if you really want some entertaining reading or just to maybe sexually fantasize, just pick up your local paper and read the personal section of the classifieds. There is some amazing reading there.

---

**I'D MARRY AGAIN IF I FOUND A MAN WHO HAD $15 MILLION AND WOULD SIGN OVER HALF OF IT TO ME BEFORE THE MARRIAGE, AND GUARANTEE HE'D BE DEAD WITHIN A YEAR.**

—*Bette Davis*

---

The bottom line is that the end of any relationship marks the potential for the beginning of another. A relationship better than the one that you had. You are smarter now, and you will most likely not repeat the same mistakes that caused the downfall of the prior relationship. You must also remember that there is nothing wrong with taking a bit of a breather in between relationships. Do not get pressured to enter another unless and until you can honestly say to yourself that you can give that new relationship your best. If the other party to the relationship cannot understand that, you have your first warning sign.

Many times during my career a client hired me because their former husband or wife had retained me in their first divorce. When their second marriage was falling apart, they remembered their experience and decided that it would be better to have me on their side the second time through the mill. Because of the inherent conflict of interest, I had to receive permission from their former spouse (my former client), because issues might remain or arise in the future between the former spouses. Permission was almost always granted. Why? If I had represented a wife against the husband, and the husband remarried and later separated from the second wife, the first wife was always particularly anxious to see the second wife get her due. What goes around comes around.

I have told you about many of the people that I was fortunate (and in some cases unfortunate) enough to have interacted with over the years. However, I really have not told you very much about my own marital history. I got married during my first year of law school to a woman I met in college. I was too young to marry, but did not know it until it was too late. When I was divorced in 1995, we agreed that matters between us were confidential and entered into an agreement confirming the same.

I believe that matters of marriage and the reasons for separation and divorce are inherently private, and should be kept that way. The famous syndicated radio personality Howard Stern has earned a reputation for his outlandish exploits on the air that has included insights into matters that would be considered extremely personal to most of us— including the miscarriage of his wife's pregnancy. I have never met Mr. Stern personally, but I have always respected his willingness to push the limit of the envelope and his fervent passion for the first amendment.

Stern had always spoken lovingly about his wife and children as he shocked the morning drive-time of our nation. Then seemingly out of the blue, he was separated. I do not know the reasons behind the divorce, but I can certainly use my imagination. Somehow, in the months following his announcement, I sensed that even when strippers were surrounding him on air that he was really somewhat sad. As if he missed what he'd had. To my knowledge, he has never spoken publicly about the details of his divorce or maligned his wife. That is the right thing to do and an example I will follow. Therefore, whoever thinks that Howard Stern does not set a good example is simply wrong—at least in this particular instance.

I certainly endured my own share of regret and pain when I divorced, especially where my children were concerned. Even so, and even given the experiences encountered in my work, I did believe I would some-day get re-married. I still had faith in marriage—mine had not been a case of institutional defect. A personal/situational defect caused the end of my marriage. Despite everything I had seen and done, I was still hopeful.

I was forging ahead in my career. I felt as if I was good at my job, and I was fortunate to have had such a rapid rise in the profession. Our firm was primarily a family law firm, and I became known for my expertise in divorce litigation. One of my first cases had been representing someone whose records I still listen to on the radio. I then represented a series of professional athletes and professional athlete's wives. Soon enough came corporate leaders, members of Congress, the wife of the owner of a professional football team, even the wife of a former Presidential Chief of Staff.

In 1989, I had met Larry King, whose radio and new cable talk show was then based in Washington DC. He came to our firm seeking representation with a divorce. (I would like to take a moment here to go on the record about something that I think is widely misperceived. So many people have this notion that Larry is some kind of serial husband, and it is just not true. In the last twenty years, he has been married twice. Hardly uncommon. He made some mistakes early on, as people tend to do when they are young. That is it.) Our first meeting was in Washington, DC, and I was late. Larry, I did not realize at the time, has what I now affectionately refer to as OED (obsessive early disorder.) Everything with Larry is live TV, so when it does not go off on time, there is a problem. With Larry, if lunch is at 12pm, show up at 10:45am, just to be on the safe side. I was 29 years old; Larry was 57. Although I was late for our first meeting, I apparently handled the matter to Larry's satisfaction, and he asked me to assist him with some other legal matters. It was the start of a great professional and personal relationship that continues to this very day.

Occasionally, when Larry has a guest on the show that I would like to meet, I drop by the studios at CNN. In 1993, I stopped by the Washington Bureau to watch Larry interview and to meet Mikhail Gorbachev. While at the studio, I could not help but notice the make-up artist attending to Larry and the former leader of the Soviet Union. She was drop-dead gorgeous. She was dressed in a couture outfit, was vivacious, had bouncing brunette hair, perfect olive skin, the best figure I had ever seen, and the features of a famous Italian actress. Quite honestly, at that time that I first saw her, I had two thoughts in mind: First, I was thinking she was going to have a tough time covering the big brown spot on Gorbachev's head, no matter how great of a makeup artist she reportedly was. Second, I knew immediately that I wanted to meet her much more than Gorbachev. There were only two small problems: Rose was married, and so was I.

A year later Rose was dealing with marital problems of her own and was looking for a divorce lawyer. She asked Larry for a recommendation, and he referred her to me. She came to the office for a consultation, and I met with her. The second time we met I took her out to lunch and agreed to represent her. The representation only lasted a week, because I had to advise her that I could no longer represent her. I liked her too much personally. Rose, of course, at that time was right in the middle of a divorce, and she needed all of this like a dieter on Atkins needs carbs.

We wound up dating for a year, and then Rose and I bought a house and moved in together. She had two children, I had two children, and the whole experience was like a tornado. Each of the four children had their own issues with the whole remarriage and the exes and the new relationships and roles; it was a challenging time, to say the least. The good thing is that I do not remember it very well now. Perhaps I have blocked out the negative aspects of the whole situation.

Before we started living together, we knew that our commitment was strong and that we would marry at some point, although no period had been set and the question had not yet been asked. I figured that when it came to proposing, I should get some advice from the master himself. Larry King and I met at the Palm Restaurant in Washington DC for dinner. We bounced around a couple of ideas.... One of things we thought about was having Bill Clinton propose to her, but I said that that would not be special enough to Rose. She was President Clinton's regular makeup artist and very close to him. We had to think up something really fun and different. Larry mentioned that he was going to be filming a segment for Warren Beatty's movie *Bulworth,* and said, "Mark, why don't we get Warren Beatty to do it?"

Warren was out in LA directing the film. Warren and I had a discussion on the phone about him proposing for me, and he was happy to do so. Rose and I flew out to LA for part of the movie shoot. We joined Larry for his regular breakfast at Nate and Al's Deli in Beverly Hills one morning, and everyone at the table knew what was going to happen that night. Everyone, of course, except for Rose.

Larry played himself in the movie, interviewing Oliver Platt. We showed up at the CNN studio where they were filming Larry's scenes in Hollywood early that evening. Chaia, Larry's daughter, was enlisted to distract Rose so I could plot the plan with Warren, so the two of them went off to grab a snack. Warren and I then had a 45-minute discussion of how he was actually going to pop the question. The plan was for Warren to hit on Rose during the filming, thereby leading up to the big moment. Warren asked me, "Well, what if she responds positively to me hitting on her?" Hey, he is Warren Beatty, it could happen. "I don't think she will," I told him. Warren retorted, "But that would certainly answer the bigger question, wouldn't it?"

---

**I AM NOT GOING TO MAKE THE SAME MISTAKE ONCE.**

*—Warren Beatty*
*(before his marriage to Annette Bening)*

---

Warren was extremely nervous about the role he was playing. He wasn't very good at this...it had sure taken a lot of years for him to ever pop the question in his own life. This was a man who had not had a lot of practice proposing marriage. Anyway, Rose returned from having Thai food and Warren started following her around, really pouring it on, hitting on her hard. It went on for a couple of hours, and we were cracking up. Rose was thinking to herself, what is this guy doing, trying to be polite, while the rest of us snickered in the background. She was being taped the whole time, though she did not know it, and it is a priceless video.

When Donald Trump saw the video on *Access Hollywood*, he stated, "One of the most impressive things I've seen recently was when Rose turned Warren Beatty down on television when he offered to marry her, and she took you over Warren! Now Warren is a friend of mine—he was very disappointed. But I will tell you, that was very impressive. You must be doing something right!" I must have been—Rose said no to Warren and yes to me, and we went out to dinner that night to celebrate with Larry, Oliver, Warren and his wife, Annette Bening. You can only imagine the reaction of our parents as Warren called them from dinner to announce that he had proposed to Rose. We were married in January 1998 in Venice, Italy and have passed the lucky seven-year mark.

So, when all said and done, should you remarry? That is up to you, and will be a question answered only after the most careful reflection on the experiences that you have in your own life and the risks you are willing to take in order to enjoy the comforts that marriage can bring. My best counsel would be to disregard the confidentiality I spoke of earlier in this chapter and undertake the most careful investigation possible about the background of your potential spouse, especially if they have been married previously. Take the trip to the courthouse and look over their file. Then, ask the hard questions. And get answers. It is better that you learn the truth before round two begins.

Be sure to take your time in making the decision to remarry, and use your common sense. Life is just too short to have to endure the misery of a divorce twice. Nevertheless, some of the very best rewards in life are bestowed upon those who take the biggest risks.

# ADVICE TO REMEMBER

$ The divorce rate for second marriages is almost 70%—in other words, two out of every three second marriages will fail.

$ Do not remarry unless you are willing to be divorced again.

$ Wait at least one year after your divorce before you consider getting married again—there is no need to rush. If you are being rushed, you are being forewarned.

$ Do not remarry without a prenuptial agreement.

$ Do not remarry the same type of person you divorced.

$ Going to the other extreme and marrying someone that is the exact opposite of your former spouse rarely works either.

$ Understand the reason why the potential spouse's first marriage failed as the same problems will most likely reappear in your own marriage.

$ You are foolish if you do not read the court file from the divorce of your potential spouse if they were married previously.

$ Make sure that if you or your potential spouse have children from a former marriage that the impact the children will have the relationship is fully explored, discussed, and discussed again.

$ If you do not really wish to act as a parental figure, do not marry someone who has minor children as the challenges faced by a step-parent are difficult and must be delicately handled.

$ If there is a crazy ex-spouse in the picture they will probably remain in the picture and do everything possible to make your relationship fail. Understand in advance the role and repercussions that such a person will have on your relationship.

$ Make certain that everything you thought was lacking in your first spouse is found in your second one.

$ Marriage is not any easier the second time. It still requires tremendous effort on the part of both parties to make it work.

# BERT FIELDS & BARBARA GUGGENHEIM
## *Much Ado about Love*

*There are several lawyers who you never want to see sitting at the table opposite you in a courtroom, and Bertram Fields is one of them. The Harvard Law Bulletin once reported, "[H]is reputation as a legendary litigator is based on stellar performances in the courtroom and at the negotiating table, in high-profile cases often involving huge sums of Hollywood money. He is also famous as the lawyer able to argue any side of the issue, for any industry party, and win..."* **Vanity Fair** *summed it up concisely, calling Bert "the most feared man in Hollywood." As one of the nation's leading entertainment lawyers, Bert has successfully represented the interests of figures like The Beatles, Tom Cruise, Warren Beatty, George Lucas, Steven Spielberg, Jeffrey Katzenberg, Michael Jackson, James Cameron, Dustin Hoffman, Mario Puzo, John Travolta, and the list just goes on and on. He also filed a $100 million suit on behalf of his client, HBO, against the head of The Soprano family, Tony Soprano (a.k.a. James Gandolfini) alleging that the actor portraying television's favorite mobster was breaching his employment contract. No one is safe around Bert Fields.*

*However, Bert was not always the Los Angeles entertainment superlawyer trained at Harvard University—his humble beginnings were in the battlefield of divorce law, where he honed many of the skills that he would later use against his opponents in the most complex litigation in the entertainment world. Bert is also a great chef (he makes the best Mediterranean salad I have ever eaten) and an accomplished author of two novels published under a pseudonym. He is also a renowned Shakespeare scholar authoring the highly acclaimed "Royal Blood: Richard III and the Mystery of the Princes" and whose new book "Players: The Shakespeare Mystery" was released earlier this year.*

*Bert met his wife, Barbara Guggenheim, while defending her in a lawsuit brought against her by Sylvester Stallone. Barbara has a doctorate in art history and is a founding principal of Guggenheim, Asher Associates, the best known firm of art consultants in the world. With offices in New York and Los Angeles, Barbara specializes in providing a comprehensive range of art advisory services, from helping individuals purchase a single work of art to guiding corporations in forming entire collections. She is also a well-known lecturer, and contributor to W and other journals. While by day, Barbara helps individuals and corporations purchase fine art, by night and on weekends, she is a collectibles junky. She has embodied some of her passion in her books "Handkerchiefs: A Collector's Guide" and the recently released "Decorating on eBay : Beautify Your Home on a Budget at Any Time of Day or Night."*

*It was with great pleasure that my wife and I, along with my editor, Julie McCarron, recently had dinner with Bert and Barbara at our home away from home in Beverly Hills, The Peninsula Hotel, to get their views on marriage and divorce. It is always great to be with Bert and Barbara, be it at a black-tie gala or taking a walk with them on the beach in Malibu. They are a wonderfully happy couple and I truly enjoyed listening to their banter about life. Rose and I truly treasure their friendship. While Bert and Barbara may own houses all over the world, there is no question that their roots are firmly grounded in love.*

## BERT

Oh, the things I used to see! The silly things people fight about in property settlements. We would have this multi-million dollar property settlement, and then the husband would say, "She wants the monkey prints that were in the dining room? Forget it! The settlement is off!" And, of course, they were absolutely worthless. The reason I stopped doing that kind of legal work was that I could truly see that it was not about money or a fair settlement—it was about hurting the other person.

Now look, in the legal arena, I do not mind hurting people, but after a while, I could not take another case where two people were out for blood. I just didn't like it. The whole monkey print thing was just an excuse to inflict pain. "I am not going to let her have those goddamned prints!" I heard so much anger and hatred.

On the other hand, though, I have told many clients: If it is a bad situation, unsalvageable and you have kids, get out of it quickly. Do not devote your life to a bad marriage. It is your life, and you only have one. You do not want to be in a situation where you are a martyr...people will spend seventy years with a woman they hated! Why do that? You do not get another shot at life—this is it. Do it when the kids are one and three, not thirteen and fifteen and they have really gotten accustomed to their living arrangement. It is so much easier than doing it when they are young.

Now, having married the *perfect* woman, I have not faced those problems myself.

This is actually my third marriage. When I was a young man I was married for a very short time. I cheated on my wife, because I was living in a novel. I was just out of law school and I thought, *This is what people do; this is how people live.* So I'd meet a pretty girl at a party and hit on her. "Let's have lunch, let's do this...." It was all just an exciting adventure. It was not so much physical attraction as it was the excitement and adventure of doing it.

I stupidly thought that this was the way intelligent, capable, worldly adults live. This is what they do. I had a very dopey, adolescent view of things for someone who was 23, a long way past adolescence. That first marriage was a very short one. I did not feel particularly guilty about infidelity then...it was all just an exciting, chancy enterprise.

That's the way I met Lydia, the woman I was married to for 26 years—I was having an affair with her. I divorced my first wife to marry Lydia without too much pain, though I will say that one of the saddest things I ever did in my life was to tell a two-year-old that Daddy was not going to live in the house any longer. That was really tough.

Lydia and I were very happily married for a quarter-century, and then she was diagnosed with cancer. When my wife was first diagnosed, I, in my arrogance, went out and bought every book I could about cancer. I am a lawyer, I'm used to doing things, taking action. I was going to beat this! I was not going to sit back passively and let something destroy us. Of course, cancer was like a huge arm that just smacked me down. We did everything to find a cure...but there wasn't one. Lydia had passed away five years before I met Barbara. I was very happy to find her – because I did not really like dating.

Barbara came to me, asking me to represent her in a legal matter. On my part, there was immediate romantic interest in her. In those days it wasn't unethical. Barbara always remembered the circumstances of our first meeting. Once we got married, Barbara did not allow me to represent young actresses anymore.

We do not have a prenuptial agreement, but I certainly advise my clients to execute one if they are someone who has a huge amount of money. If I have an instinct that the marriage may not last forever, I certainly try to urge them to sign one. It's just a gut feeling I get sometimes, with a 65-year-old billionaire and, say, a 23-year-old supermodel.

The secret to a successful relationship? I think to myself that I am responsible for Barbara's happiness. I want to behave in a manner that reflects that. I would never want to betray that responsibility. It helps a lot if you do not fight about many silly little things. Why would I want to make her unhappy? Pick your fights. You do not have to call someone on every time they are wrong, or you think they are wrong, or they do something you do not like. Take it easy, let the little things go. Finally, what really works for us is literally to take a hike. We walk every day, sometimes up to 15 miles! You have to talk while you are walking with someone.

I do not have a textbook definition of love, but for me it is really very simple: Whatever I'm going to do, I want to do it with my wife. I just want to be with her. So much of it has to do with companionship, friendship, being married. A girl you meet in a bar is a different story. However, married love, I think, is that feeling of warm companionship, that this is your best friend in the world. When Barbara is away, I do not feel complete. Nothing is really wrong, but I just don't feel whole. I think that is what love is: you want to spend your life with someone…and it is a *wonderful thing* when you find that *right person*.

## BARBARA

I was 44 and never before married when I met Bert. As I told him during our honeymoon on the beach in Mexico looking at the most beautiful moonlight, "You know, if I had known it was going to turn out like this, I would have had a much better time along the way."

I did not know if I would ever get married or not. I had a very full life in New York City and lots of friends. Sometimes, of course, we would talk about boyfriends and marriage. I had one girlfriend who used to tell me that the person you want to be with is the person who gets on your nerves the least. I had another friend who got married five times, and I asked her once, "How did you know when you weren't in love with that guy anymore?" She said, "When I accept a marriage proposal from someone else."

I actually met Bert because I got sued, and a friend of mine told me, "If you can afford Bert Fields, get him." So I called and made an appointment for legal advice. The interview was going on and on, and he had mentioned theater tickets that evening when I first arrived.

Eventually the phone on his desk rang and I heard him tell a woman, "You go ahead and go, and I'll meet you at the theater." I did not know if he had already seen the play three times or what. However, he seemed reluctant to end the meeting.

Widowers were a whole category of men I had not even considered until I met Bert. The thing about widowers is if they were happily married before, they want to be happily married again. My mother was the funniest. After she found out I was dating a lawyer, she literally chased me out of the house and down the path one day as I left, crying out, "Just be sure he doesn't charge you for the hours you sleep!"

After we got married I went through his whole roster of clients...Faye Dunaway, for example...she had to go!

Very early in our marriage we went to a wedding...and in the middle of the ceremony, at some point the minister said, "I want you to remember that you are responsible for the well-being and happiness of this other person." What he was saying, in so many words, was that if you wake up in a foul mood you do not have the right to take it out on the other person. I sat up and did a double take. It really struck a chord within me. Every morning when we are brushing our teeth, we acknowledge that fact.

If I had to spell out some rules of marital happiness that work for us, I would say this: One: remember that you are responsible for the other person's happiness. Two: Bury your crankiness. Keep work problems at work. Remember, you are here to make the other person happy, not to complain and complain. I love coming home and saying, "Do you want to hear what she said to me today?" However, not to overload him with complaining.

The other day I read an article on marriage about a man who said, "When I look back on this marriage at the end of my life, I will be very sad because of the ten days I wasn't with my wife that I could have spent with her." This sentiment really moved me, and I told my business partner what the man had said. And my partner Abigail pointed out, "Bert feels that way about *you.*" And I realized yes, that's right, he does. *It truly is the most wonderful feeling.*

# A FEW WORDS OF THANKS

It is hard for me to acknowledge (or for that matter blame) all of those who are responsible for giving me the experiences in my life that have enabled me to write this book. I am certain that I will leave someone out that I should have included, and to each of you I apologize.

I must first thank my Mother and my late Father for all of the sacrifices that you made to provide me with my formal education, allowing me to graduate from law school without a penny of debt. Of course, you also provided me so much more, and I am not talented enough to embody their gifts in mere words.

I must next thank my wife Rose for her patience and understanding during the writing of this book; well, for that matter, during the entirety of our marriage. I can be difficult to live with but I deny that I love my laptop more than you; although the Blackberry sometimes runs neck and neck.

Andrew and Alec, my wonderful boys, you know how proud I am of you, and I know how glad you are that this project is finished. Thank you for letting me spend so much time writing. Yes, we can play some video games now.

My other children, Georgie and Priscilla, I know the ride has not been easy. Both of you can reach any goal you seek. Your mom and I are always here to help.

My in-laws, Rose and Al Procopio, deserve special thanks for accepting me and making me a part of the family. Al, one day I would like to write a book just about you. I envision it as a multi-volume work. I am living proof that there is an ass for every seat.

Professionally, they are many who have touched my life. Special thanks to Mark B. Sandground and Glenn C. Lewis, the two people who helped define my career path. I owe a substantial debt of gratitude to Bob Shapiro, Skip Miller, Peter Weil, Patty Glaser, Barry Fink and Terry Christensen for giving me the chance to become a part of such a first-class team.

Bert Fields, thank you for being there whenever I need you.

There are not enough words to extend my gratitude to Larry King. You changed my life in so many ways and I can never repay you. I love you, Shawn, and all of the children. Can't wait for the next rocket launch.

Montel, you know how important our friendship is. Thanks for everything you do for me personally, as well as for all of the men and women battling MS.

Lewis, you never say no. I want to be the President of your fan club. Gordon, thanks for always being there. You and Diana are as reliable as a precise timepiece. Donald, thanks for all of your support. I know I can always count on you and Norma. PK and Dick, you know how much I respect you both. Gene and Shannon, you guys are amazing. Hope we can go bowling someday soon. Fred, you should be President. Stan, you always tell it like it is, with amazing clarity. Barbara, Linell and Sherry, your husbands certainly did "marry up." Joanne, I only wish that all Judges had your style.

Phil, your advice was just perfect. Thanks for all of your incredible support and letting me stalk Chandler so much.

Wendy Walker, you are the best, and you know that I love you. Thanks for helping me so much and always being a true friend.

Melanie McLaughlin, your unique candor qualifies you as my honorary sister. Let's fight again soon.

So many others have helped me and I make mention of their names—each one of you knows the importance of your role within this book and the play called my life: David P. Barondess, Nile Rodgers, Nancy Hunt, David Duff, Ron Cherry, Joe Forman, Nancy Davis, VADM Al Konetzni, Patty Leoni, Joe Novello, M.D., Peter Max, Gene Luntz, Bill Margaritis, Steve & Fran Rotter, Rod Langway, John Crawford, Sandy Ain, Mike Johnston, Diane & Leonard Brown, Peaches, Bart Tessler, David Rosenfeld, Paul & Deborah Lankford, Len Kuntz, Judy Lynch, Harry Rauner, Valerie Volpe, Steve Parnell, Clark & Holly Lee, Norma & Russ Ramsey, Penny Yerks, Larry Jeffries, Bob Gurnee, The Engemann Family, Sen. Walter Stosch, Suzanne Clarke Schaar, Bruce Jamerson, Gary Pate, Tommy Jacomo and the guys at The Washington, DC Palm, Chris Berry, Rick & Amy Levy, Cheryl M. New, Adam Kaplin, M.D., Peter Calabresi, M.D., Steven Hauser, M.D. and Ali Kasicki and everyone at our second home, the best hotel in the world, The Peninsula Beverly Hills.

There are others who have left this world that had such an impact on my life including my Dad, my Aunt Diane, Horace Cistola and Mattie Stepanek. I miss you so much.

This book would not have been possible without the opportunity afforded to me by Michael Viner, my publisher. Even while confronted with personal adversity that would bring down most of us, you withstood the challenges and will come out on top. Thank you for standing behind this project and making it happen.

Julie McCarron, my editor, you are unbelievable. I am sorry I made you cry, and hope you enjoyed the laughs. At least you don't have to live with me, and yes, that was a contraction, just for you, and here's another. Can't wait to see your new house in the country. You deserve it. Thank you so much. Your support, guidance and common sense are the backbone of this book.

Many thanks to Suzanne Wickham-Beaird, my publicist. I am sure that by the time our book tour is completed that you and Julie will have much more to commiserate about.

And a big thank you to my book designer Sonia Fiore. I appreciate all your hard work and creativity...oh, and Sonia, I have just one more change on that cover....

Finally, thank you to all of the clients that endured my representation over the years. It was a pleasure to be of service to you, and I hope that life has brought you everything you desire.